Top Cow Productions Presents...

ST. MERCY

VOLUME ONE

Created By
JOHN ZUUR PLATTEN

Published by Top Cow Productions, Inc.
Los Angeles

For Top Cow Productions, Inc.
Marc Silvestri - CEO
Matt Hawkins - President & COO
Elena Salcedo - Vice President of Operations
Vincent Valentine - Production Manager

To find the comic shop
nearest you, call:
1-888-COMICBOOK

Want more info? Check out
www.topcow.com
for news & exclusive Top Cow merchandise

IMAGE COMICS, INC. • **Robert Kirkman**: Chief Operating Officer • **Erik Larsen**: Chief Financial Officer • **Todd McFarlane**: President • **Marc Silvestri**: Chief Executive Officer • **Jim Valentino**: Vice President • **Eric Stephenson**: Publisher / Chief Creative Officer • **Nicole Lapalme**: Controller • **Leanna Caunter**: Accounting Analyst • **Sue Korpela**: Accounting & HR Manager • **Marla Eizik**: Talent Liaison • **Jeff Boison**: Director of Sales & Publishing Planning • **Lorelei Bunjes**: Director of Digital Services • **Dirk Wood**: Director of International Sales & Licensing • **Alex Cox**: Director of Direct Market Sales • **Chloe Ramos**: Book Market & Library Sales Manager • **Emilio Bautista**: Digital Sales Coordinator • **Jon Schlaffman**: Specialty Sales Coordinator • **Kat Salazar**: Director of PR & Marketing • **Drew Fitzgerald**: Marketing Content Associate • **Heather Doornink**: Production Director • **Drew Gill**: Art Director • **Hilary DiLoreto**: Print Manager • **Tricia Ramos**: Traffic Manager • **Melissa Gifford**: Content Manager • **Erika Schnatz**: Senior Production Artist • **Ryan Brewer**: Production Artist • **Deanna Phelps**: Production Artist • **IMAGECOMICS.COM**

Top Cow Productions Presents...

ST. MERCY

VOLUME ONE

Written By
JOHN ZUUR PLATTEN

Art By
ATILIO ROJO

Letters By
TROY PETERI
ALW STUDIOS

Edited by
ELENA SALCEDO

Cover By
ATILIO ROJO

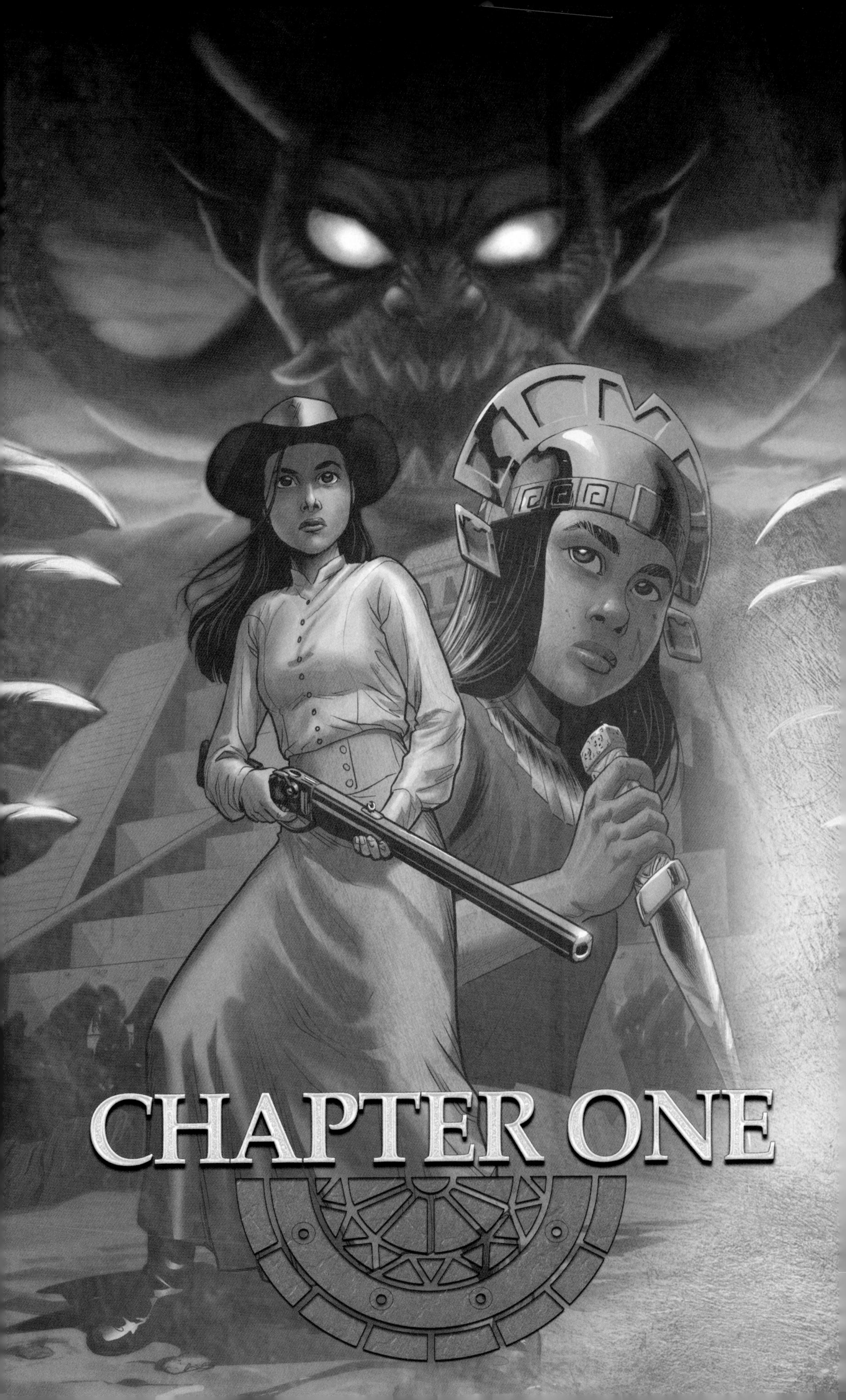

CHAPTER ONE

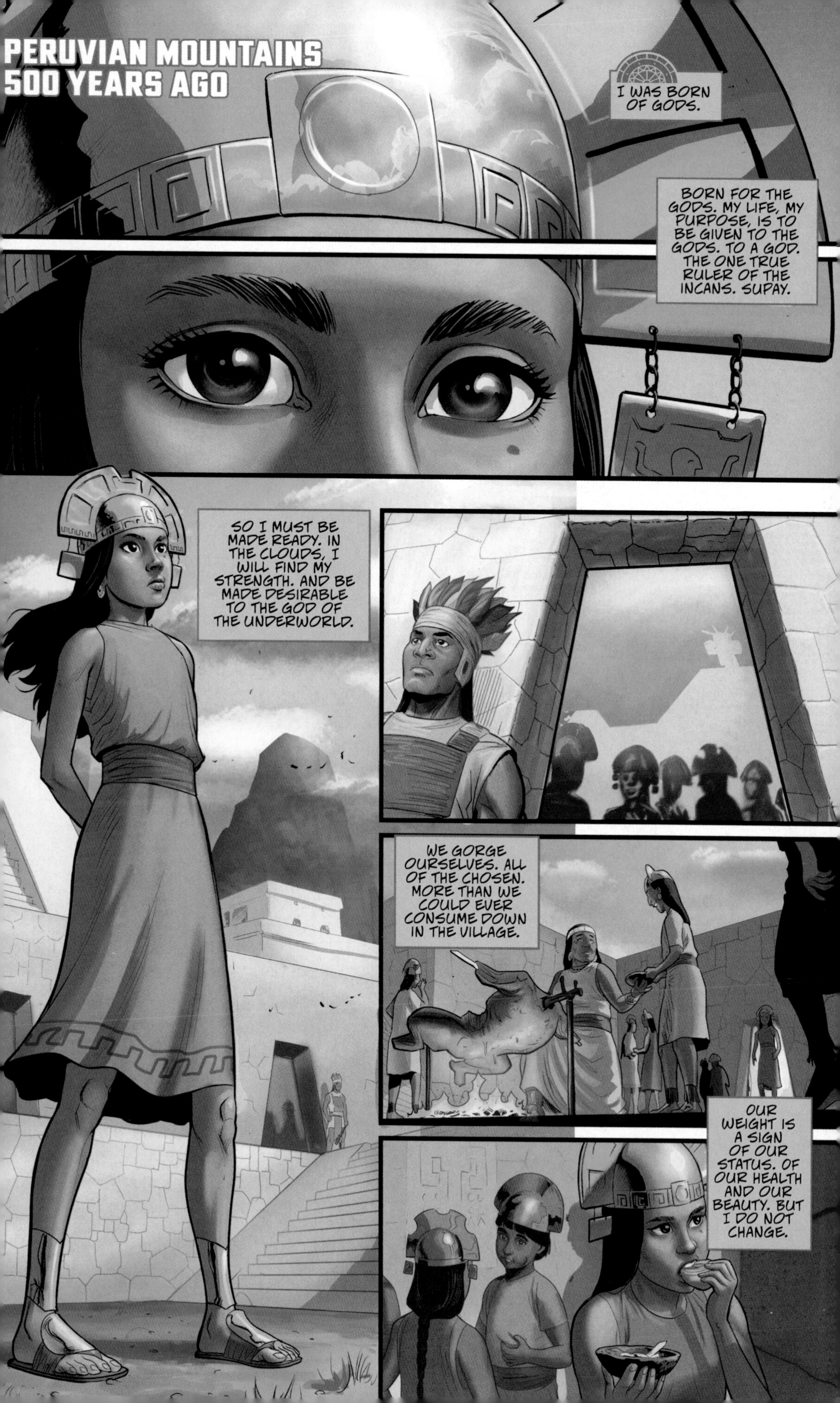

PERUVIAN MOUNTAINS
500 YEARS AGO
I WAS BORN OF GODS.
BORN FOR THE GODS. MY LIFE, MY PURPOSE, IS TO BE GIVEN TO THE GODS. TO A GOD. THE ONE TRUE RULER OF THE INCANS. SUPAY.
SO I MUST BE MADE READY. IN THE CLOUDS, I WILL FIND MY STRENGTH. AND BE MADE DESIRABLE TO THE GOD OF THE UNDERWORLD.
WE GORGE OURSELVES. ALL OF THE CHOSEN. MORE THAN WE COULD EVER CONSUME DOWN IN THE VILLAGE.
OUR WEIGHT IS A SIGN OF OUR STATUS. OF OUR HEALTH AND OUR BEAUTY. BUT I DO NOT CHANGE.

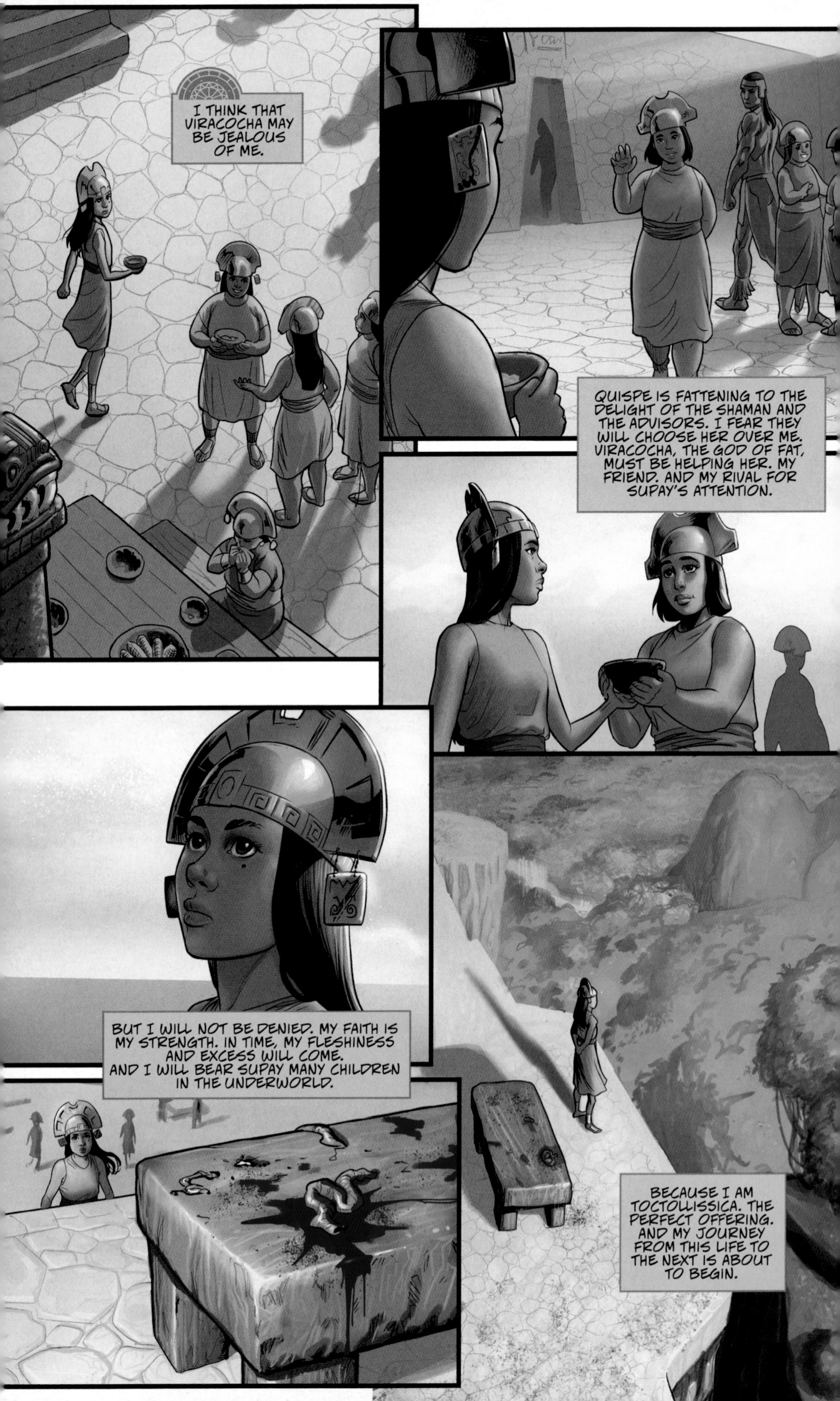
I THINK THAT VIRACOCHA MAY BE JEALOUS OF ME.
QUISPE IS FATTENING TO THE DELIGHT OF THE SHAMAN AND THE ADVISORS. I FEAR THEY WILL CHOOSE HER OVER ME. VIRACOCHA, THE GOD OF FAT, MUST BE HELPING HER. MY FRIEND. AND MY RIVAL FOR SUPAY'S ATTENTION.
BUT I WILL NOT BE DENIED. MY FAITH IS MY STRENGTH. IN TIME, MY FLESHINESS AND EXCESS WILL COME. AND I WILL BEAR SUPAY MANY CHILDREN IN THE UNDERWORLD.
BECAUSE I AM TOCTOLLISSICA. THE PERFECT OFFERING. AND MY JOURNEY FROM THIS LIFE TO THE NEXT IS ABOUT TO BEGIN.

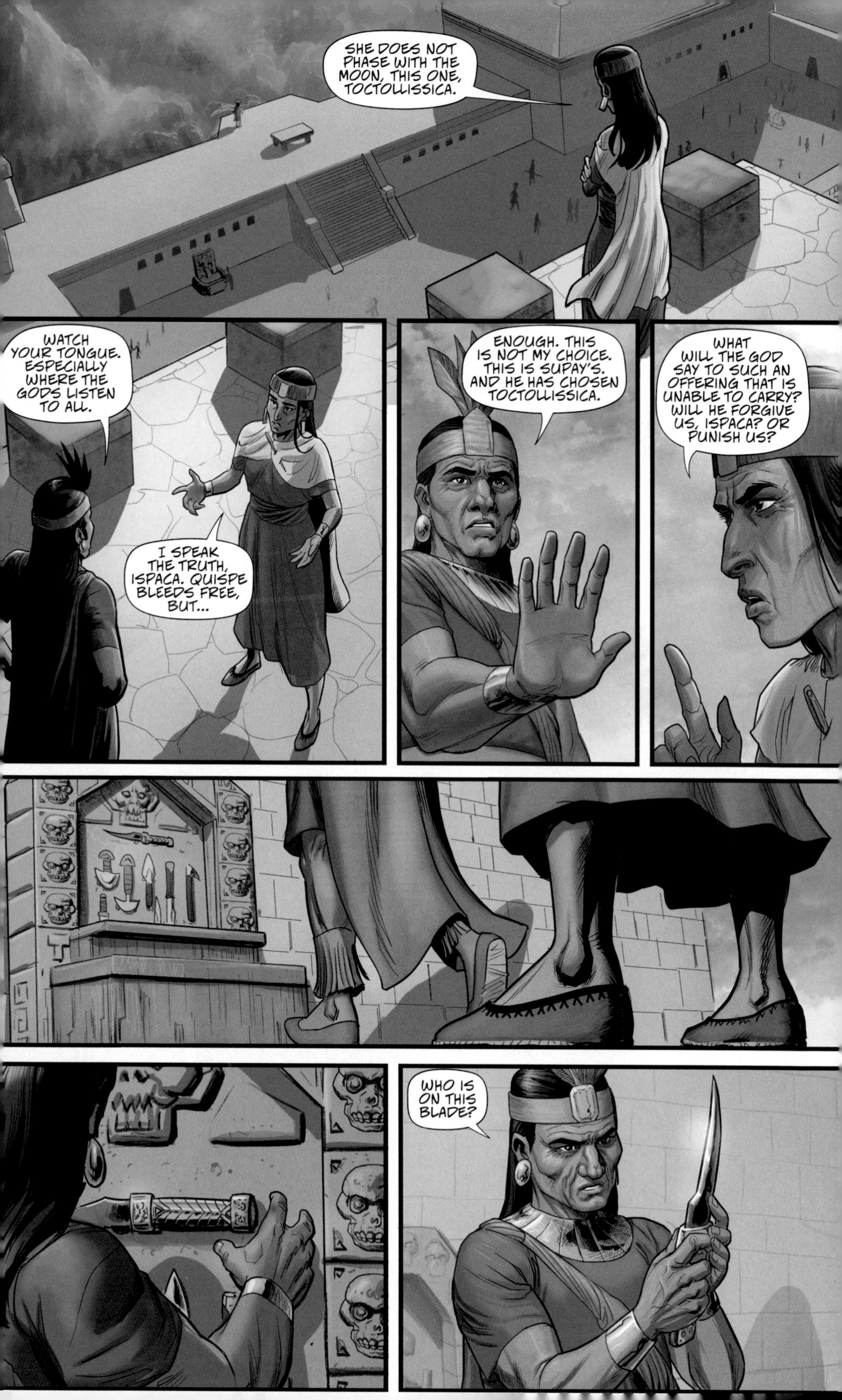
SHE DOES NOT PHASE WITH THE MOON, THIS ONE, TOCTOLLISSICA.
WATCH YOUR TONGUE. ESPECIALLY WHERE THE GODS LISTEN TO ALL.
I SPEAK THE TRUTH, ISPACA. QUISPE BLEEDS FREE, BUT...
ENOUGH. THIS IS NOT MY CHOICE. THIS IS SUPAY'S. AND HE HAS CHOSEN TOCTOLLISSICA.
WHAT WILL THE GOD SAY TO SUCH AN OFFERING THAT IS UNABLE TO CARRY? WILL HE FORGIVE US, ISPACA? OR PUNISH US?
WHO IS ON THIS BLADE?

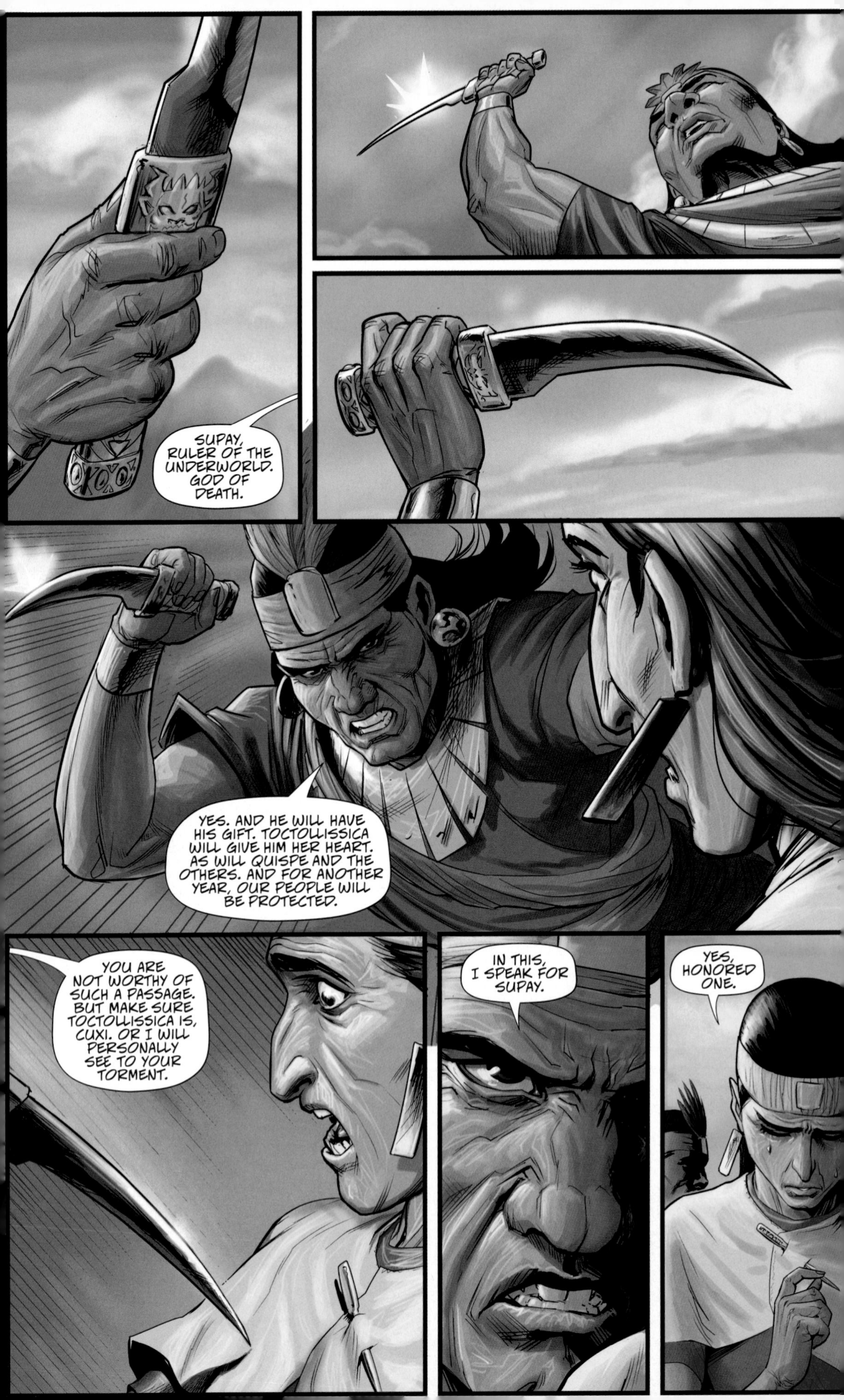
SUPAY, RULER OF THE UNDERWORLD. GOD OF DEATH.
YES. AND HE WILL HAVE HIS GIFT. TOCTOLLISSICA WILL GIVE HIM HER HEART. AS WILL QUISPE AND THE OTHERS. AND FOR ANOTHER YEAR, OUR PEOPLE WILL BE PROTECTED.
YOU ARE NOT WORTHY OF SUCH A PASSAGE. BUT MAKE SURE TOCTOLLISSICA IS, CUXI. OR I WILL PERSONALLY SEE TO YOUR TORMENT.
IN THIS, I SPEAK FOR SUPAY.
YES, HONORED ONE.

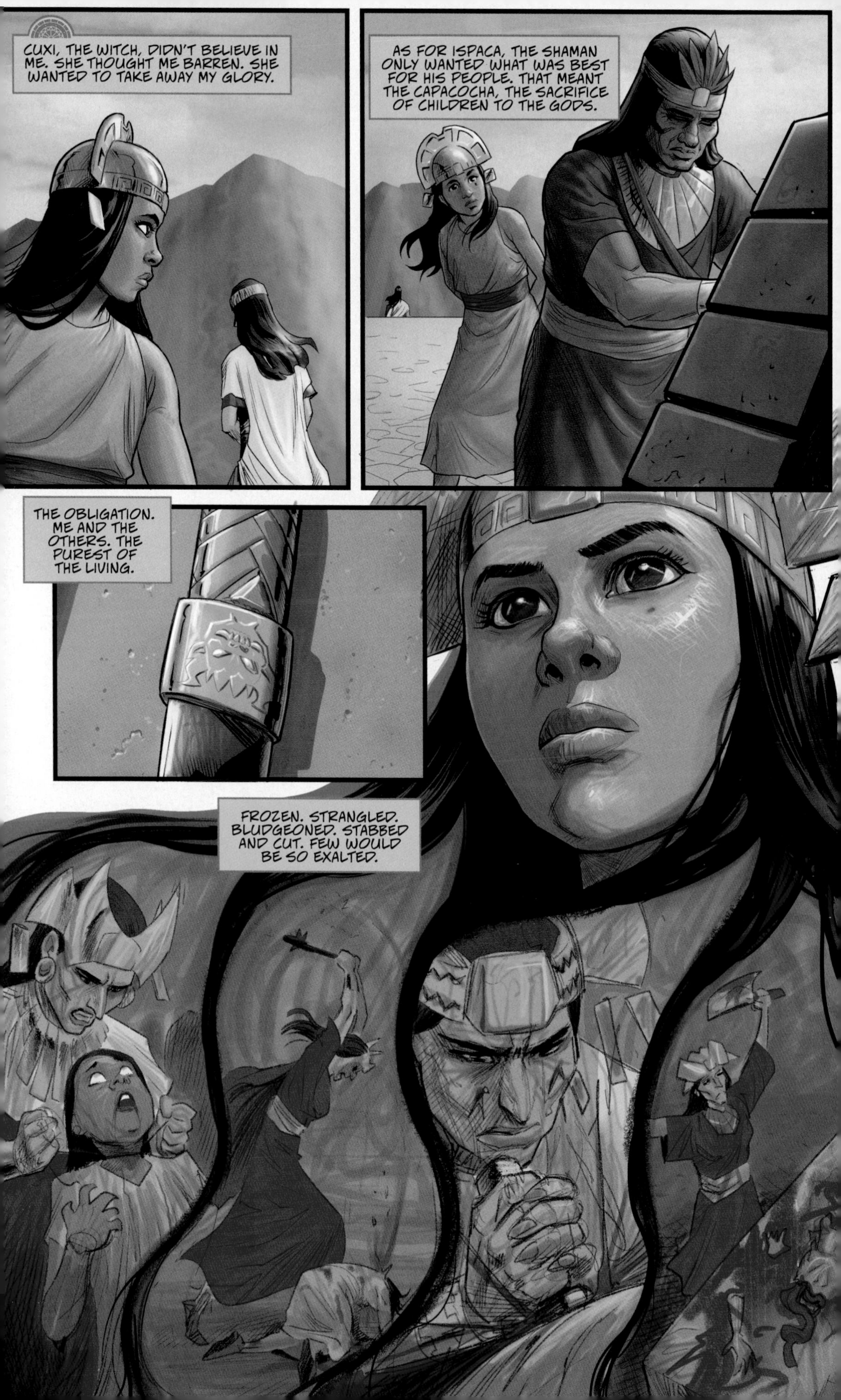
CUXI, THE WITCH, DIDN'T BELIEVE IN ME. SHE THOUGHT ME BARREN. SHE WANTED TO TAKE AWAY MY GLORY.
AS FOR ISPACA, THE SHAMAN ONLY WANTED WHAT WAS BEST FOR HIS PEOPLE. THAT MEANT THE CAPACOCHA, THE SACRIFICE OF CHILDREN TO THE GODS.
THE OBLIGATION. ME AND THE OTHERS. THE PUREST OF THE LIVING.
FROZEN. STRANGLED. BLUDGEONED. STABBED AND CUT. FEW WOULD BE SO EXALTED.

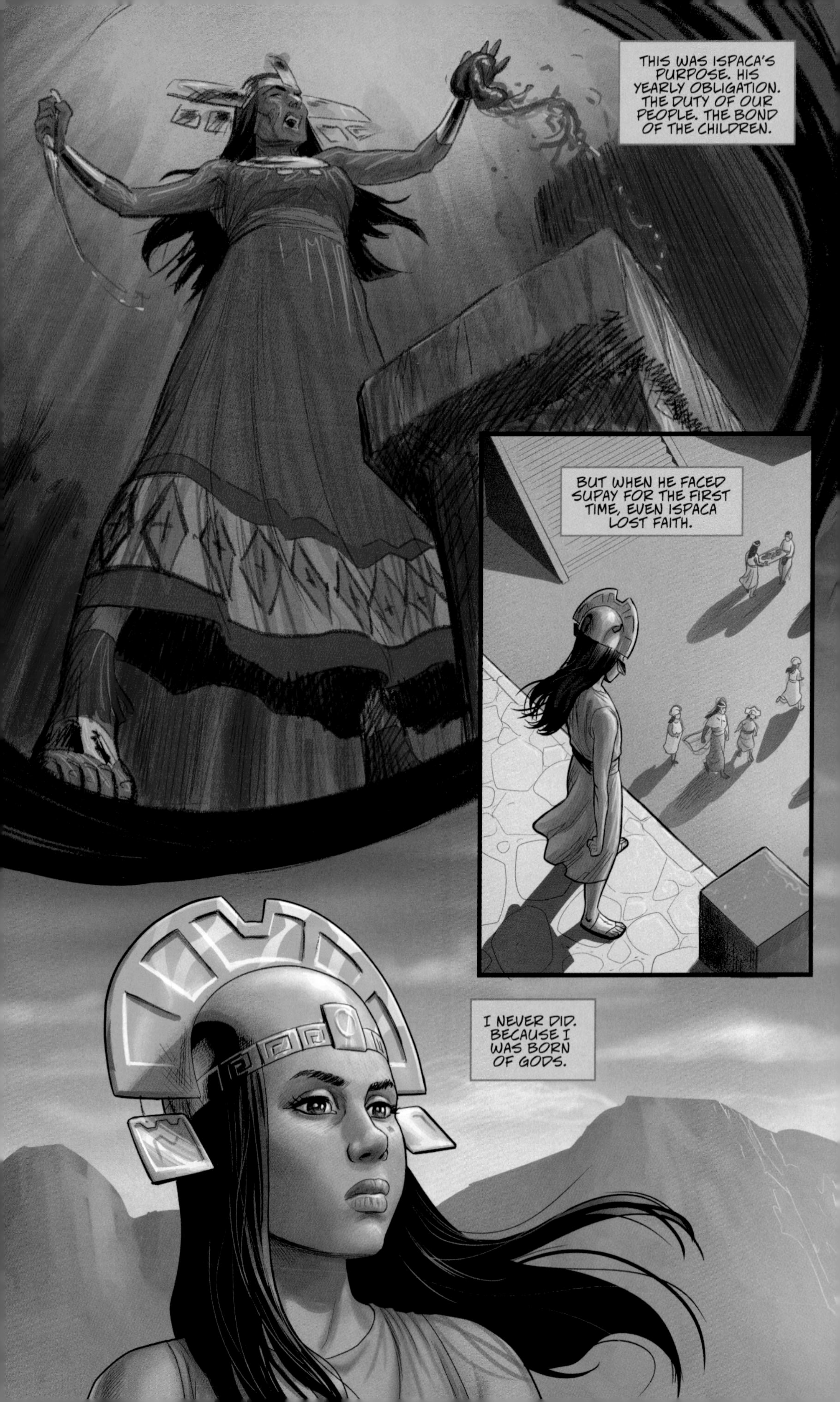
THIS WAS ISPACA'S PURPOSE. HIS YEARLY OBLIGATION. THE DUTY OF OUR PEOPLE. THE BOND OF THE CHILDREN.
BUT WHEN HE FACED SUPAY FOR THE FIRST TIME, EVEN ISPACA LOST FAITH.
I NEVER DID. BECAUSE I WAS BORN OF GODS.

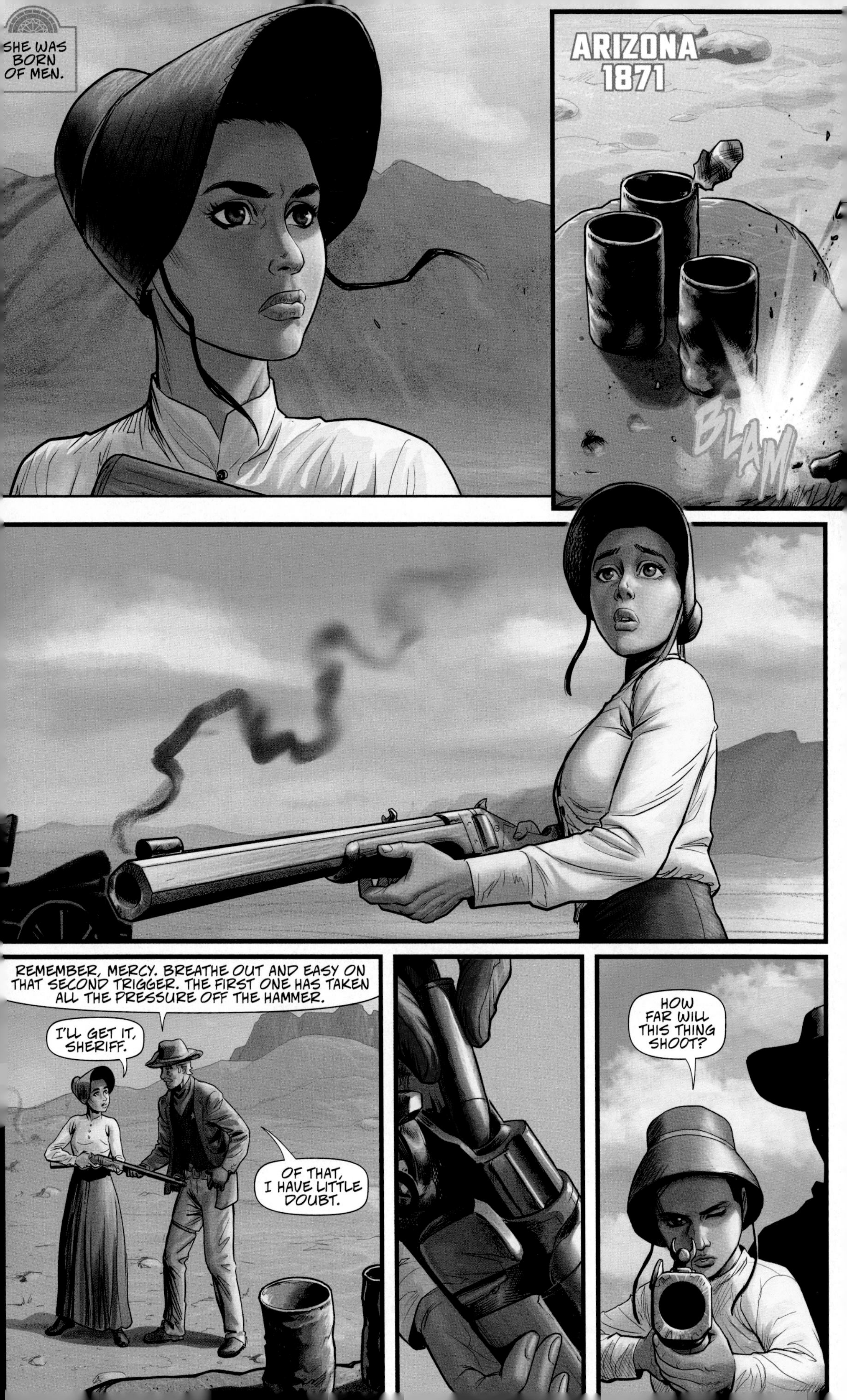
SHE WAS BORN OF MEN.
ARIZONA 1871
BLAM
REMEMBER, MERCY. BREATHE OUT AND EASY ON THAT SECOND TRIGGER. THE FIRST ONE HAS TAKEN ALL THE PRESSURE OFF THE HAMMER.
I'LL GET IT, SHERIFF.
OF THAT, I HAVE LITTLE DOUBT.
HOW FAR WILL THIS THING SHOOT?

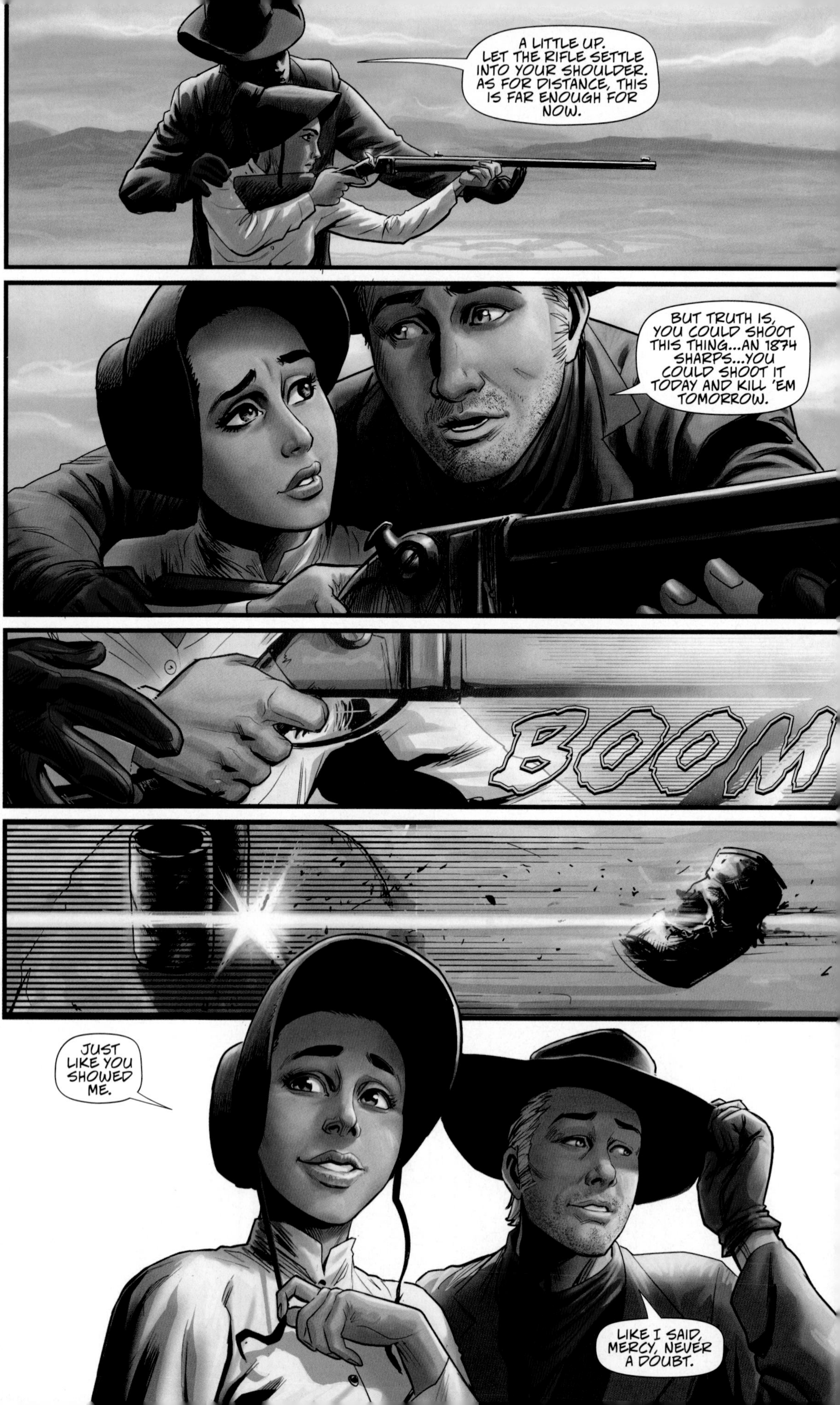
A LITTLE UP. LET THE RIFLE SETTLE INTO YOUR SHOULDER. AS FOR DISTANCE, THIS IS FAR ENOUGH FOR NOW.
BUT TRUTH IS, YOU COULD SHOOT THIS THING...AN 1874 SHARPS...YOU COULD SHOOT IT TODAY AND KILL 'EM TOMORROW.
BOOM
JUST LIKE YOU SHOWED ME.
LIKE I SAID, MERCY, NEVER A DOUBT.

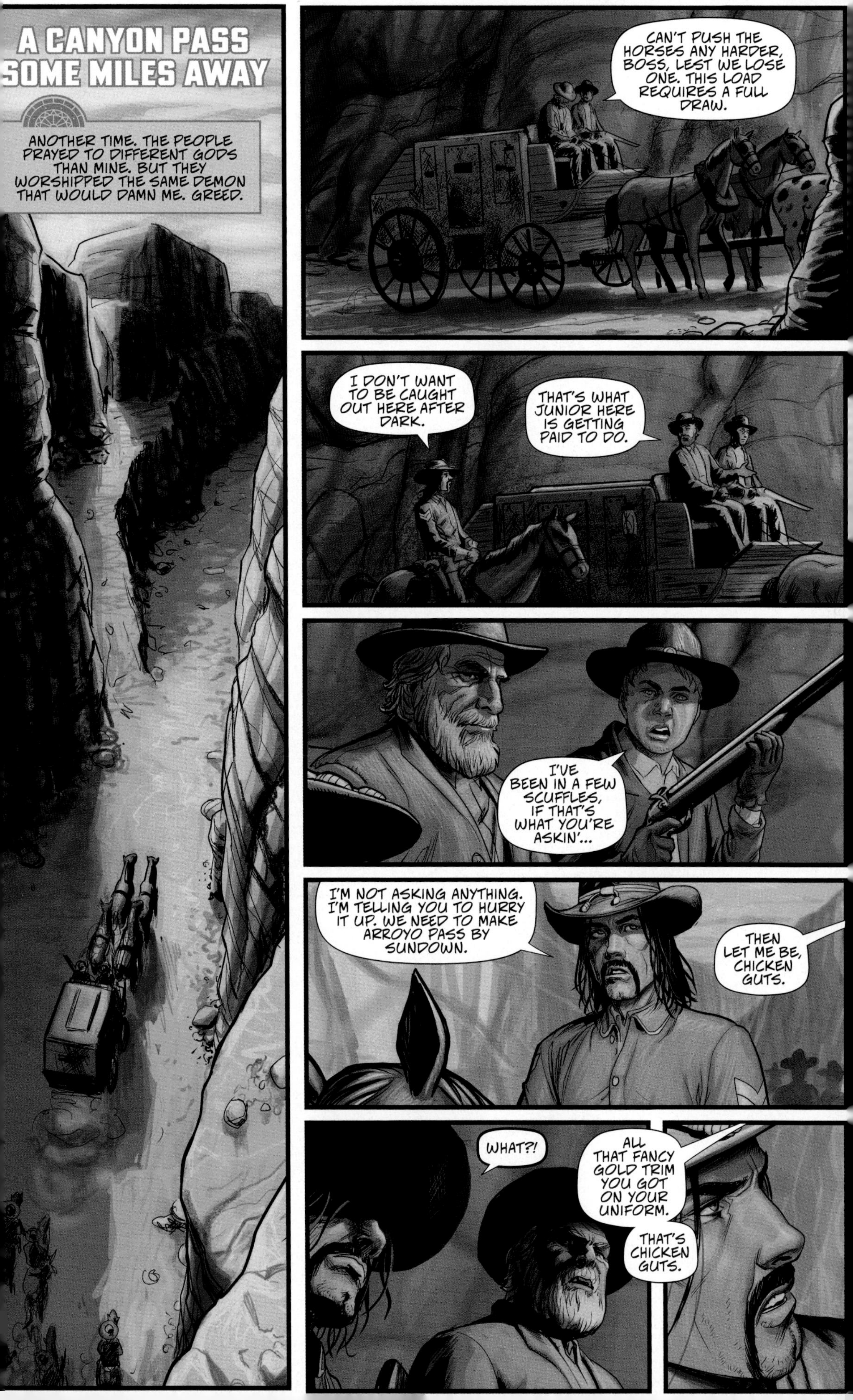
A CANYON PASS SOME MILES AWAY
ANOTHER TIME. THE PEOPLE PRAYED TO DIFFERENT GODS THAN MINE. BUT THEY WORSHIPPED THE SAME DEMON THAT WOULD DAMN ME. GREED.
CAN'T PUSH THE HORSES ANY HARDER, BOSS, LEST WE LOSE ONE. THIS LOAD REQUIRES A FULL DRAW.
I DON'T WANT TO BE CAUGHT OUT HERE AFTER DARK.
THAT'S WHAT JUNIOR HERE IS GETTING PAID TO DO.
I'VE BEEN IN A FEW SCUFFLES, IF THAT'S WHAT YOU'RE ASKIN'...
I'M NOT ASKING ANYTHING. I'M TELLING YOU TO HURRY IT UP. WE NEED TO MAKE ARROYO PASS BY SUNDOWN.
THEN LET ME BE, CHICKEN GUTS.
WHAT?!
ALL THAT FANCY GOLD TRIM YOU GOT ON YOUR UNIFORM.
THAT'S CHICKEN GUTS.

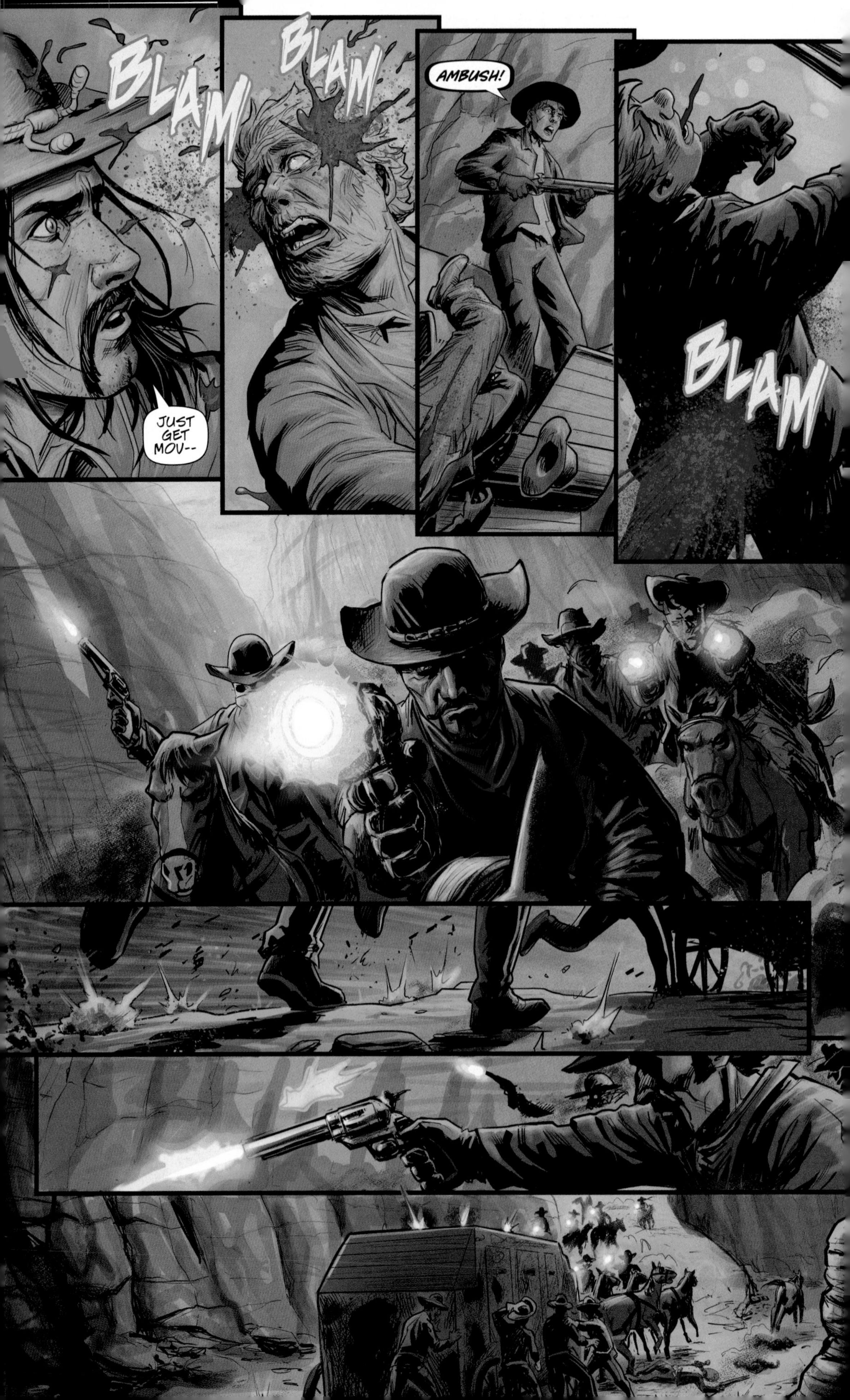
BLAM
JUST GET MOU--
BLAM
AMBUSH!
BLAM

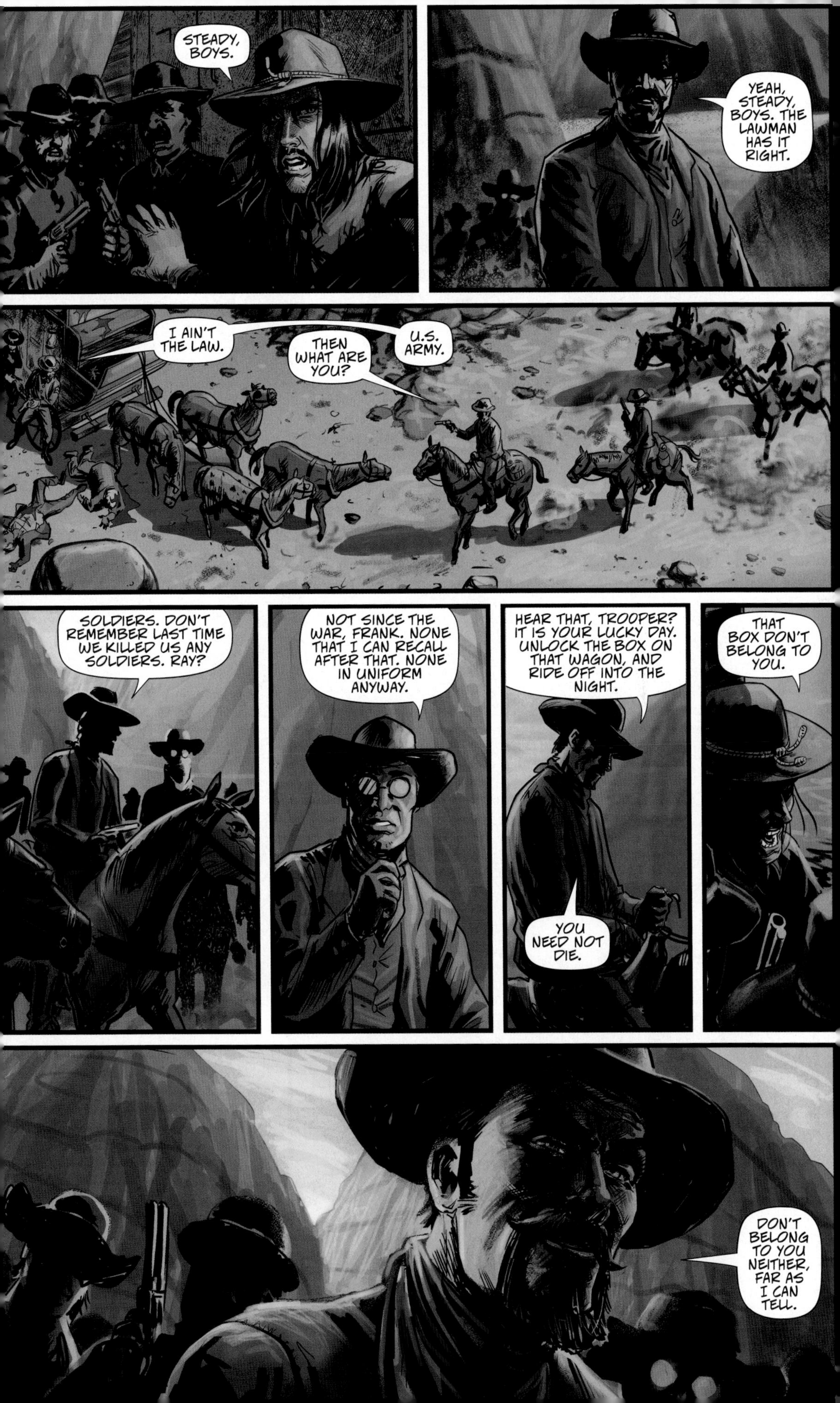
STEADY, BOYS.
YEAH, STEADY, BOYS. THE LAWMAN HAS IT RIGHT.
I AIN'T THE LAW.
THEN WHAT ARE YOU?
U.S. ARMY.
SOLDIERS. DON'T REMEMBER LAST TIME WE KILLED US ANY SOLDIERS. RAY?
NOT SINCE THE WAR, FRANK. NONE THAT I CAN RECALL AFTER THAT. NONE IN UNIFORM ANYWAY.
HEAR THAT, TROOPER? IT IS YOUR LUCKY DAY. UNLOCK THE BOX ON THAT WAGON, AND RIDE OFF INTO THE NIGHT.
YOU NEED NOT DIE.
THAT BOX DON'T BELONG TO YOU.
DON'T BELONG TO YOU NEITHER, FAR AS I CAN TELL.

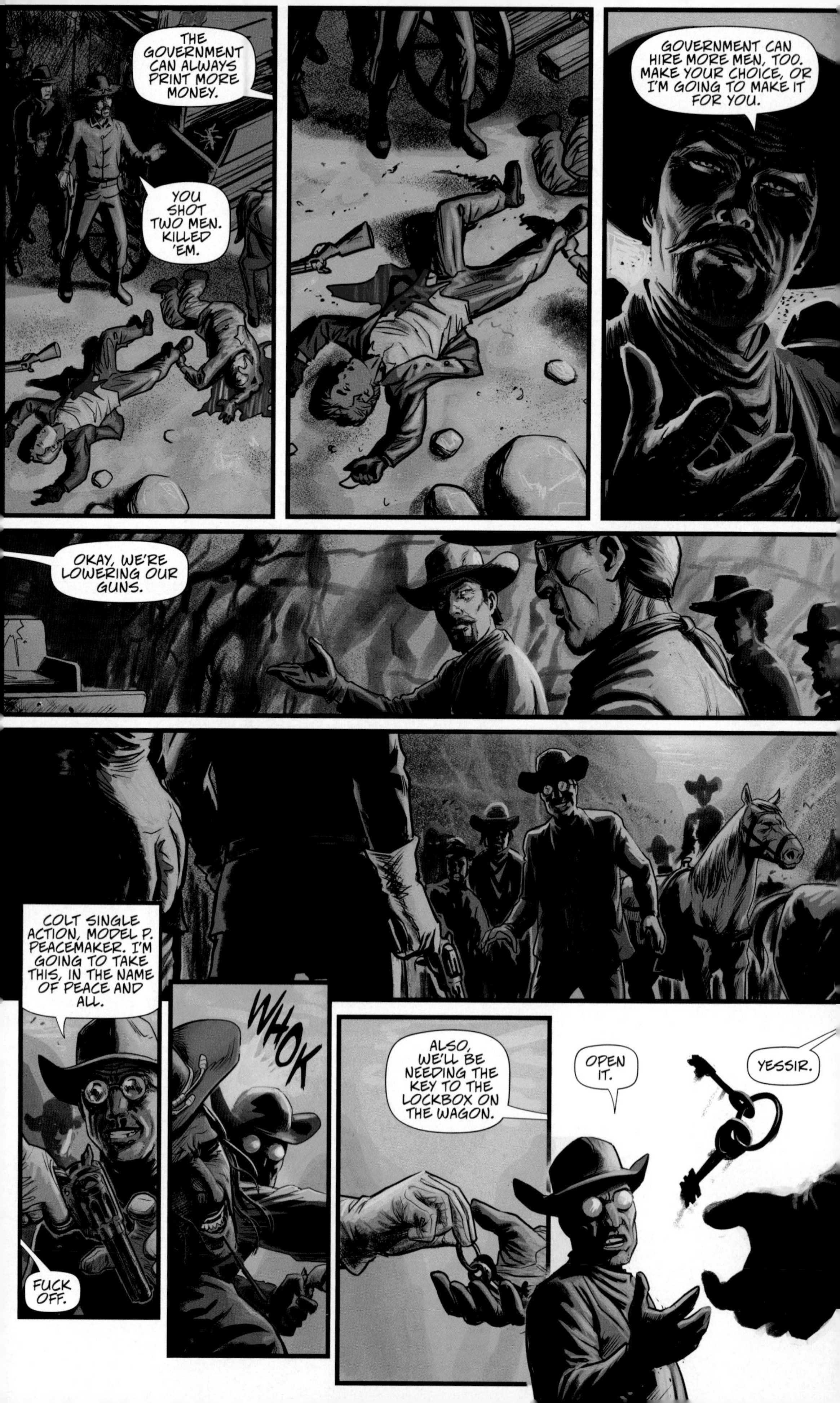
THE GOVERNMENT CAN ALWAYS PRINT MORE MONEY.
YOU SHOT TWO MEN. KILLED 'EM.
GOVERNMENT CAN HIRE MORE MEN, TOO. MAKE YOUR CHOICE, OR I'M GOING TO MAKE IT FOR YOU.
OKAY, WE'RE LOWERING OUR GUNS.
COLT SINGLE ACTION, MODEL P. PEACEMAKER. I'M GOING TO TAKE THIS, IN THE NAME OF PEACE AND ALL.
FUCK OFF.
WHOK
ALSO, WE'LL BE NEEDING THE KEY TO THE LOCKBOX ON THE WAGON.
OPEN IT.
YESSIR.

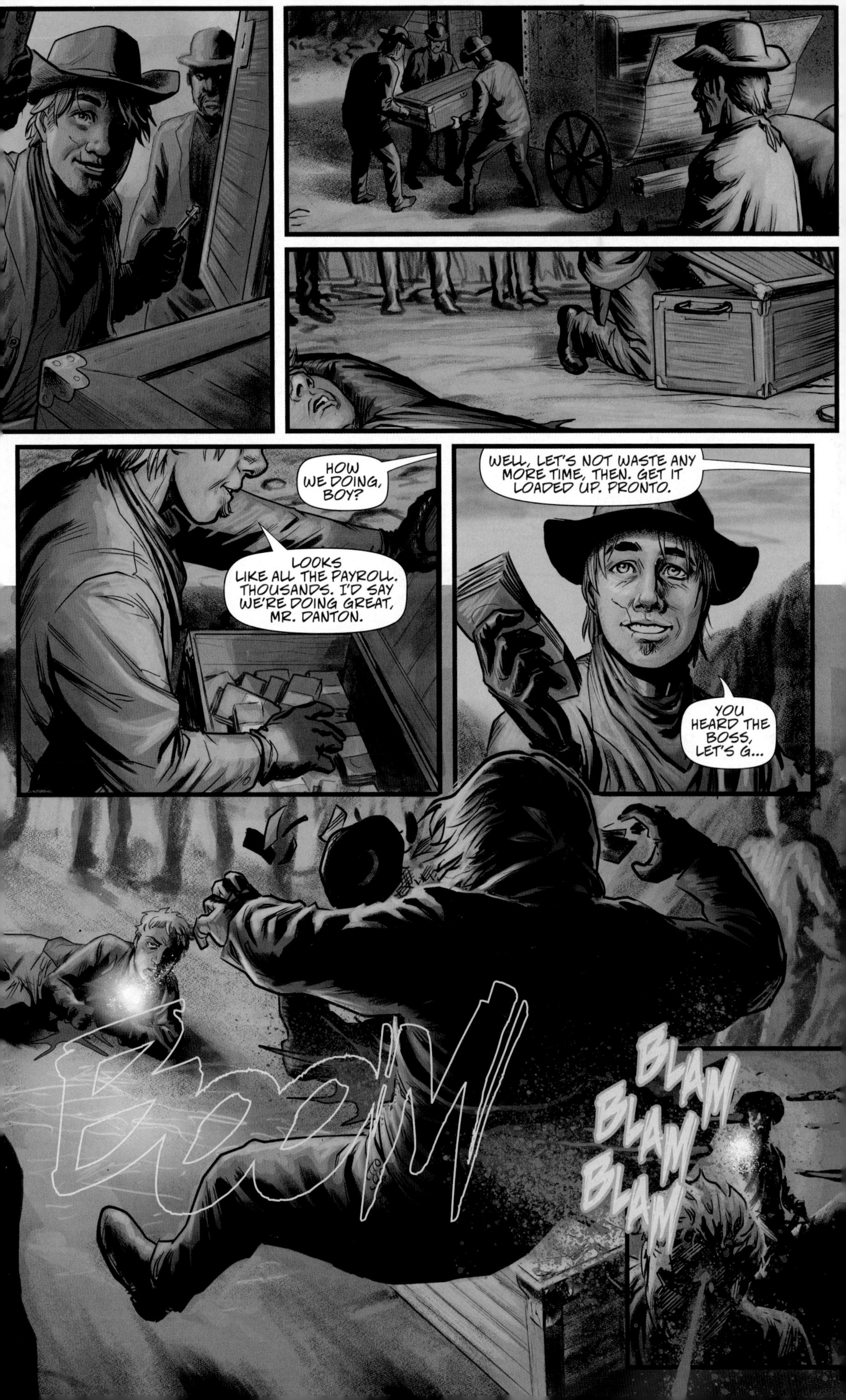
HOW WE DOING, BOY?
LOOKS LIKE ALL THE PAYROLL. THOUSANDS. I'D SAY WE'RE DOING GREAT, MR. DANTON.
WELL, LET'S NOT WASTE ANY MORE TIME, THEN. GET IT LOADED UP. PRONTO.
YOU HEARD THE BOSS, LET'S G...
BOOM
BLAM
BLAM
BLAM

WE THOUGHT HE WAS DEAD. WE DIDN'T KNOW.

HERE'S THE THING. I BELIEVE YOU.

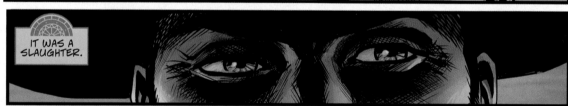

IT WAS A SLAUGHTER.

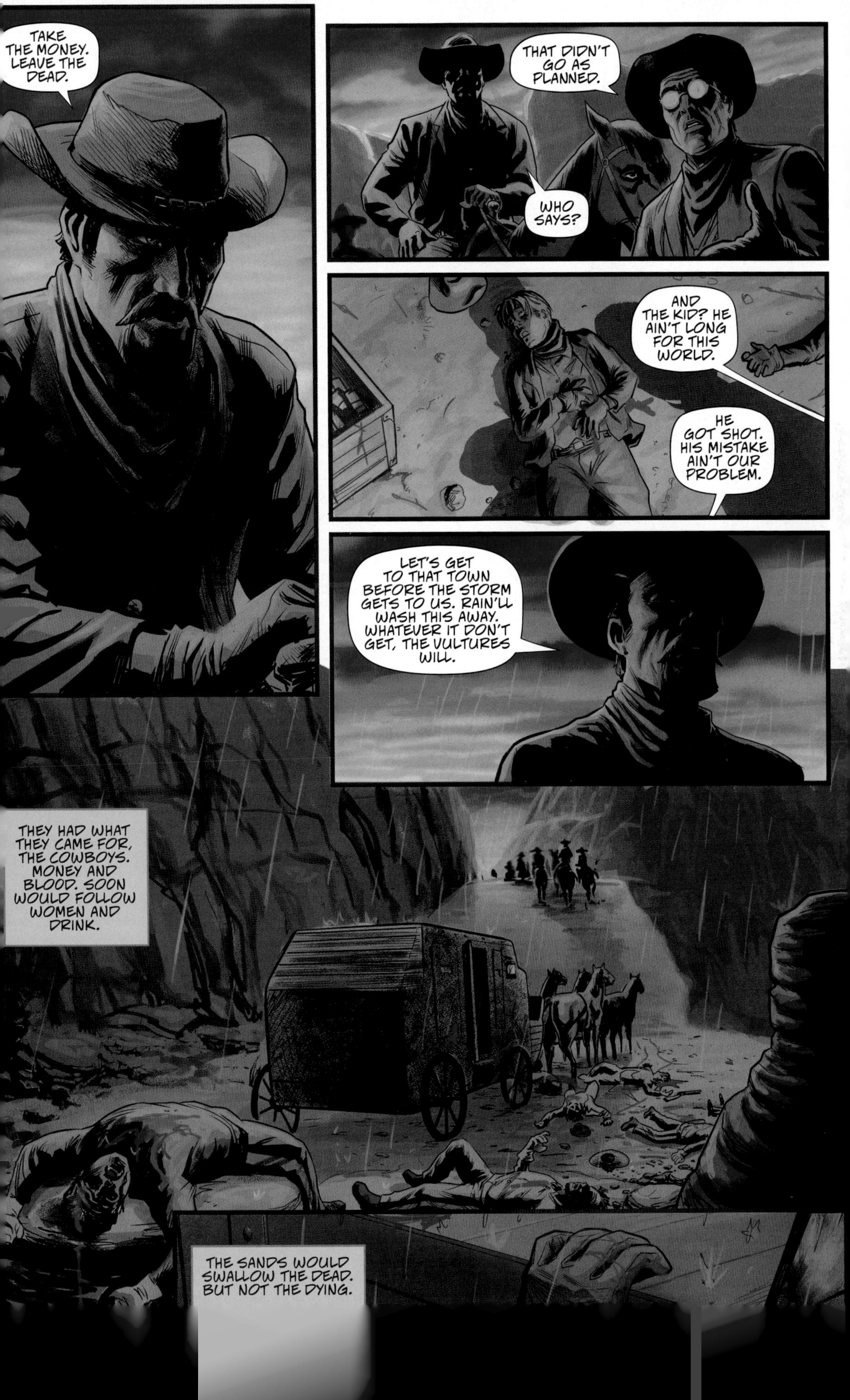
TAKE THE MONEY. LEAVE THE DEAD.
THAT DIDN'T GO AS PLANNED.
WHO SAYS?
AND THE KID? HE AIN'T LONG FOR THIS WORLD.
HE GOT SHOT. HIS MISTAKE AIN'T OUR PROBLEM.
LET'S GET TO THAT TOWN BEFORE THE STORM GETS TO US. RAIN'LL WASH THIS AWAY. WHATEVER IT DON'T GET, THE VULTURES WILL.
THEY HAD WHAT THEY CAME FOR, THE COWBOYS. MONEY AND BLOOD. SOON WOULD FOLLOW WOMEN AND DRINK.
THE SANDS WOULD SWALLOW THE DEAD. BUT NOT THE DYING.

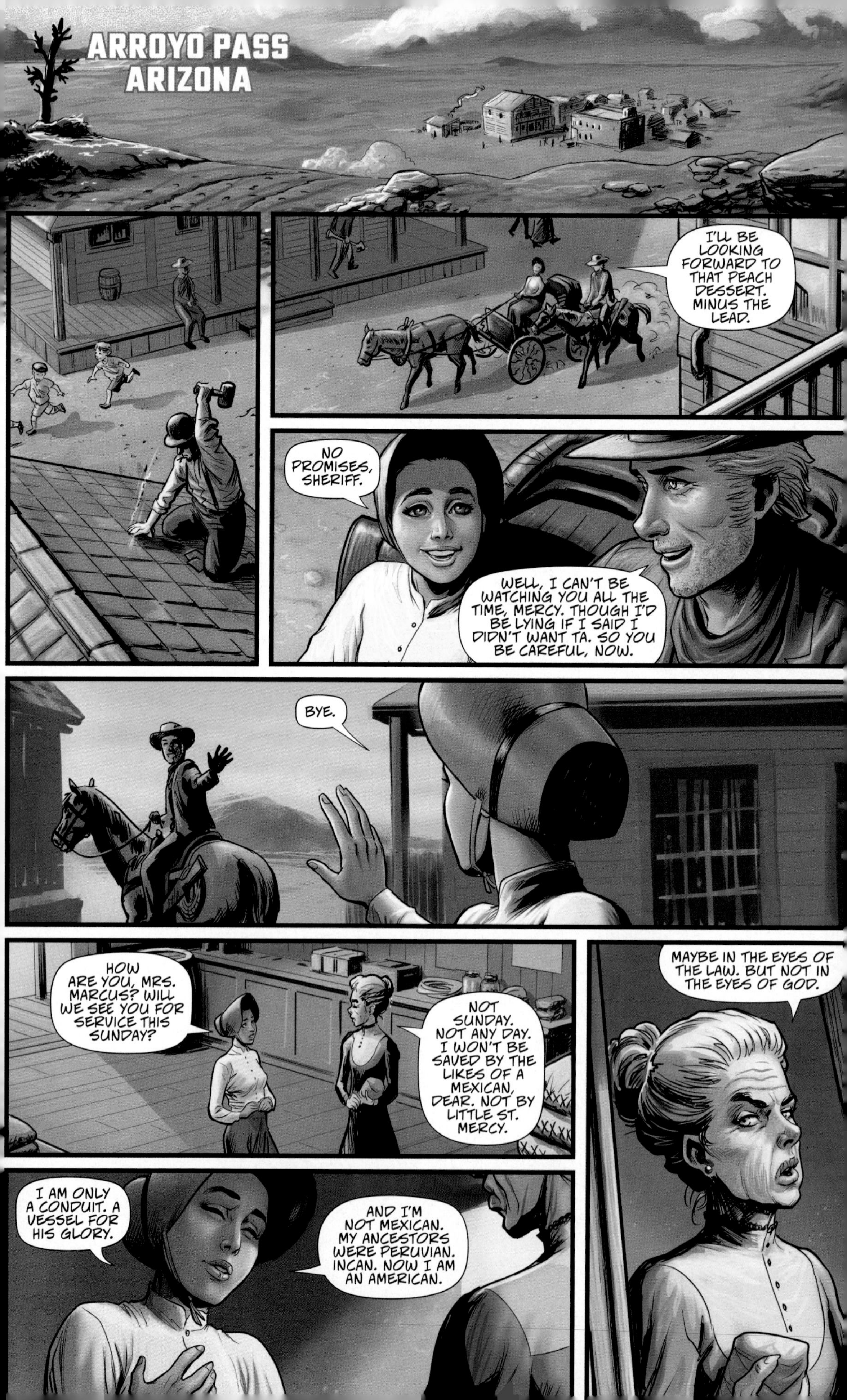
ARROYO PASS ARIZONA
I'LL BE LOOKING FORWARD TO THAT PEACH DESSERT. MINUS THE LEAD.
NO PROMISES, SHERIFF.
WELL, I CAN'T BE WATCHING YOU ALL THE TIME, MERCY. THOUGH I'D BE LYING IF I SAID I DIDN'T WANT TA. SO YOU BE CAREFUL, NOW.
BYE.
HOW ARE YOU, MRS. MARCUS? WILL WE SEE YOU FOR SERVICE THIS SUNDAY?
NOT SUNDAY. NOT ANY DAY. I WON'T BE SAVED BY THE LIKES OF A MEXICAN, DEAR. NOT BY LITTLE ST. MERCY.
I AM ONLY A CONDUIT. A VESSEL FOR HIS GLORY.
AND I'M NOT MEXICAN. MY ANCESTORS WERE PERUVIAN. INCAN. NOW I AM AN AMERICAN.
MAYBE IN THE EYES OF THE LAW. BUT NOT IN THE EYES OF GOD.

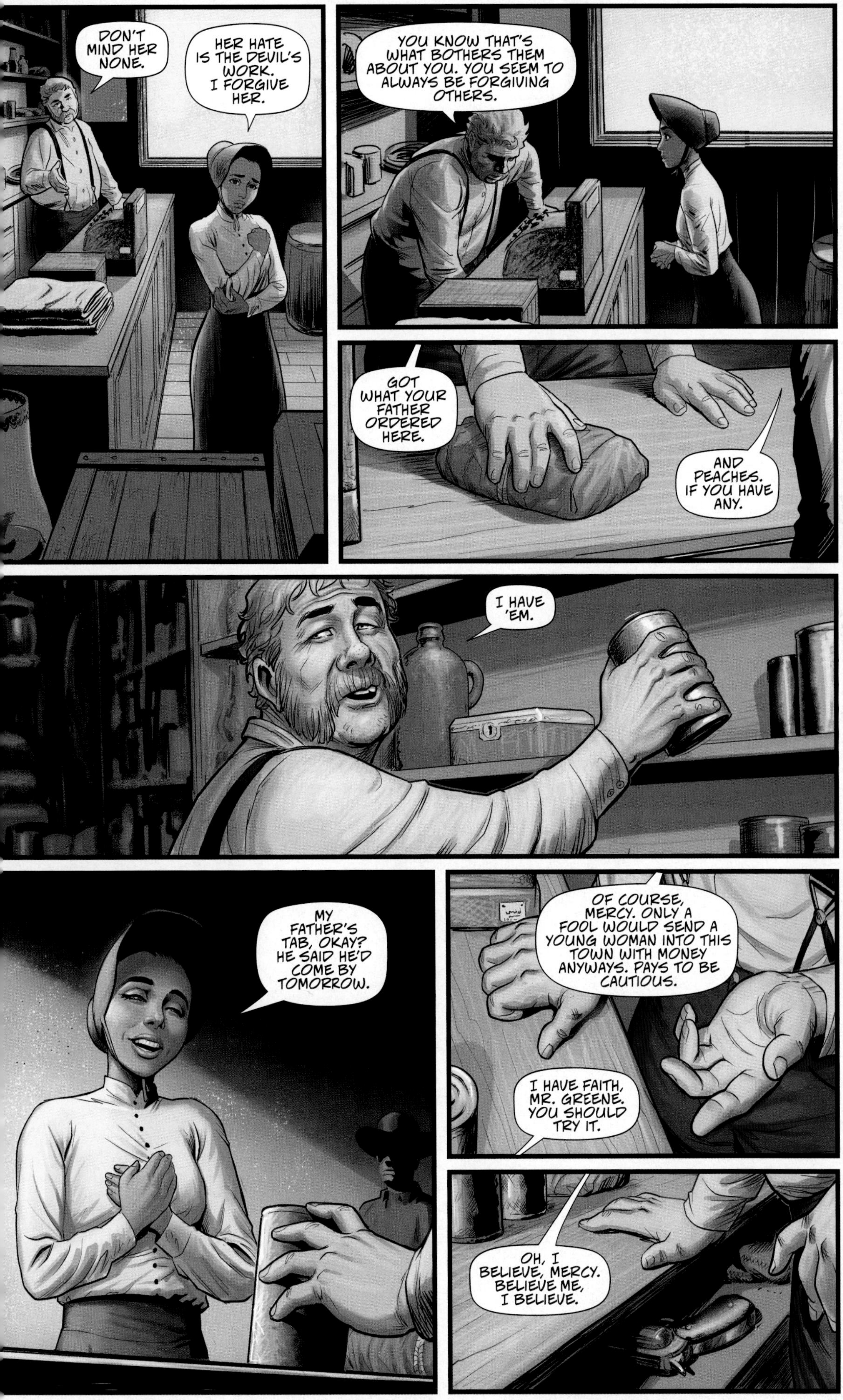
DON'T MIND HER NONE.
HER HATE IS THE DEVIL'S WORK. I FORGIVE HER.
YOU KNOW THAT'S WHAT BOTHERS THEM ABOUT YOU. YOU SEEM TO ALWAYS BE FORGIVING OTHERS.
GOT WHAT YOUR FATHER ORDERED HERE.
AND PEACHES. IF YOU HAVE ANY.
I HAVE 'EM.
MY FATHER'S TAB, OKAY? HE SAID HE'D COME BY TOMORROW.
OF COURSE, MERCY. ONLY A FOOL WOULD SEND A YOUNG WOMAN INTO THIS TOWN WITH MONEY ANYWAYS. PAYS TO BE CAUTIOUS.
I HAVE FAITH, MR. GREENE. YOU SHOULD TRY IT.
OH, I BELIEVE, MERCY. BELIEVE ME, I BELIEVE.

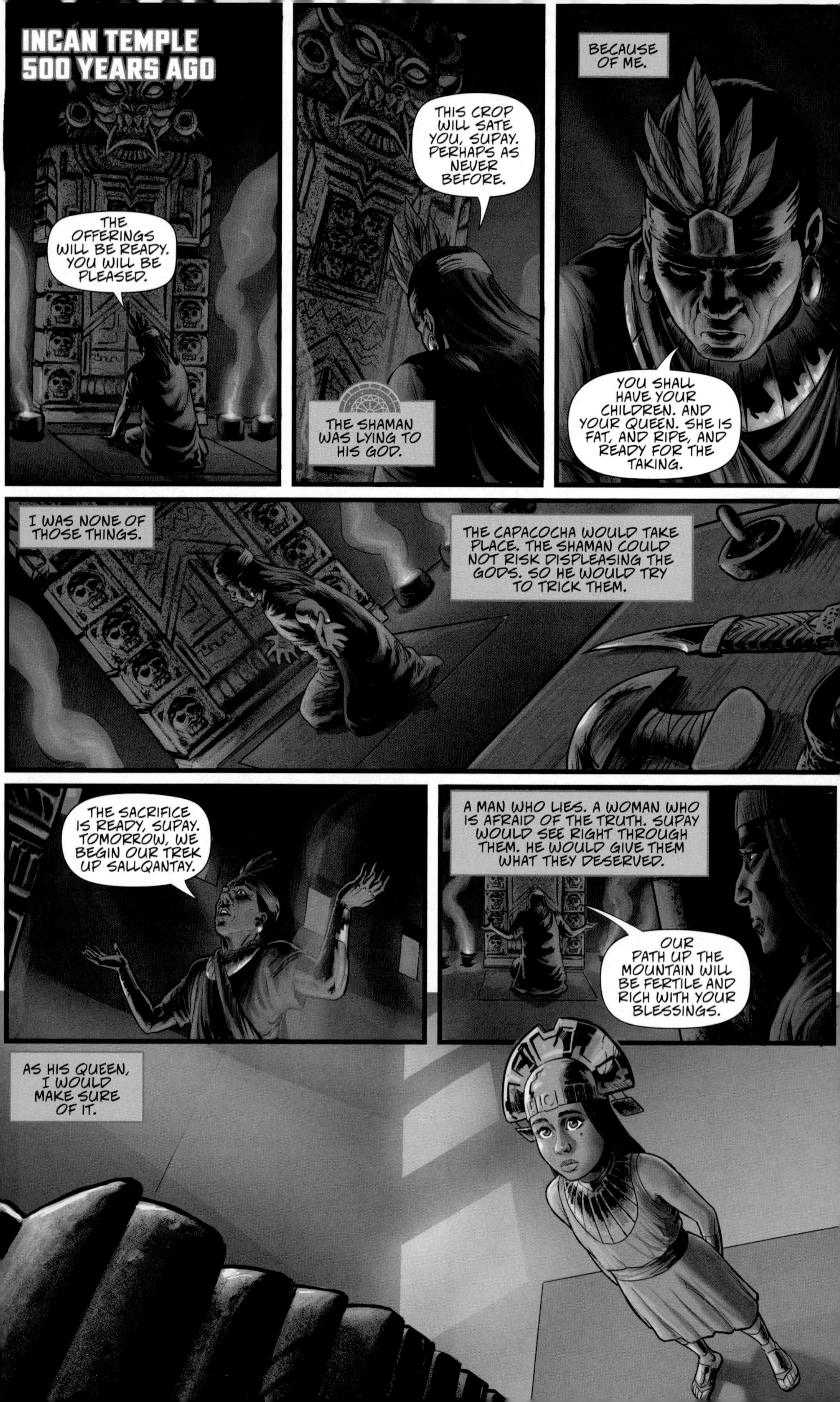
INCAN TEMPLE
500 YEARS AGO
THE OFFERINGS WILL BE READY. YOU WILL BE PLEASED.
THIS CROP WILL SATE YOU, SUPAY. PERHAPS AS NEVER BEFORE.
THE SHAMAN WAS LYING TO HIS GOD.
BECAUSE OF ME.
YOU SHALL HAVE YOUR CHILDREN. AND YOUR QUEEN. SHE IS FAT, AND RIPE, AND READY FOR THE TAKING.
I WAS NONE OF THOSE THINGS.
THE CAPACOCHA WOULD TAKE PLACE. THE SHAMAN COULD NOT RISK DISPLEASING THE GODS. SO HE WOULD TRY TO TRICK THEM.
THE SACRIFICE IS READY, SUPAY. TOMORROW, WE BEGIN OUR TREK UP SALLQANTAY.
A MAN WHO LIES. A WOMAN WHO IS AFRAID OF THE TRUTH. SUPAY WOULD SEE RIGHT THROUGH THEM. HE WOULD GIVE THEM WHAT THEY DESERVED.
OUR PATH UP THE MOUNTAIN WILL BE FERTILE AND RICH WITH YOUR BLESSINGS.
AS HIS QUEEN, I WOULD MAKE SURE OF IT.

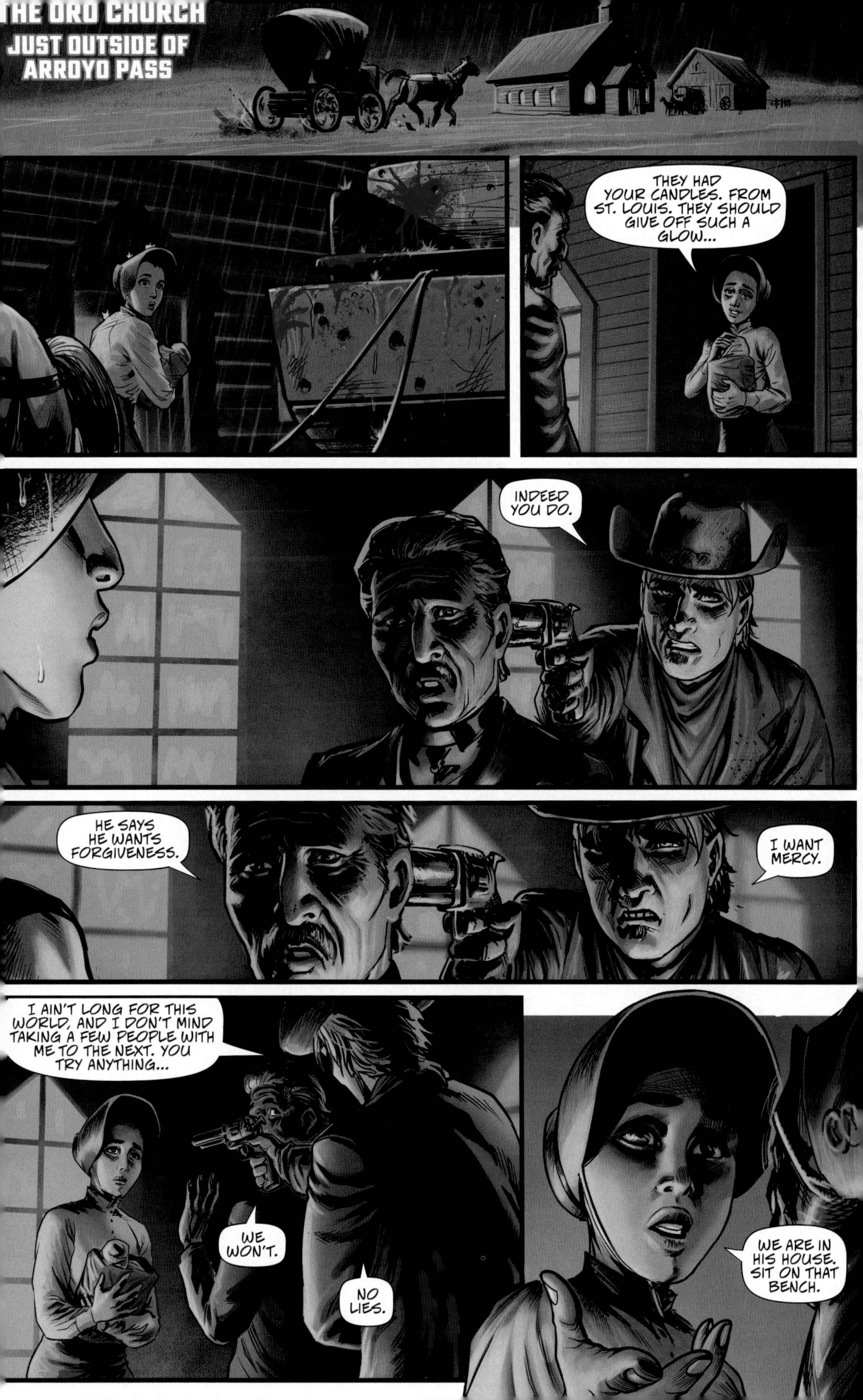
THE ORO CHURCH
JUST OUTSIDE OF ARROYO PASS
THEY HAD YOUR CANDLES. FROM ST. LOUIS. THEY SHOULD GIVE OFF SUCH A GLOW...
INDEED YOU DO.
HE SAYS HE WANTS FORGIVENESS.
I WANT MERCY.
I AIN'T LONG FOR THIS WORLD, AND I DON'T MIND TAKING A FEW PEOPLE WITH ME TO THE NEXT. YOU TRY ANYTHING...
WE WON'T.
NO LIES.
WE ARE IN HIS HOUSE. SIT ON THAT BENCH.

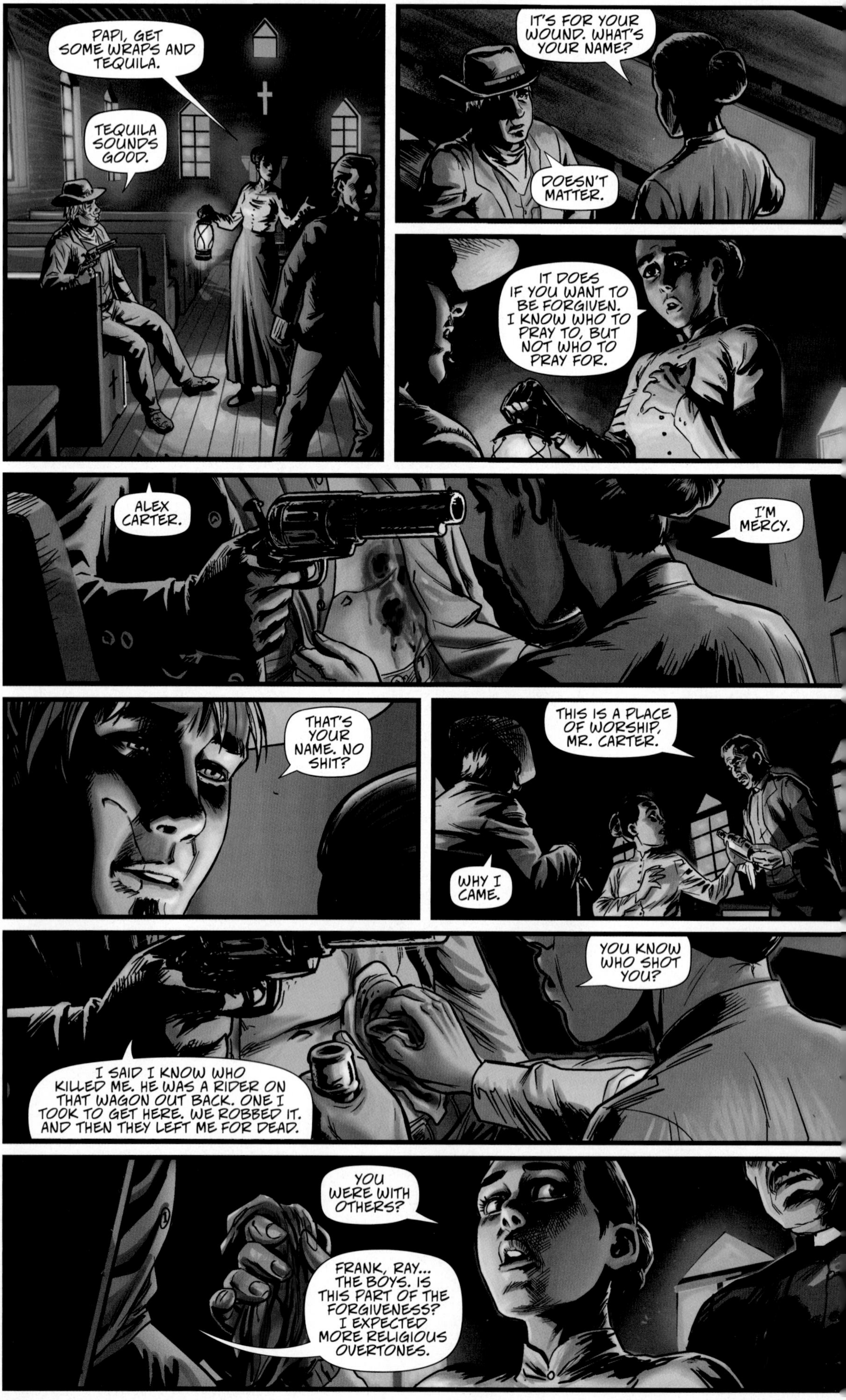
PAPI, GET SOME WRAPS AND TEQUILA.
TEQUILA SOUNDS GOOD.
IT'S FOR YOUR WOUND. WHAT'S YOUR NAME?
DOESN'T MATTER.
IT DOES IF YOU WANT TO BE FORGIVEN. I KNOW WHO TO PRAY TO, BUT NOT WHO TO PRAY FOR.
ALEX CARTER.
I'M MERCY.
THAT'S YOUR NAME. NO SHIT?
THIS IS A PLACE OF WORSHIP, MR. CARTER.
WHY I CAME.
YOU KNOW WHO SHOT YOU?
I SAID I KNOW WHO KILLED ME. HE WAS A RIDER ON THAT WAGON OUT BACK. ONE I TOOK TO GET HERE. WE ROBBED IT. AND THEN THEY LEFT ME FOR DEAD.
YOU WERE WITH OTHERS?
FRANK, RAY... THE BOYS. IS THIS PART OF THE FORGIVENESS? I EXPECTED MORE RELIGIOUS OVERTONES.

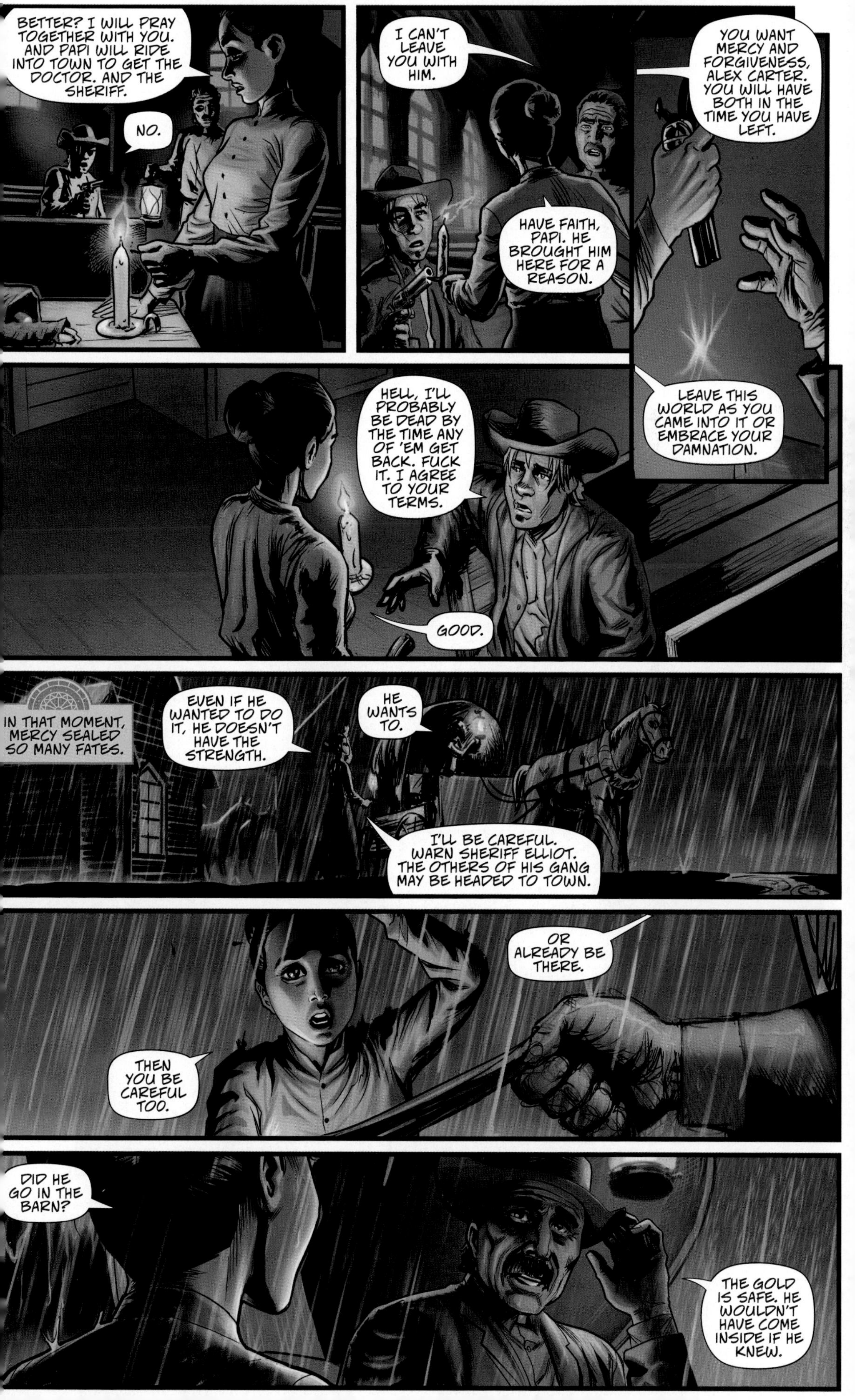
BETTER? I WILL PRAY TOGETHER WITH YOU. AND PAPI WILL RIDE INTO TOWN TO GET THE DOCTOR. AND THE SHERIFF.
NO.
I CAN'T LEAVE YOU WITH HIM.
HAVE FAITH, PAPI. HE BROUGHT HIM HERE FOR A REASON.
YOU WANT MERCY AND FORGIVENESS, ALEX CARTER. YOU WILL HAVE BOTH IN THE TIME YOU HAVE LEFT.
LEAVE THIS WORLD AS YOU CAME INTO IT OR EMBRACE YOUR DAMNATION.
HELL, I'LL PROBABLY BE DEAD BY THE TIME ANY OF 'EM GET BACK. FUCK IT. I AGREE TO YOUR TERMS.
GOOD.
IN THAT MOMENT, MERCY SEALED SO MANY FATES.
EVEN IF HE WANTED TO DO IT, HE DOESN'T HAVE THE STRENGTH.
HE WANTS TO.
I'LL BE CAREFUL. WARN SHERIFF ELLIOT. THE OTHERS OF HIS GANG MAY BE HEADED TO TOWN.
OR ALREADY BE THERE.
THEN YOU BE CAREFUL TOO.
DID HE GO IN THE BARN?
THE GOLD IS SAFE. HE WOULDN'T HAVE COME INSIDE IF HE KNEW.

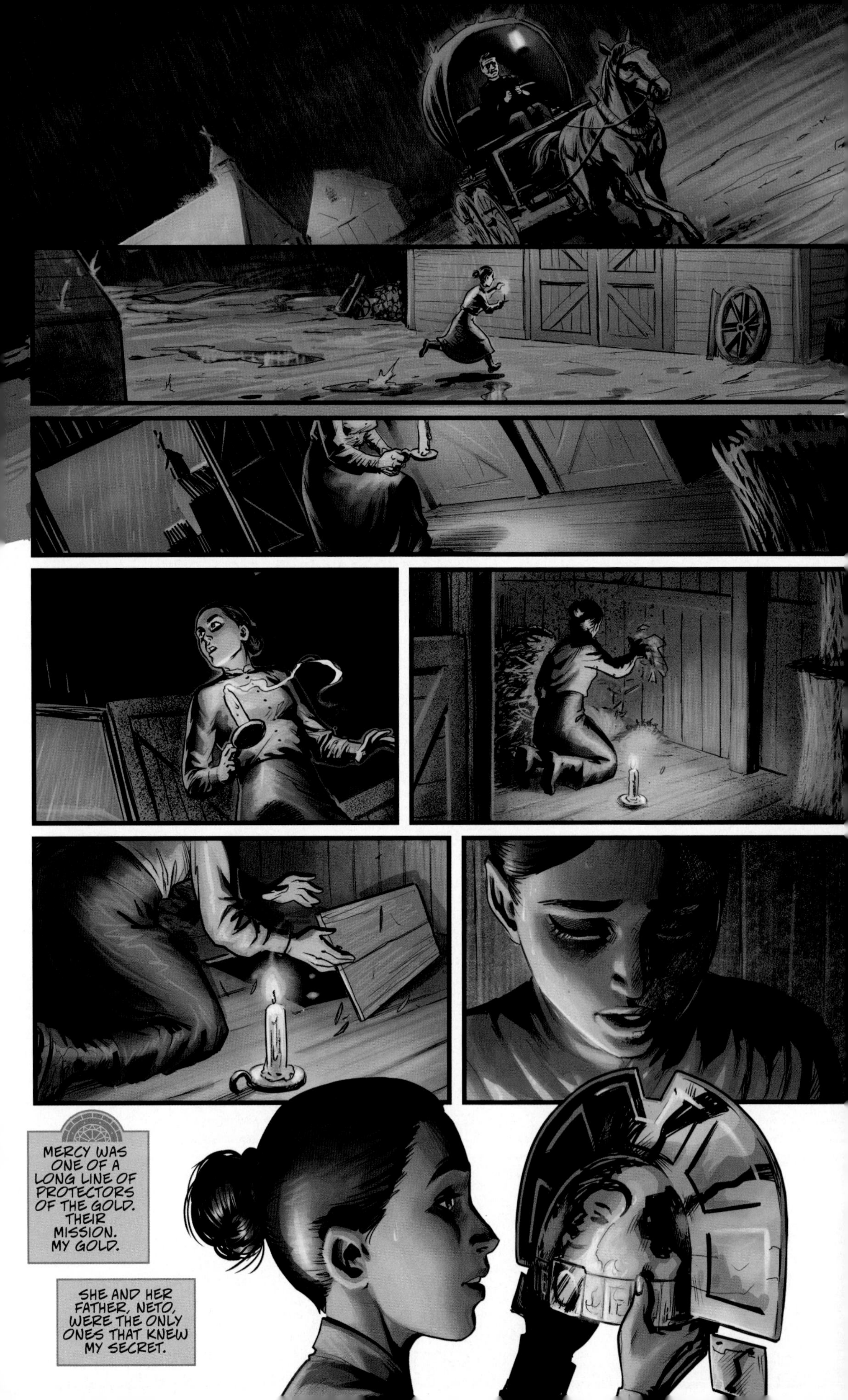
MERCY WAS ONE OF A LONG LINE OF PROTECTORS OF THE GOLD. THEIR MISSION. MY GOLD.
SHE AND HER FATHER, NETO, WERE THE ONLY ONES THAT KNEW MY SECRET.

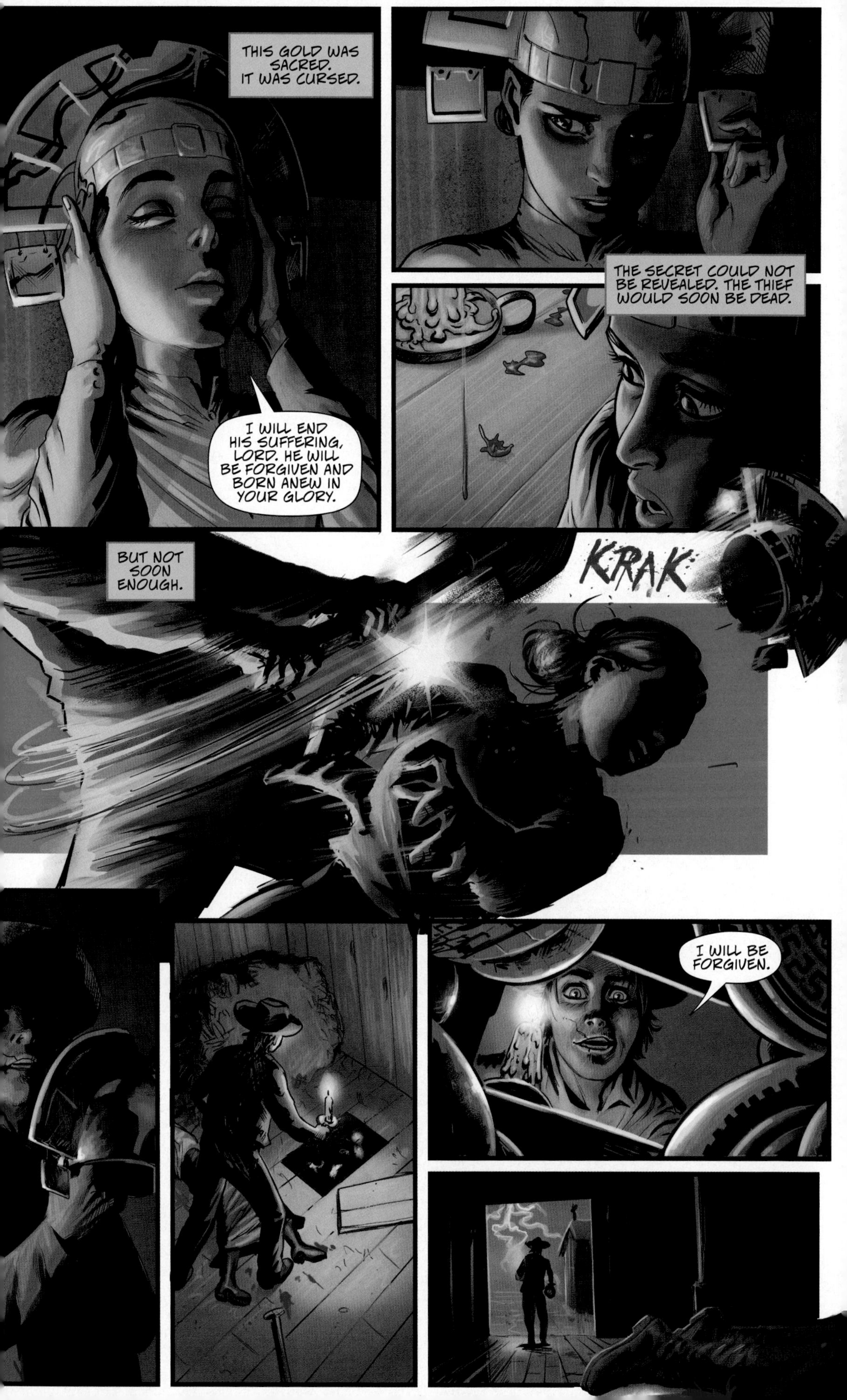

THIS GOLD WAS SACRED. IT WAS CURSED.
I WILL END HIS SUFFERING, LORD. HE WILL BE FORGIVEN AND BORN ANEW IN YOUR GLORY.
THE SECRET COULD NOT BE REVEALED. THE THIEF WOULD SOON BE DEAD.
BUT NOT SOON ENOUGH.
KRAK
I WILL BE FORGIVEN.

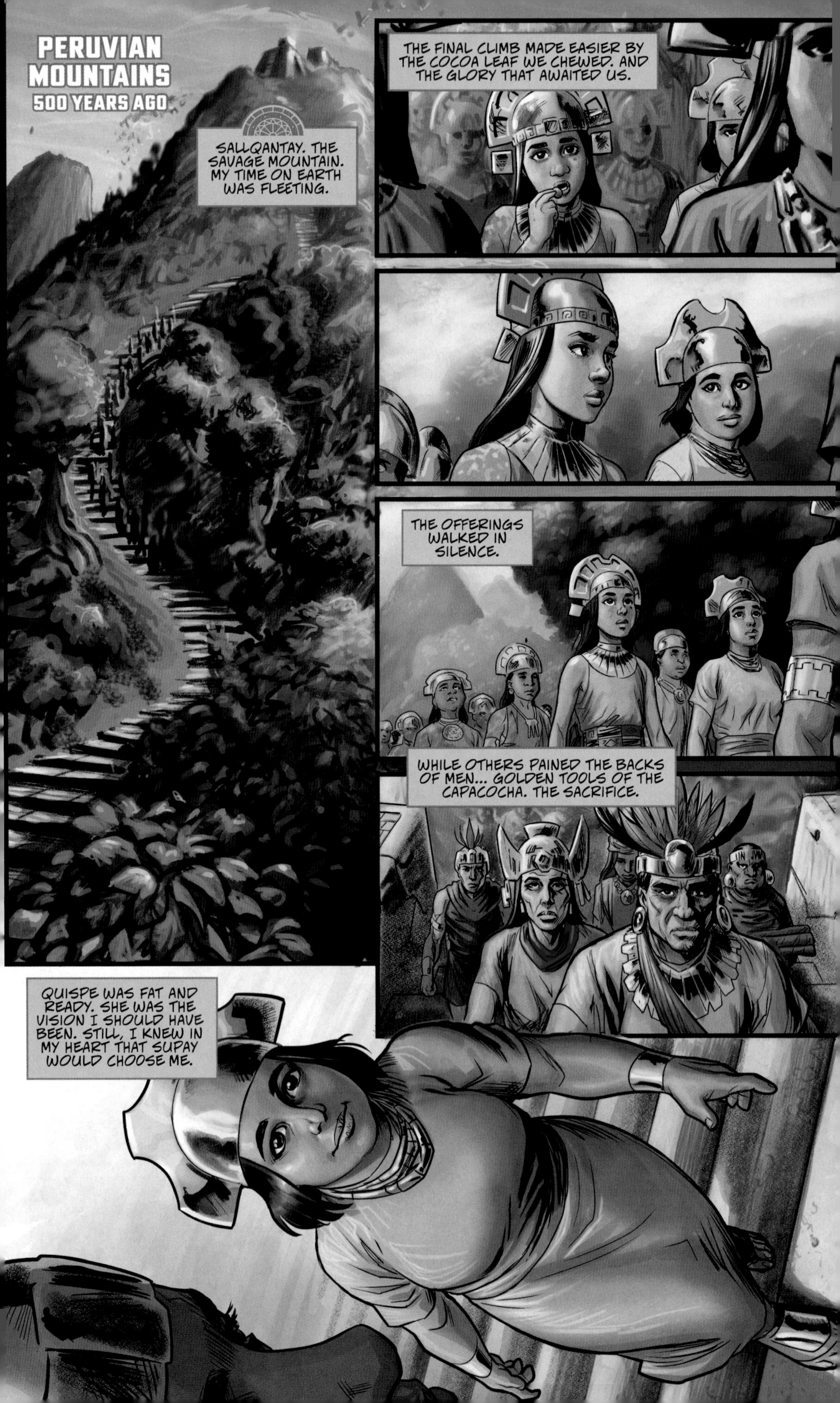
PERUVIAN MOUNTAINS
500 YEARS AGO
SALLQANTAY. THE SAVAGE MOUNTAIN. MY TIME ON EARTH WAS FLEETING.
THE FINAL CLIMB MADE EASIER BY THE COCOA LEAF WE CHEWED. AND THE GLORY THAT AWAITED US.
THE OFFERINGS WALKED IN SILENCE.
WHILE OTHERS PAINED THE BACKS OF MEN... GOLDEN TOOLS OF THE CAPACOCHA. THE SACRIFICE.
QUISPE WAS FAT AND READY. SHE WAS THE VISION I SHOULD HAVE BEEN. STILL, I KNEW IN MY HEART THAT SUPAY WOULD CHOOSE ME.

BECAUSE MORE THAN ANYTHING, I BELIEVED. I HAD PREPARED MYSELF FOR THIS MOMENT. I WAS THE ONE THAT WOULD SATISFY THE GOD AND SAVE MY PEOPLE. I WASN'T AFRAID.

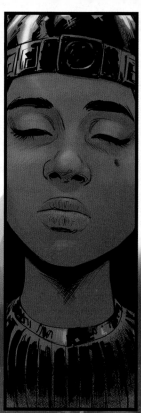

BUT I WAS WRONG.

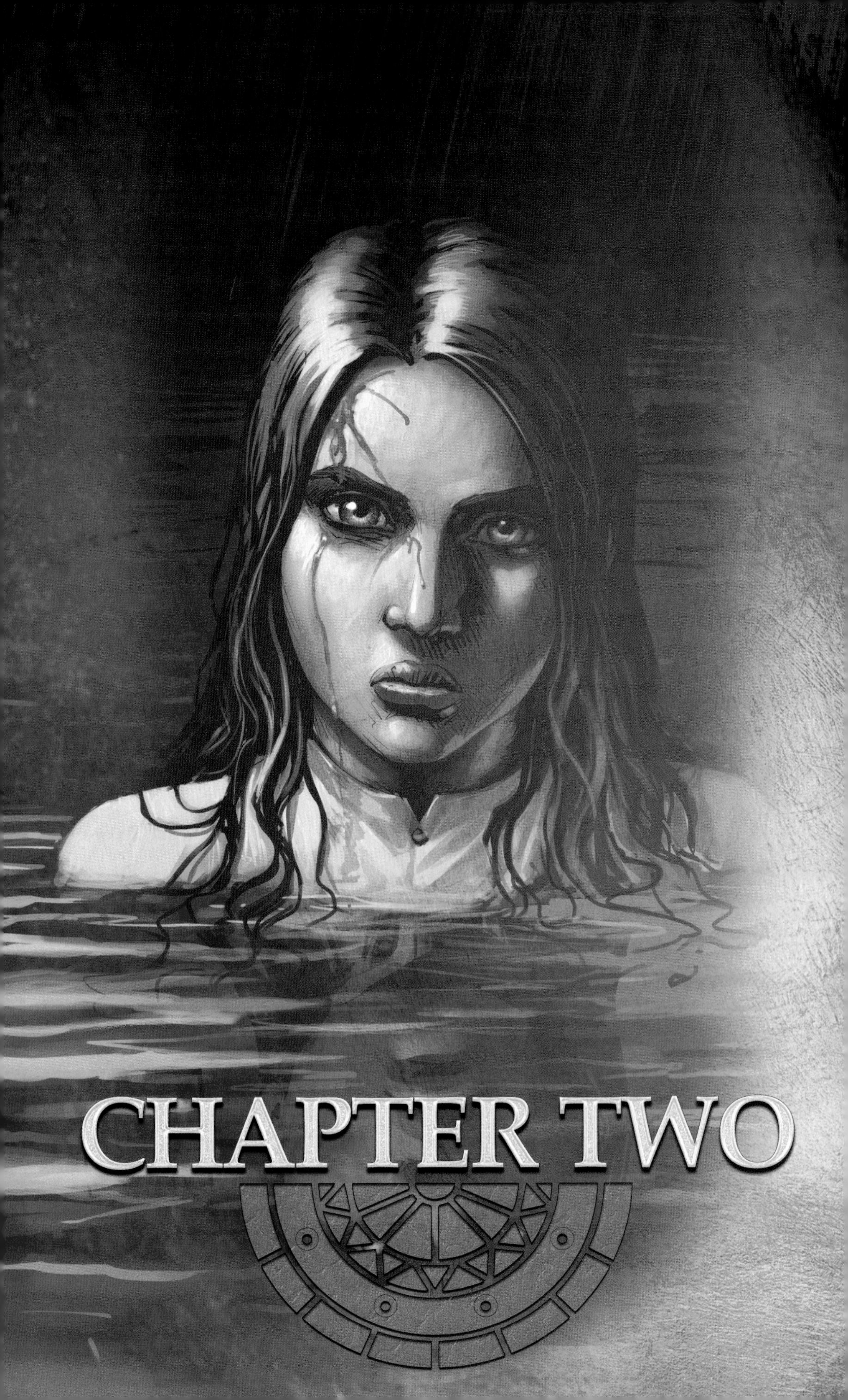
CHAPTER TWO

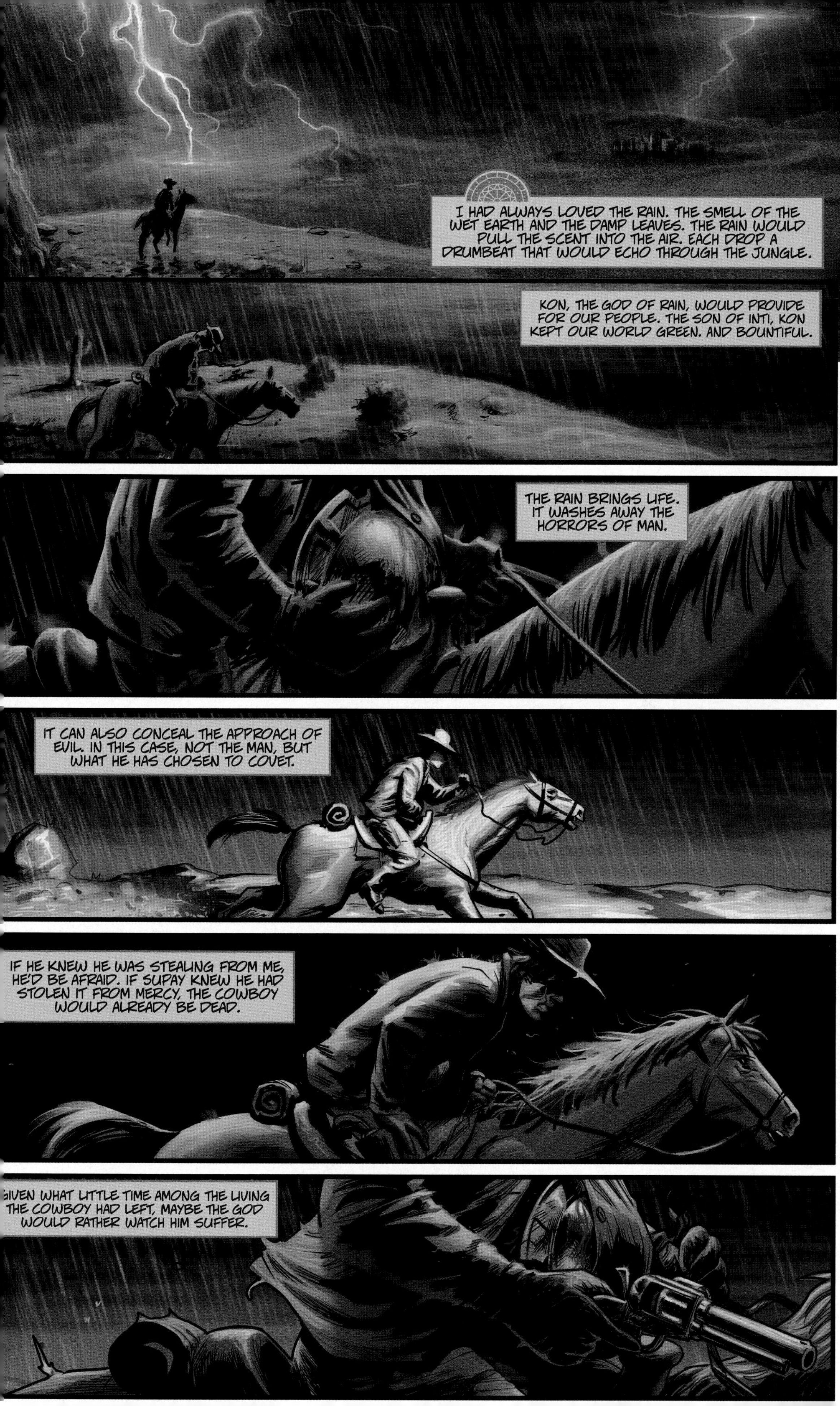
I HAD ALWAYS LOVED THE RAIN. THE SMELL OF THE WET EARTH AND THE DAMP LEAVES. THE RAIN WOULD PULL THE SCENT INTO THE AIR. EACH DROP A DRUMBEAT THAT WOULD ECHO THROUGH THE JUNGLE.
KON, THE GOD OF RAIN, WOULD PROVIDE FOR OUR PEOPLE. THE SON OF INTI, KON KEPT OUR WORLD GREEN. AND BOUNTIFUL.
THE RAIN BRINGS LIFE. IT WASHES AWAY THE HORRORS OF MAN.
IT CAN ALSO CONCEAL THE APPROACH OF EVIL. IN THIS CASE, NOT THE MAN, BUT WHAT HE HAS CHOSEN TO COVET.
IF HE KNEW HE WAS STEALING FROM ME, HE'D BE AFRAID. IF SUPAY KNEW HE HAD STOLEN IT FROM MERCY, THE COWBOY WOULD ALREADY BE DEAD.
GIVEN WHAT LITTLE TIME AMONG THE LIVING THE COWBOY HAD LEFT, MAYBE THE GOD WOULD RATHER WATCH HIM SUFFER.

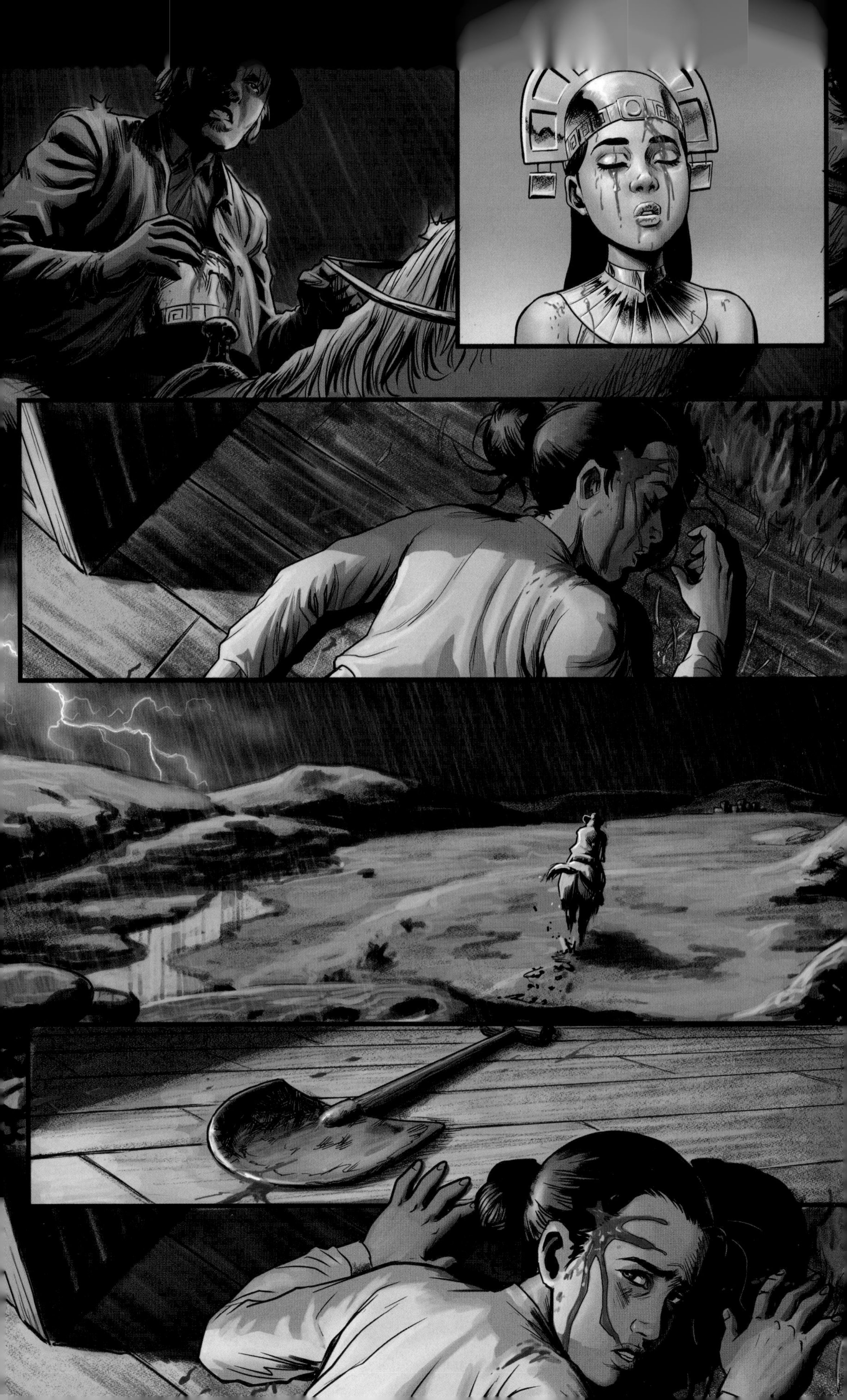

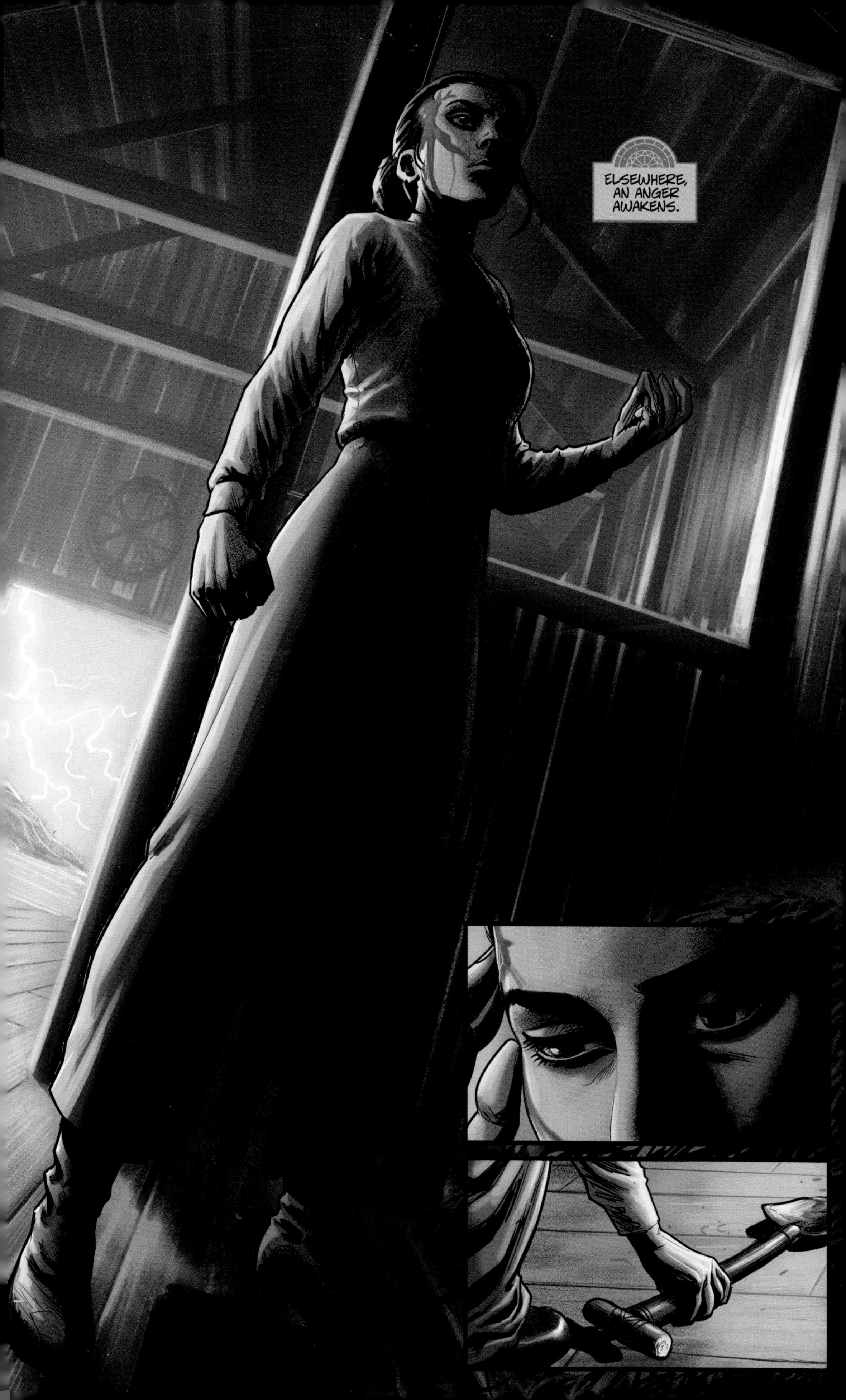
ELSEWHERE, AN ANGER AWAKENS.

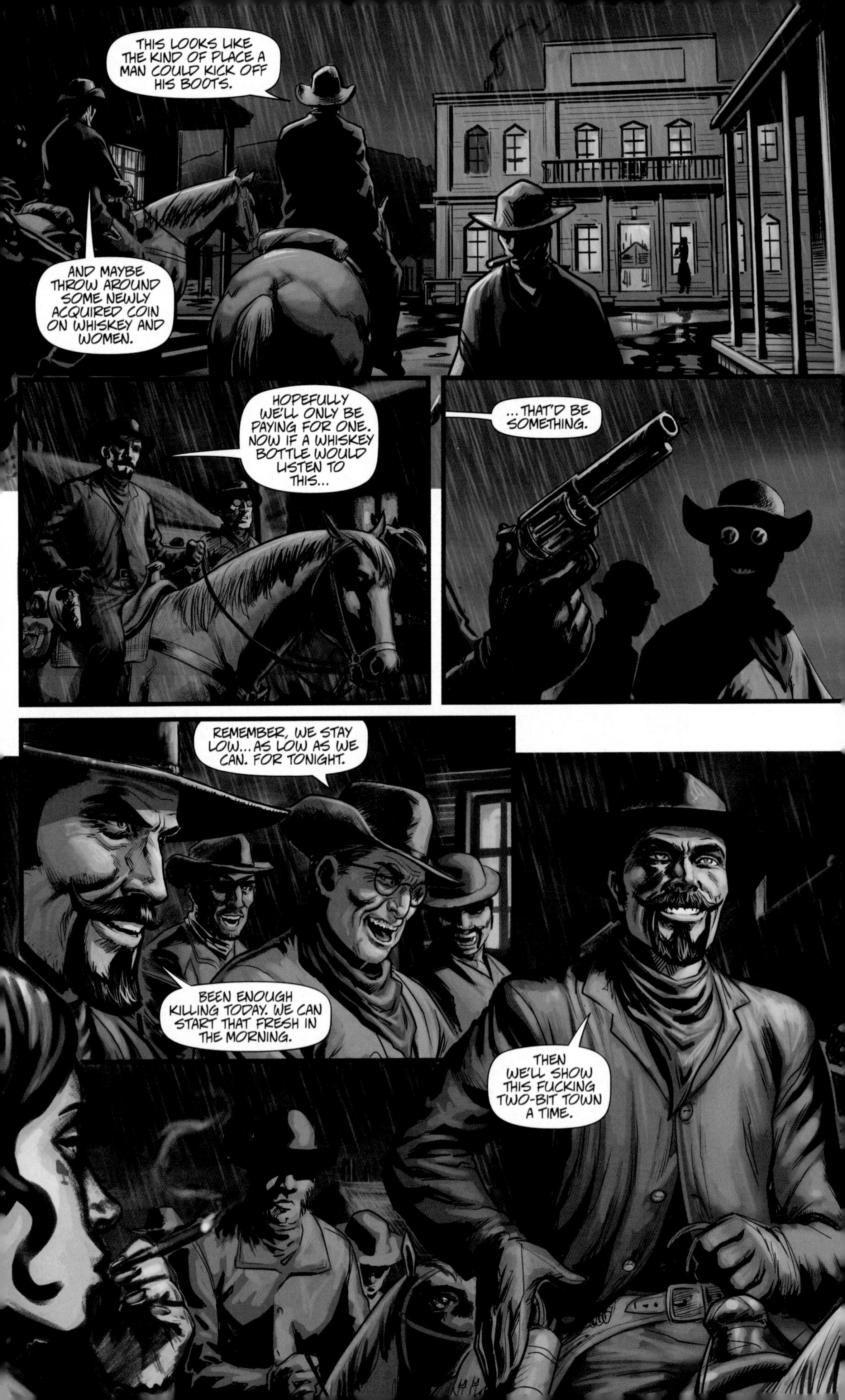
THIS LOOKS LIKE THE KIND OF PLACE A MAN COULD KICK OFF HIS BOOTS.
AND MAYBE THROW AROUND SOME NEWLY ACQUIRED COIN ON WHISKEY AND WOMEN.
HOPEFULLY WE'LL ONLY BE PAYING FOR ONE. NOW IF A WHISKEY BOTTLE WOULD LISTEN TO THIS...
...THAT'D BE SOMETHING.
REMEMBER, WE STAY LOW...AS LOW AS WE CAN. FOR TONIGHT.
BEEN ENOUGH KILLING TODAY. WE CAN START THAT FRESH IN THE MORNING.
THEN WE'LL SHOW THIS FUCKING TWO-BIT TOWN A TIME.

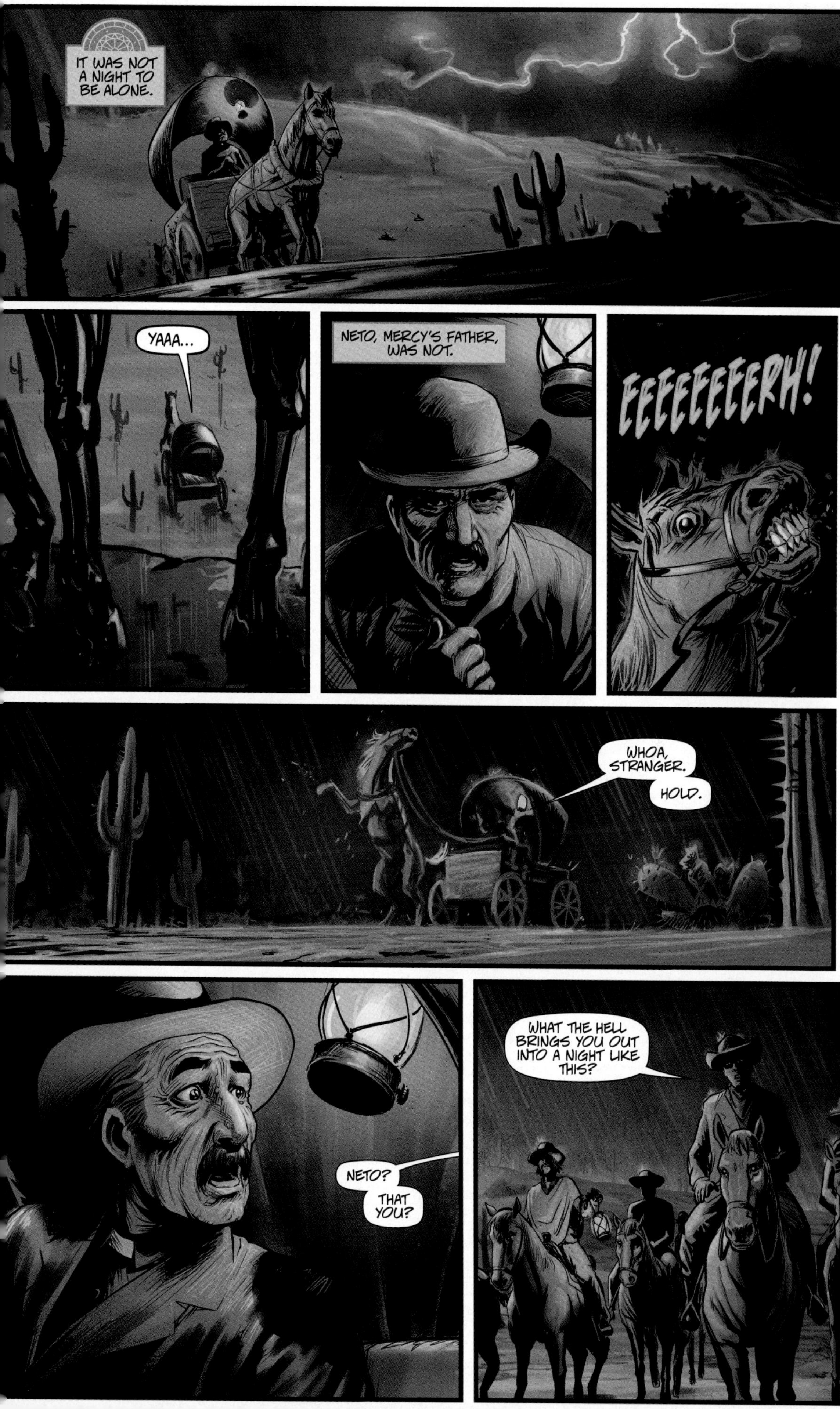

IT WAS NOT A NIGHT TO BE ALONE.
YAAA...
NETO, MERCY'S FATHER, WAS NOT.
EEEEEEEERH!
WHOA, STRANGER.
HOLD.
NETO?
THAT YOU?
WHAT THE HELL BRINGS YOU OUT INTO A NIGHT LIKE THIS?

SHERIFF?

ONE AND THE SAME.

THANK GOD. HE IS WITH ME.

I'D PREFER NOT TO REPEAT MYSELF, NETO. ABOUT THE REASON YOU'RE OUT, I MEAN.

THERE IS A MAN... BARELY DONE BEING A BOY. HE'S BEEN SHOT. BAD. GUT STRAIGHT THROUGH. CAME TO THE CHURCH. ASKING ME AND MERCY TO HELP HIM FIND FORGIVENESS.

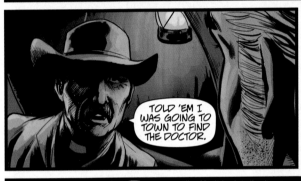

TOLD 'EM I WAS GOING TO TOWN TO FIND THE DOCTOR.

DOC CAN HELP HIM?

NOT LIKELY. TRUTH IS, I WAS COMING FOR YOU.

HE'S GONNA BE ONE OF THE BOYS WE'RE LOOKING FOR.

PAYROLL WAGON GOT HIT EARLIER. WASN'T PRETTY WHAT THEY DONE.

MERCY.

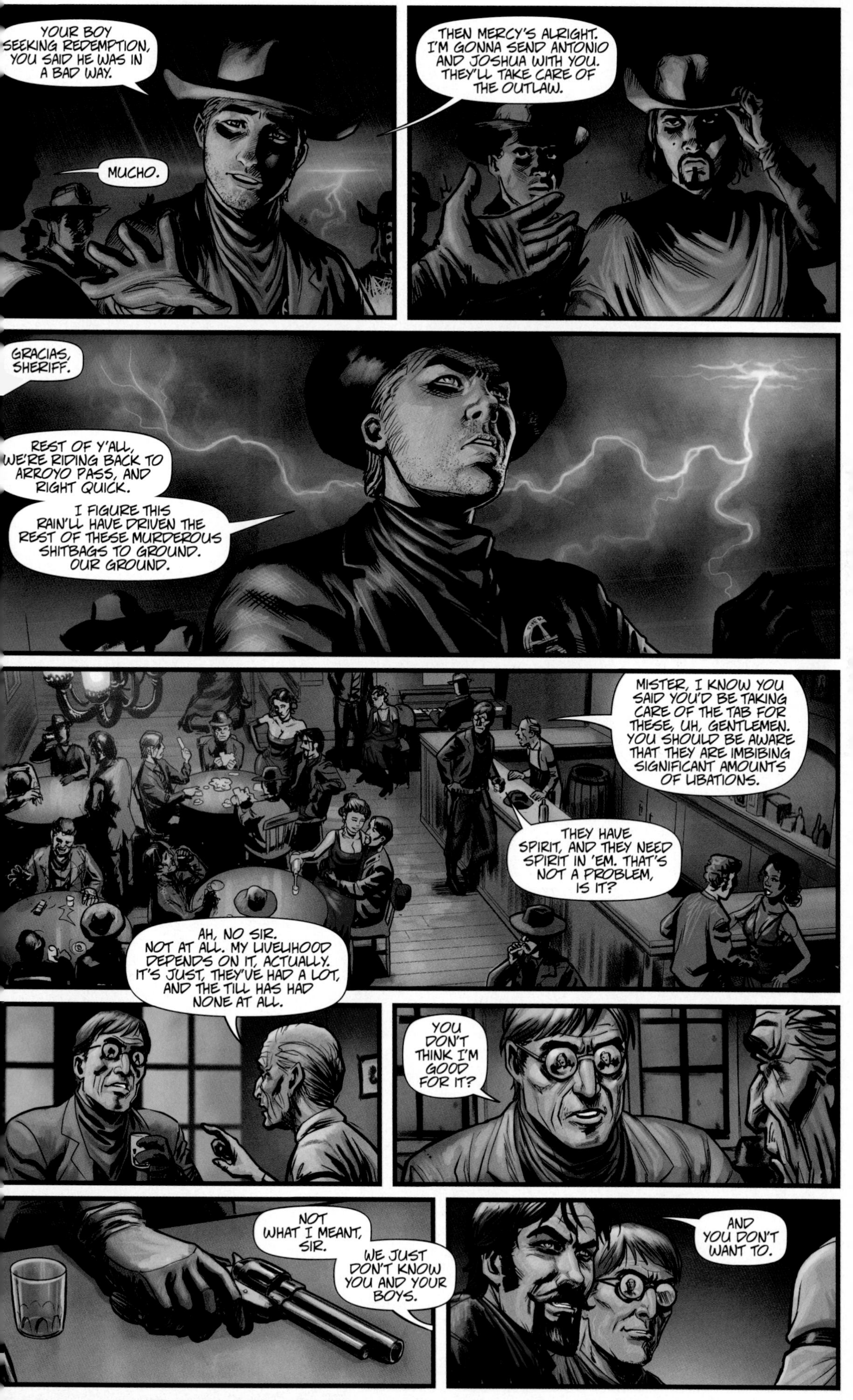
YOUR BOY SEEKING REDEMPTION, YOU SAID HE WAS IN A BAD WAY.
MUCHO.
THEN MERCY'S ALRIGHT. I'M GONNA SEND ANTONIO AND JOSHUA WITH YOU. THEY'LL TAKE CARE OF THE OUTLAW.
GRACIAS, SHERIFF.
REST OF Y'ALL, WE'RE RIDING BACK TO ARROYO PASS, AND RIGHT QUICK.
I FIGURE THIS RAIN'LL HAVE DRIVEN THE REST OF THESE MURDEROUS SHITBAGS TO GROUND. OUR GROUND.
MISTER, I KNOW YOU SAID YOU'D BE TAKING CARE OF THE TAB FOR THESE, UH, GENTLEMEN. YOU SHOULD BE AWARE THAT THEY ARE IMBIBING SIGNIFICANT AMOUNTS OF LIBATIONS.
THEY HAVE SPIRIT, AND THEY NEED SPIRIT IN 'EM. THAT'S NOT A PROBLEM, IS IT?
AH, NO SIR. NOT AT ALL. MY LIVELIHOOD DEPENDS ON IT, ACTUALLY. IT'S JUST, THEY'VE HAD A LOT, AND THE TILL HAS HAD NONE AT ALL.
YOU DON'T THINK I'M GOOD FOR IT?
NOT WHAT I MEANT, SIR.
WE JUST DON'T KNOW YOU AND YOUR BOYS.
AND YOU DON'T WANT TO.

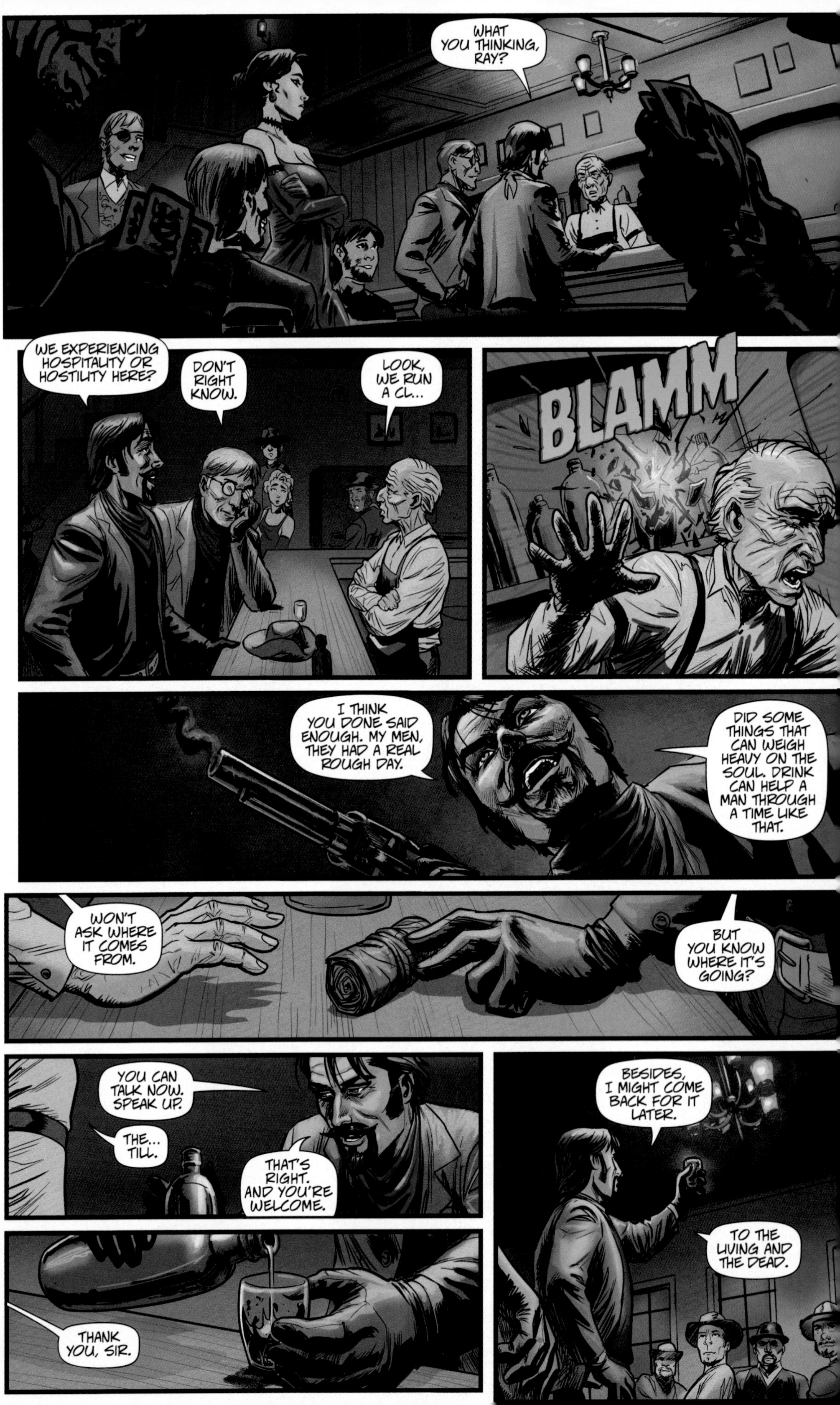
WHAT YOU THINKING, RAY?
WE EXPERIENCING HOSPITALITY OR HOSTILITY HERE?
DON'T RIGHT KNOW.
LOOK, WE RUN A CL...
BLAMM
I THINK YOU DONE SAID ENOUGH. MY MEN, THEY HAD A REAL ROUGH DAY.
DID SOME THINGS THAT CAN WEIGH HEAVY ON THE SOUL. DRINK CAN HELP A MAN THROUGH A TIME LIKE THAT.
WON'T ASK WHERE IT COMES FROM.
BUT YOU KNOW WHERE IT'S GOING?
YOU CAN TALK NOW. SPEAK UP.
THE... TILL.
THAT'S RIGHT. AND YOU'RE WELCOME.
THANK YOU, SIR.
BESIDES, I MIGHT COME BACK FOR IT LATER.
TO THE LIVING AND THE DEAD.

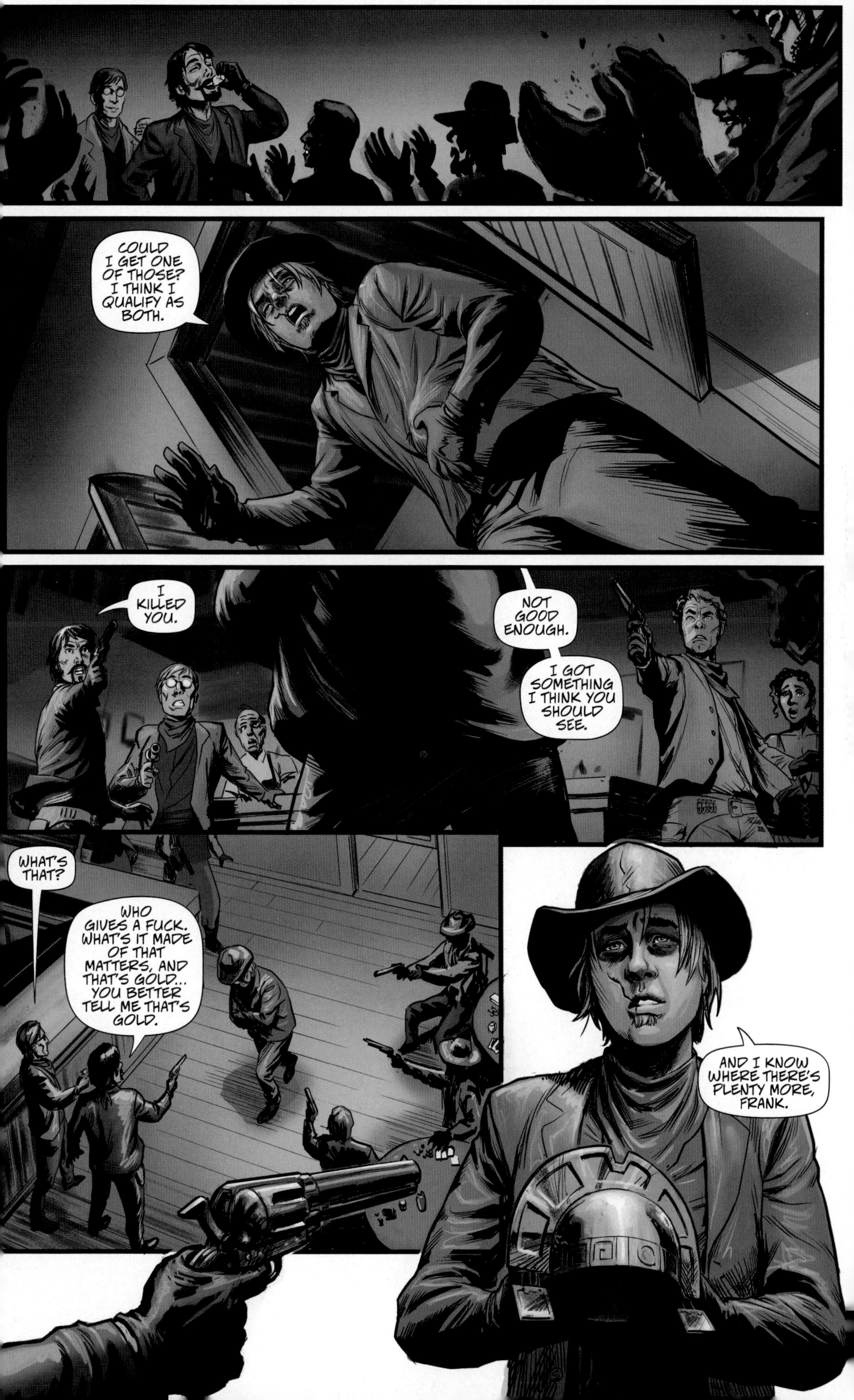
COULD I GET ONE OF THOSE? I THINK I QUALIFY AS BOTH.
I KILLED YOU.
NOT GOOD ENOUGH.
I GOT SOMETHING I THINK YOU SHOULD SEE.
WHAT'S THAT?
WHO GIVES A FUCK. WHAT'S IT MADE OF THAT MATTERS, AND THAT'S GOLD... YOU BETTER TELL ME THAT'S GOLD.
AND I KNOW WHERE THERE'S PLENTY MORE, FRANK.

WHAT YOU WANT IN RETURN, ALEX?

A DOCTOR. AND TO RIDE WITH THE GANG AGAIN.

YOU'D HOLD US BACK.

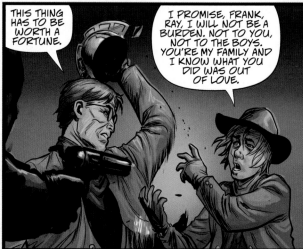

THIS THING HAS TO BE WORTH A FORTUNE.

I PROMISE, FRANK, RAY, I WILL NOT BE A BURDEN. NOT TO YOU, NOT TO THE BOYS. YOU'RE MY FAMILY AND I KNOW WHAT YOU DID WAS OUT OF LOVE.

I THINK YOU DONE CONFUSED LOVE WITH NECESSITY. STILL, YOU LOOK PRETTY GOOD FOR A DEAD MAN. RAY?

I'M INTERESTED.

BARTENDER, GET MY FRIEND HERE WHATEVER HE WANTS.

AND WE NEED THE DOCTOR TO COME AROUND PROMPTLY. SEND SOMEONE. ONE OF MY BOYS WILL ACCOMPANY.

RIGHT AWAY, SIR.

WELCOME BACK HOME, ALEX.

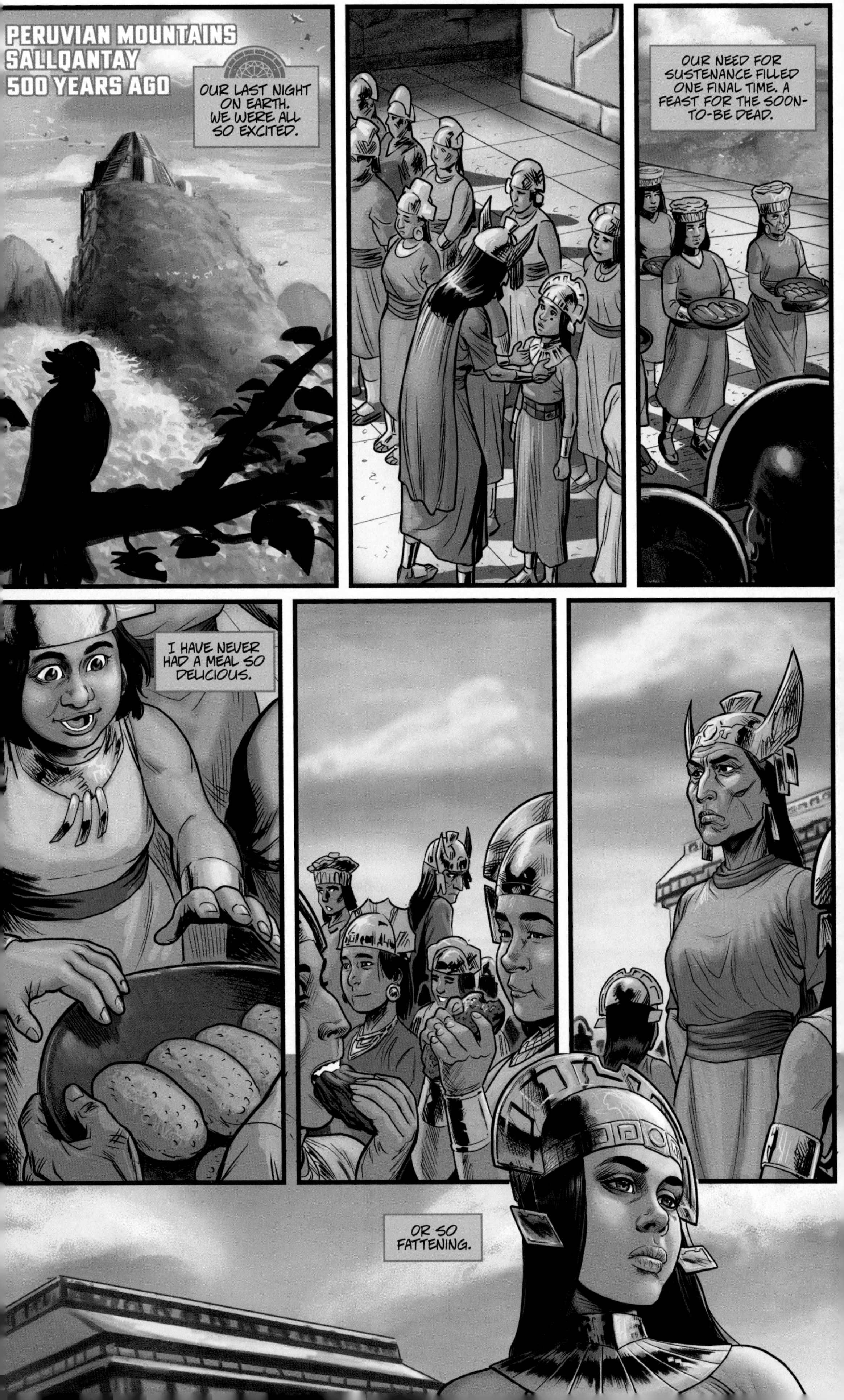
PERUVIAN MOUNTAINS
SALLQANTAY
500 YEARS AGO
OUR LAST NIGHT ON EARTH. WE WERE ALL SO EXCITED.
OUR NEED FOR SUSTENANCE FILLED ONE FINAL TIME. A FEAST FOR THE SOON-TO-BE DEAD.
I HAVE NEVER HAD A MEAL SO DELICIOUS.
OR SO FATTENING.

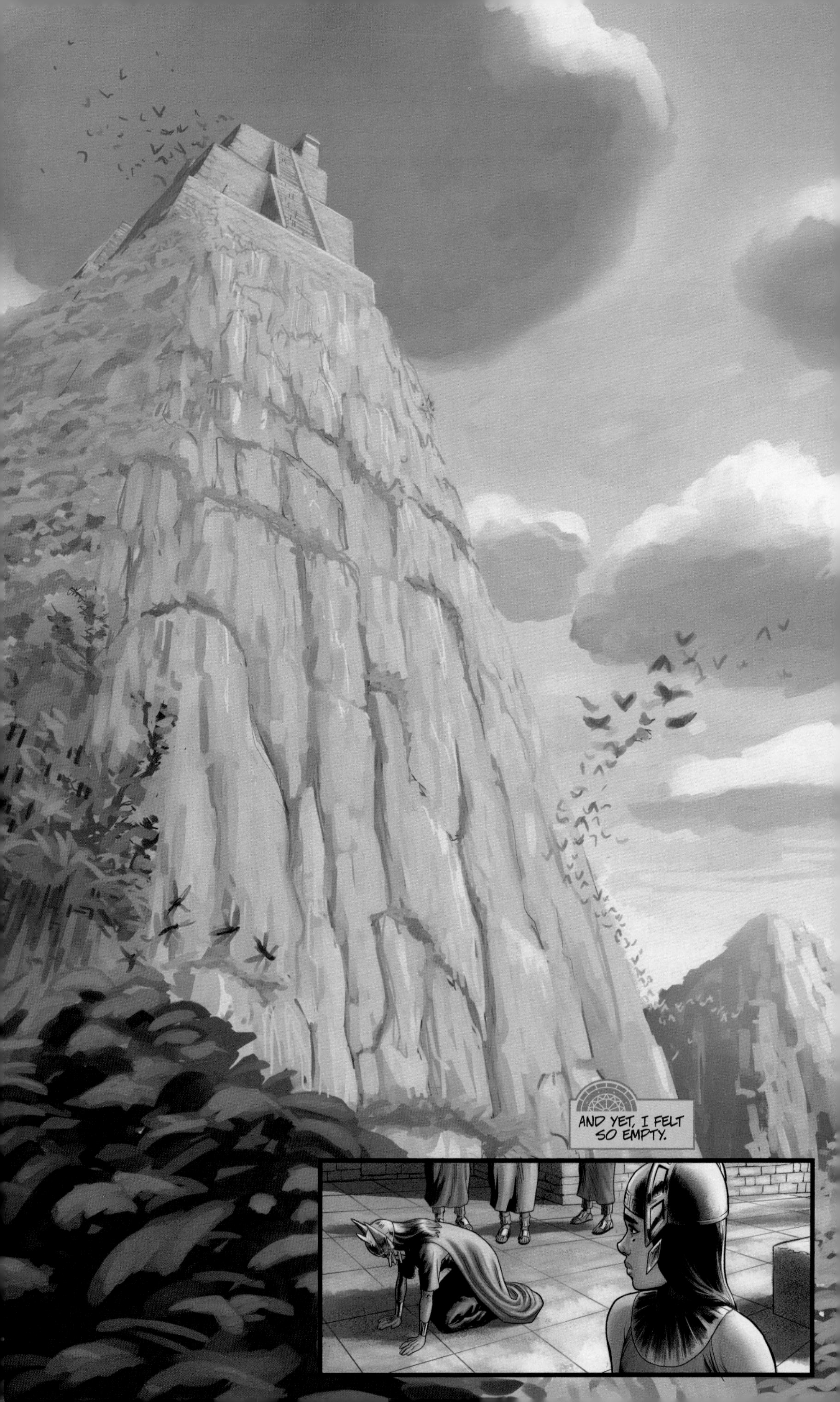
AND YET, I FELT SO EMPTY.

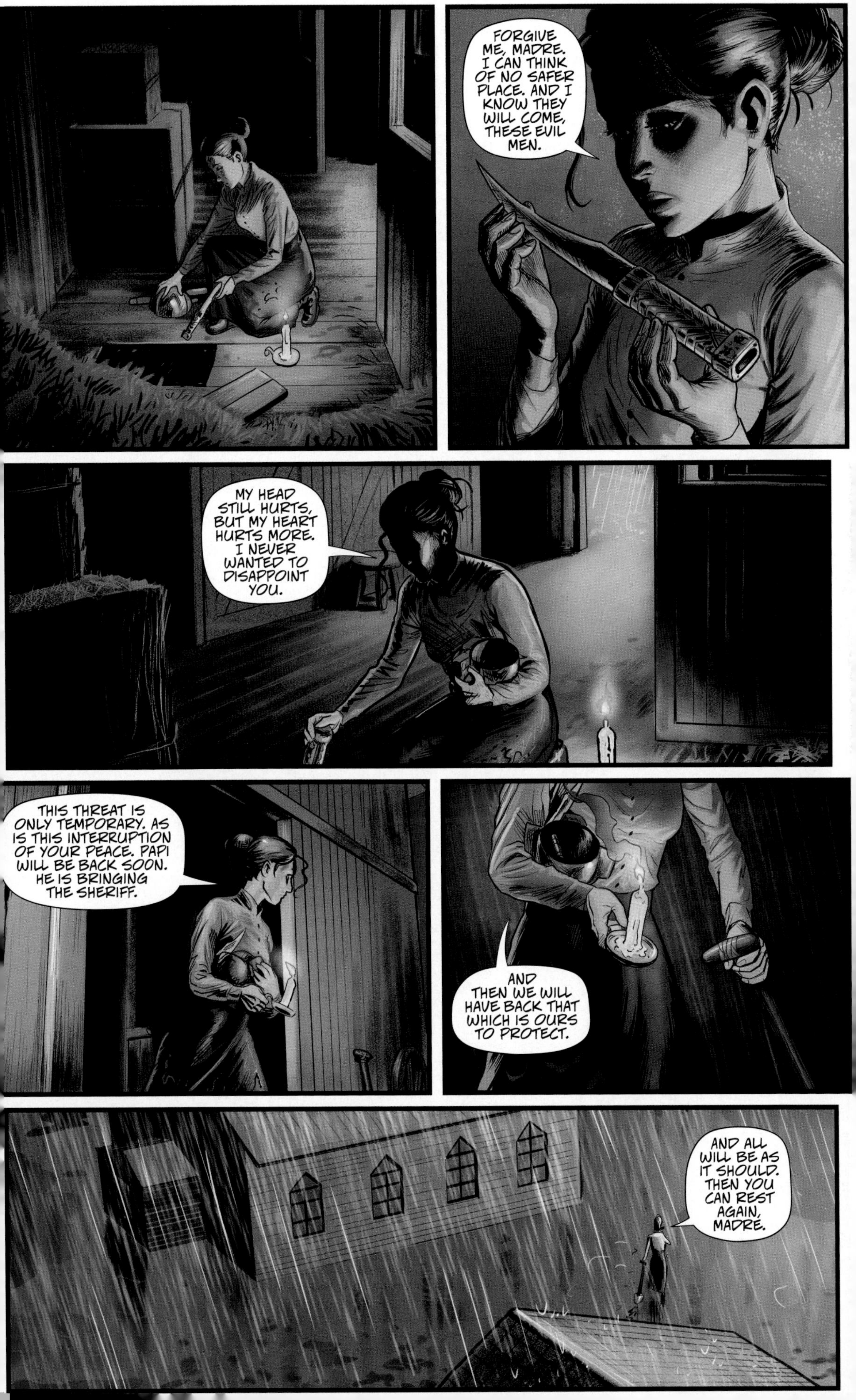

FORGIVE ME, MADRE. I CAN THINK OF NO SAFER PLACE. AND I KNOW THEY WILL COME, THESE EVIL MEN.
MY HEAD STILL HURTS, BUT MY HEART HURTS MORE. I NEVER WANTED TO DISAPPOINT YOU.
THIS THREAT IS ONLY TEMPORARY. AS IS THIS INTERRUPTION OF YOUR PEACE. PAPI WILL BE BACK SOON. HE IS BRINGING THE SHERIFF.
AND THEN WE WILL HAVE BACK THAT WHICH IS OURS TO PROTECT.
AND ALL WILL BE AS IT SHOULD. THEN YOU CAN REST AGAIN, MADRE.

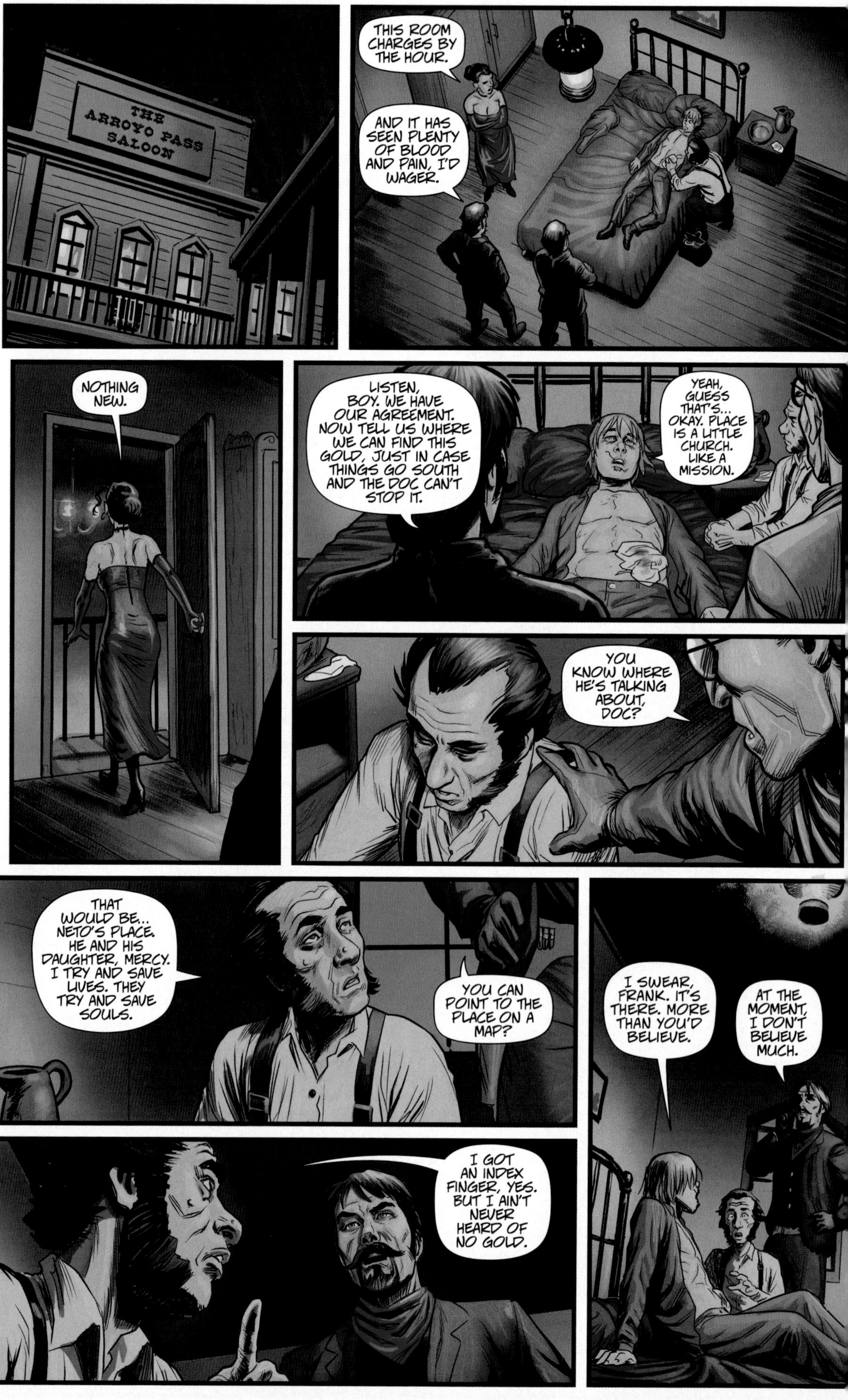
THE ARROYO PASS SALOON
THIS ROOM CHARGES BY THE HOUR.
AND IT HAS SEEN PLENTY OF BLOOD AND PAIN, I'D WAGER.
NOTHING NEW.
LISTEN, BOY. WE HAVE OUR AGREEMENT. NOW TELL US WHERE WE CAN FIND THIS GOLD, JUST IN CASE THINGS GO SOUTH AND THE DOC CAN'T STOP IT.
YEAH, GUESS THAT'S... OKAY. PLACE IS A LITTLE CHURCH. LIKE A MISSION.
YOU KNOW WHERE HE'S TALKING ABOUT, DOC?
THAT WOULD BE... NETO'S PLACE. HE AND HIS DAUGHTER, MERCY. I TRY AND SAVE LIVES. THEY TRY AND SAVE SOULS.
YOU CAN POINT TO THE PLACE ON A MAP?
I GOT AN INDEX FINGER, YES. BUT I AIN'T NEVER HEARD OF NO GOLD.
I SWEAR, FRANK. IT'S THERE. MORE THAN YOU'D BELIEVE.
AT THE MOMENT, I DON'T BELIEVE MUCH.

IT'S IN THE BARN. THERE'S A HIDDEN SPACE UNDER. A PLACE YOU CAN CRAWL INTO. DOOR TO IT IS IN THE FLOOR AT THE BACK. I SWEAR.

HE SWEARS, FRANK.

SO WHAT'S THE PROGNOSIS, DOC? HOW MUCH TO FIX HIM?

HE'S HURT BAD, MISTER...

DANTON.

STILL ASSESSING WHAT WE'RE UP AGAINST. GUT SHOTS ARE A HELL OF A THING TO DEAL WITH. IT'LL BE EXPENSIVE, AND I CAN PROVIDE NO GUARANTEE OF SUCCESS.

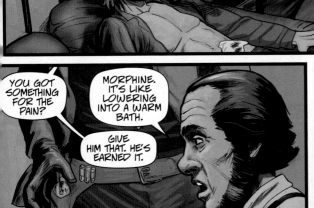

YOU GOT SOMETHING FOR THE PAIN?

MORPHINE. IT'S LIKE LOWERING INTO A WARM BATH.

GIVE HIM THAT. HE'S EARNED IT.

YOU CAN'T GO RUNNING OFF AT THE MOUTH TO THE SHERIFF ABOUT THIS, IF WE DIDN'T MAKE THAT OBVIOUS.

HIPPOCRATIC OATH. MY LOYALTY IS TO MY PATIENT.

YEAH, THAT'S IT.

BLAM BLAM BLAM

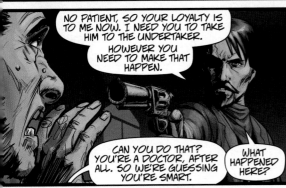

NO PATIENT, SO YOUR LOYALTY IS TO ME NOW. I NEED YOU TO TAKE HIM TO THE UNDERTAKER. HOWEVER YOU NEED TO MAKE THAT HAPPEN.

CAN YOU DO THAT? YOU'RE A DOCTOR, AFTER ALL. SO WE'RE GUESSING YOU'RE SMART.

WHAT HAPPENED HERE?

A MAN DIED OF HIS INJURIES. THERE WAS NOTHING THAT COULD BE DONE. SO I... EASED HIS PAIN. THEN HE WAS GONE.

THAT'S GOOD, DOC. REAL GOOD.

BUT WE'RE GOING TO LEAVE SOME MEN TO WATCH THAT THINGS GET DONE AS MR. DANTON WANTS.

AND TO DEAL WITH THE SHERIFF IF HE GETS BACK BEFORE WE DO.

ENOUGH?

IT'LL DO NICELY.

I'M EXPECTING, DOC, THAT YOU WILL AS WELL.

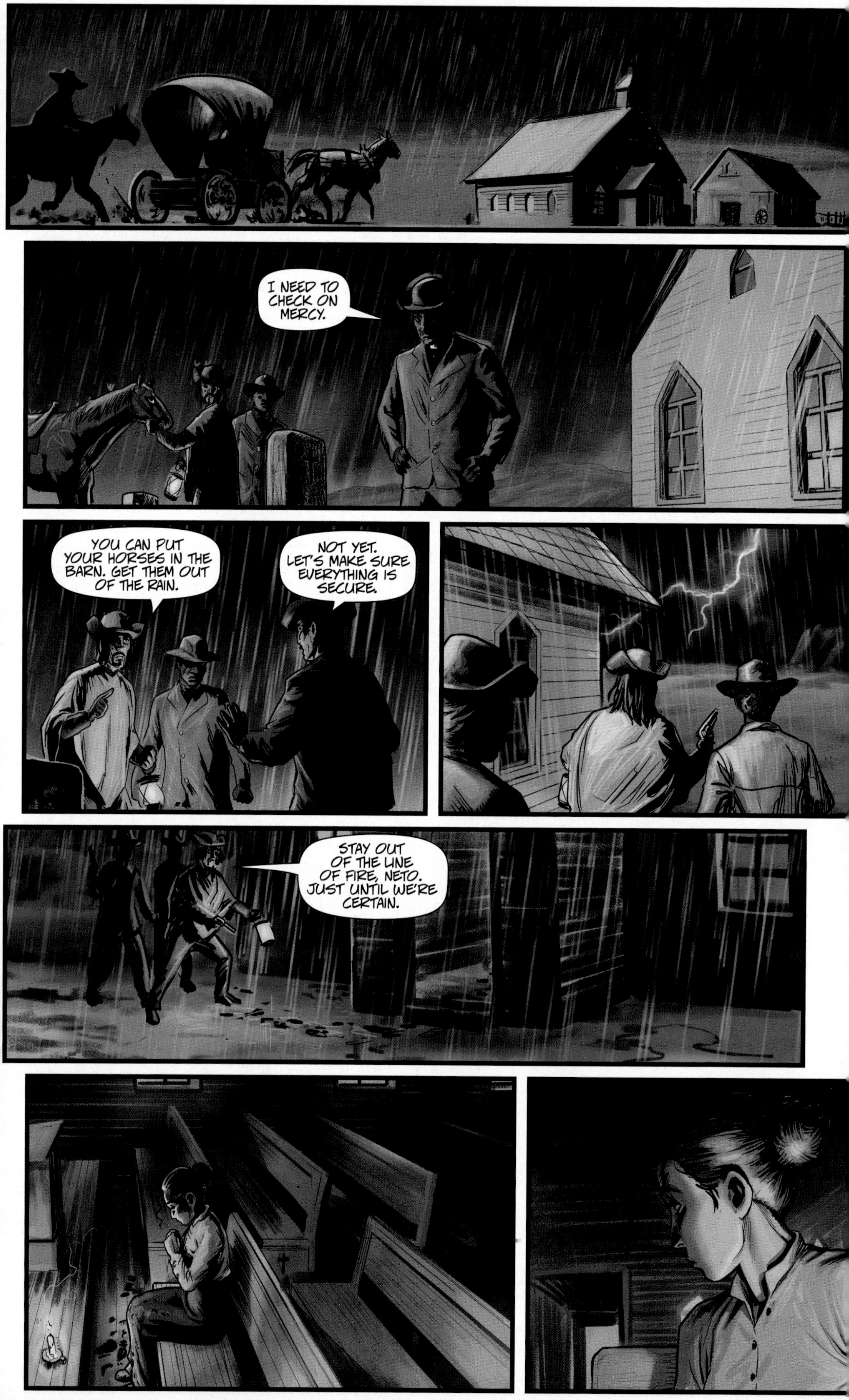
I NEED TO CHECK ON MERCY.
YOU CAN PUT YOUR HORSES IN THE BARN. GET THEM OUT OF THE RAIN.
NOT YET. LET'S MAKE SURE EVERYTHING IS SECURE.
STAY OUT OF THE LINE OF FIRE, NETO. JUST UNTIL WE'RE CERTAIN.

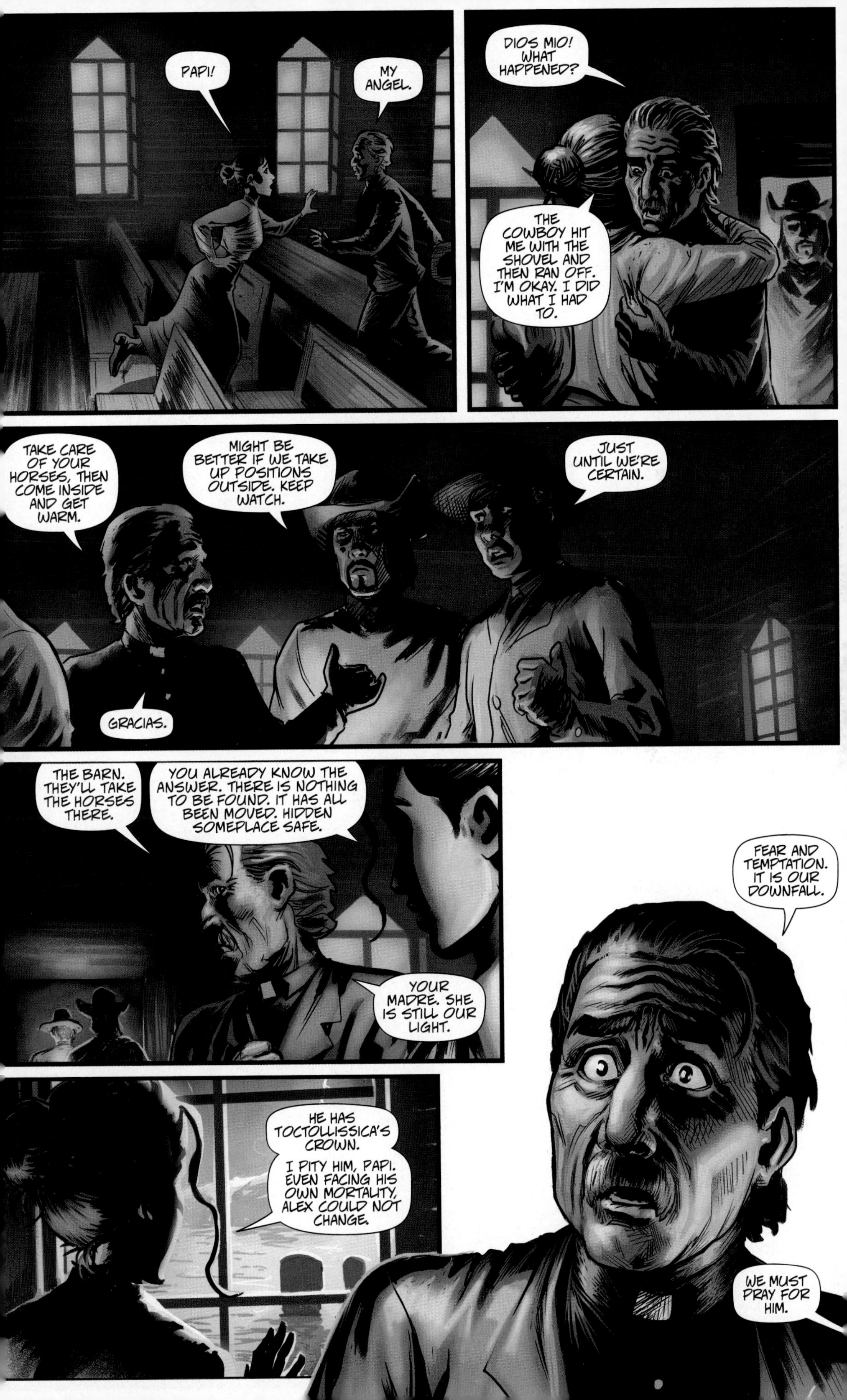
PAPI!
MY ANGEL.
DIOS MIO! WHAT HAPPENED?
THE COWBOY HIT ME WITH THE SHOVEL AND THEN RAN OFF. I'M OKAY. I DID WHAT I HAD TO.
TAKE CARE OF YOUR HORSES, THEN COME INSIDE AND GET WARM.
MIGHT BE BETTER IF WE TAKE UP POSITIONS OUTSIDE. KEEP WATCH.
JUST UNTIL WE'RE CERTAIN.
GRACIAS.
THE BARN. THEY'LL TAKE THE HORSES THERE.
YOU ALREADY KNOW THE ANSWER. THERE IS NOTHING TO BE FOUND. IT HAS ALL BEEN MOVED. HIDDEN SOMEPLACE SAFE.
YOUR MADRE. SHE IS STILL OUR LIGHT.
HE HAS TOCTOLLISSICA'S CROWN.
I PITY HIM, PAPI. EVEN FACING HIS OWN MORTALITY, ALEX COULD NOT CHANGE.
FEAR AND TEMPTATION. IT IS OUR DOWNFALL.
WE MUST PRAY FOR HIM.

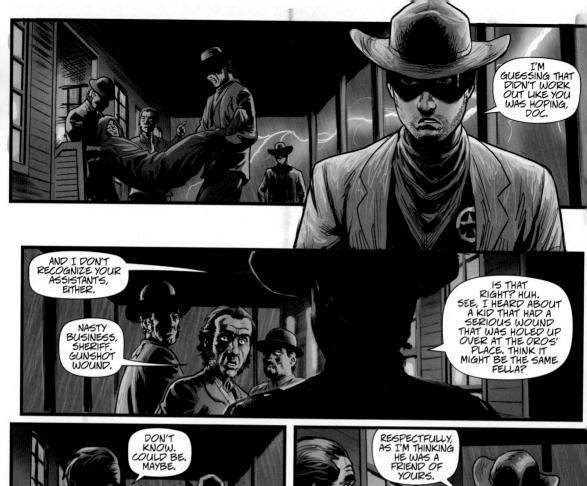

I'M GUESSING THAT DIDN'T WORK OUT LIKE YOU WAS HOPING, DOC.

AND I DON'T RECOGNIZE YOUR ASSISTANTS, EITHER.

NASTY BUSINESS, SHERIFF. GUNSHOT WOUND.

IS THAT RIGHT? HUH. SEE, I HEARD ABOUT A KID THAT HAD A SERIOUS WOUND THAT WAS HOLED UP OVER AT THE OROS' PLACE. THINK IT MIGHT BE THE SAME FELLA?

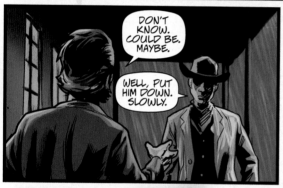

DON'T KNOW. COULD BE. MAYBE.

WELL, PUT HIM DOWN. SLOWLY.

RESPECTFULLY, AS I'M THINKING HE WAS A FRIEND OF YOURS.

WASN'T A FRIEND.

HARDLY KNEW HIM.

THEN YOU WON'T MIND LEAVING HIM RIGHT THERE AND STEPPING BACK, CAREFUL LIKE.

WHERE'S YOUR POSSE?

EXCUSE ME?

STEP AWAY, DOC. OR YOU MAY BE FIXING YOURSELF. OR WORSE.

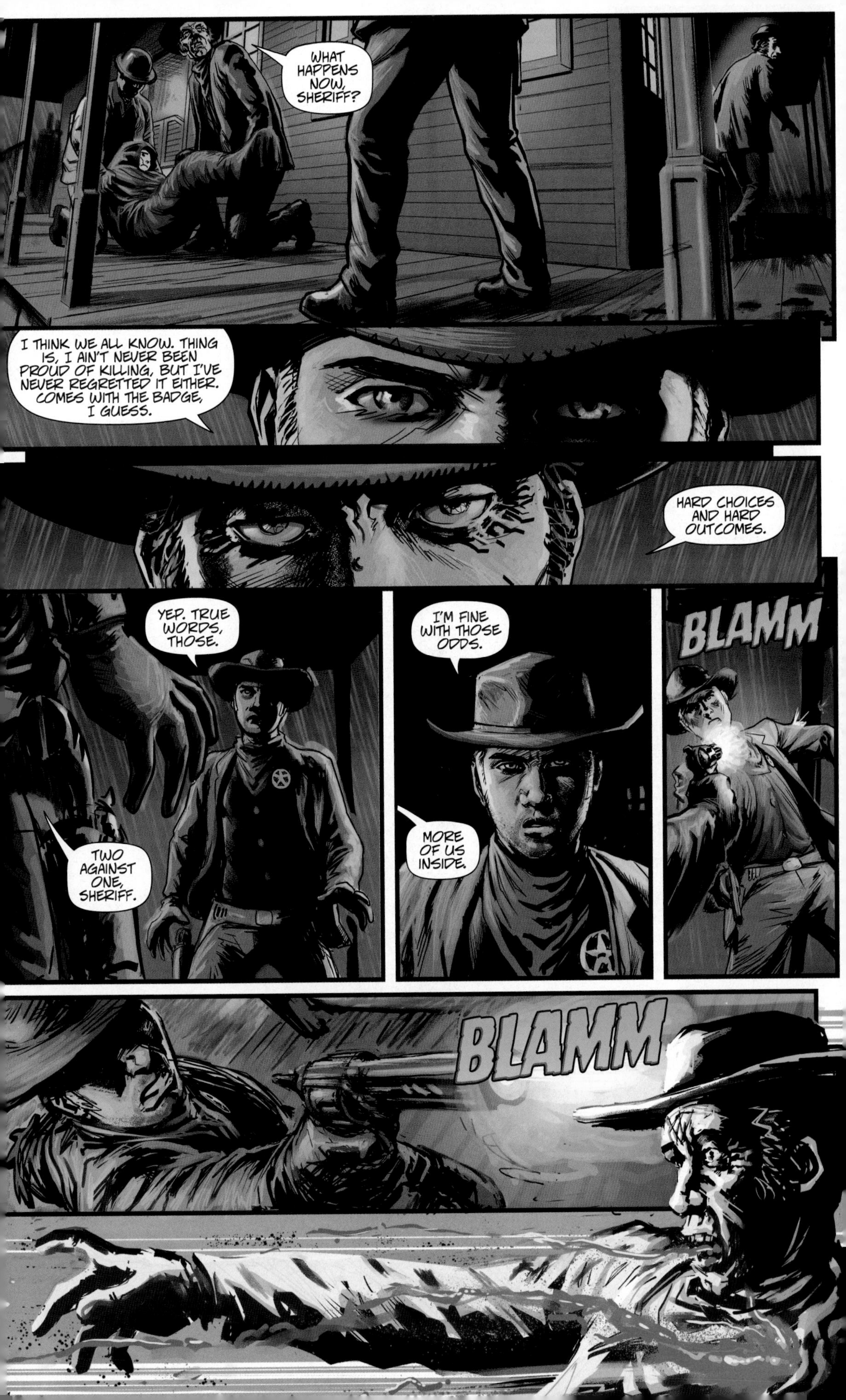
WHAT HAPPENS NOW, SHERIFF?
I THINK WE ALL KNOW. THING IS, I AIN'T NEVER BEEN PROUD OF KILLING, BUT I'VE NEVER REGRETTED IT EITHER. COMES WITH THE BADGE, I GUESS.
HARD CHOICES AND HARD OUTCOMES.
YEP. TRUE WORDS, THOSE.
TWO AGAINST ONE, SHERIFF.
I'M FINE WITH THOSE ODDS.
MORE OF US INSIDE.
BLAMM
BLAMM

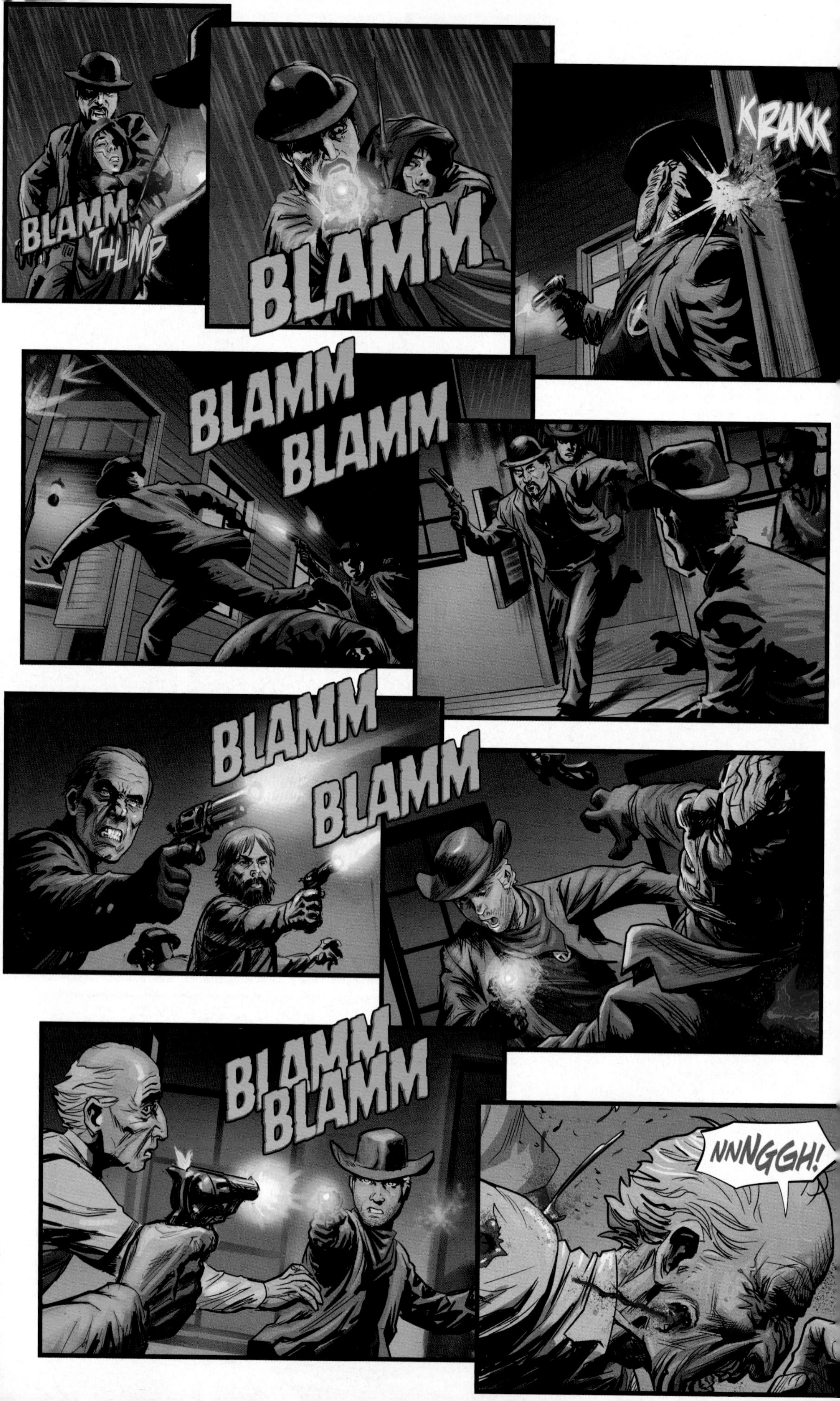
BLAMM
THUMP
BLAMM
KRAKK
BLAMM
BLAMM
BLAMM
BLAMM
BLAMM
BLAMM
NNNGGH!

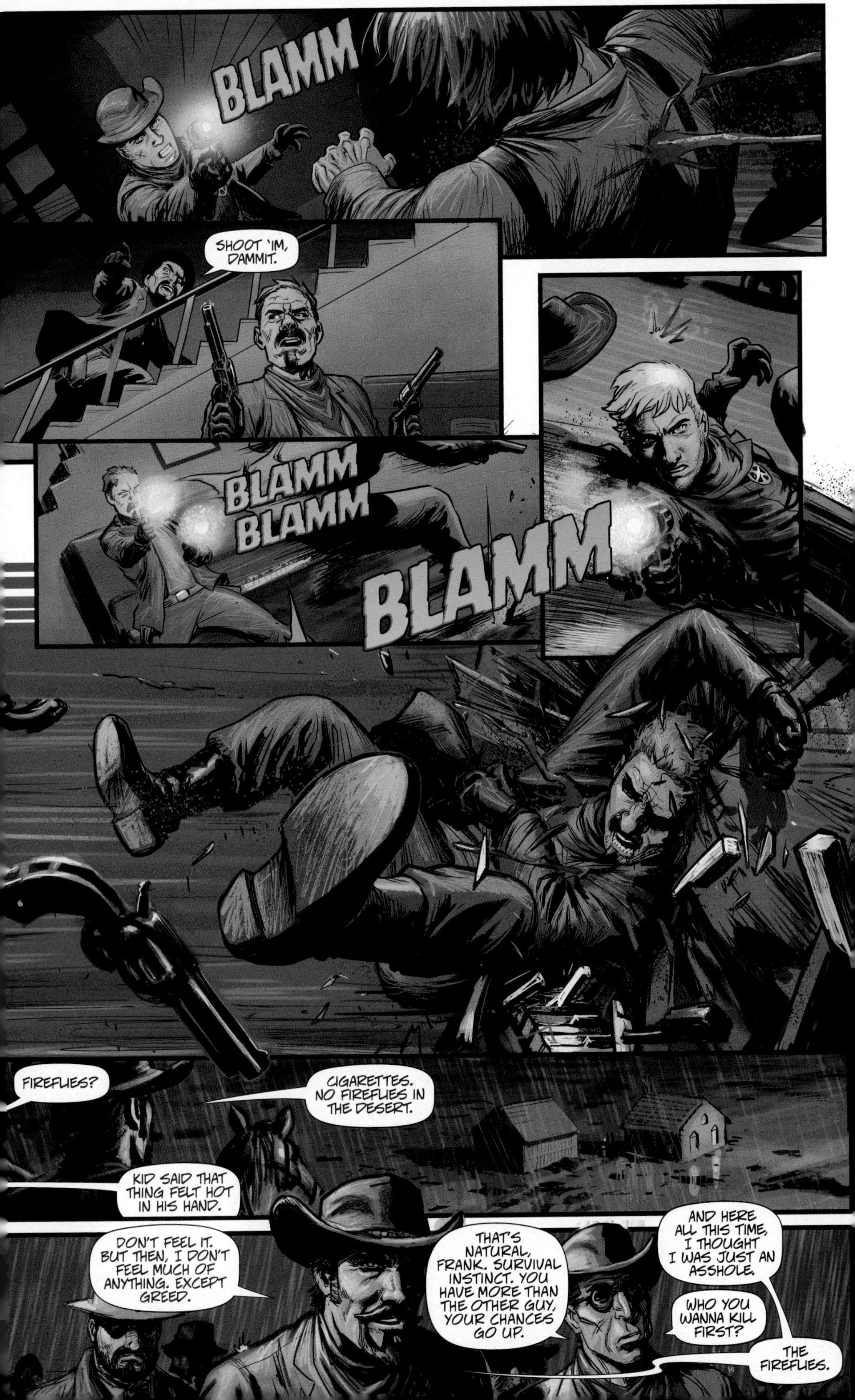
BLAMM
SHOOT 'IM, DAMMIT.
BLAMM BLAMM
BLAMM
FIREFLIES?
CIGARETTES. NO FIREFLIES IN THE DESERT.
KID SAID THAT THING FELT HOT IN HIS HAND.
DON'T FEEL IT. BUT THEN, I DON'T FEEL MUCH OF ANYTHING. EXCEPT GREED.
THAT'S NATURAL, FRANK. SURVIVAL INSTINCT. YOU HAVE MORE THAN THE OTHER GUY, YOUR CHANCES GO UP.
AND HERE ALL THIS TIME, I THOUGHT I WAS JUST AN ASSHOLE.
WHO YOU WANNA KILL FIRST?
THE FIREFLIES.

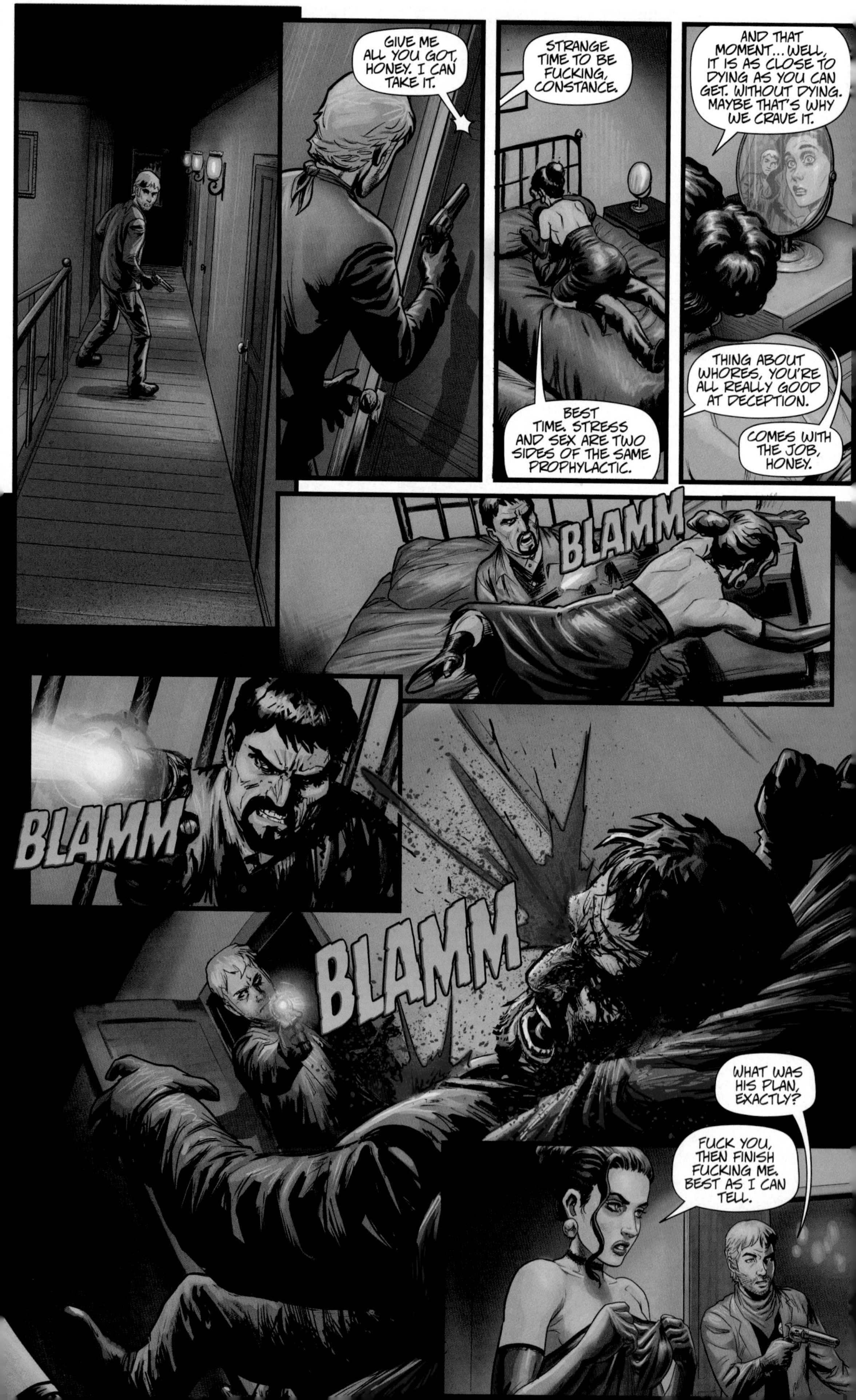
GIVE ME ALL YOU GOT, HONEY. I CAN TAKE IT.
STRANGE TIME TO BE FUCKING, CONSTANCE.
BEST TIME. STRESS AND SEX ARE TWO SIDES OF THE SAME PROPHYLACTIC.
AND THAT MOMENT... WELL, IT IS AS CLOSE TO DYING AS YOU CAN GET. WITHOUT DYING. MAYBE THAT'S WHY WE CRAVE IT.
THING ABOUT WHORES, YOU'RE ALL REALLY GOOD AT DECEPTION.
COMES WITH THE JOB, HONEY.
BLAMM
BLAMM
BLAMM
WHAT WAS HIS PLAN, EXACTLY?
FUCK YOU, THEN FINISH FUCKING ME. BEST AS I CAN TELL.

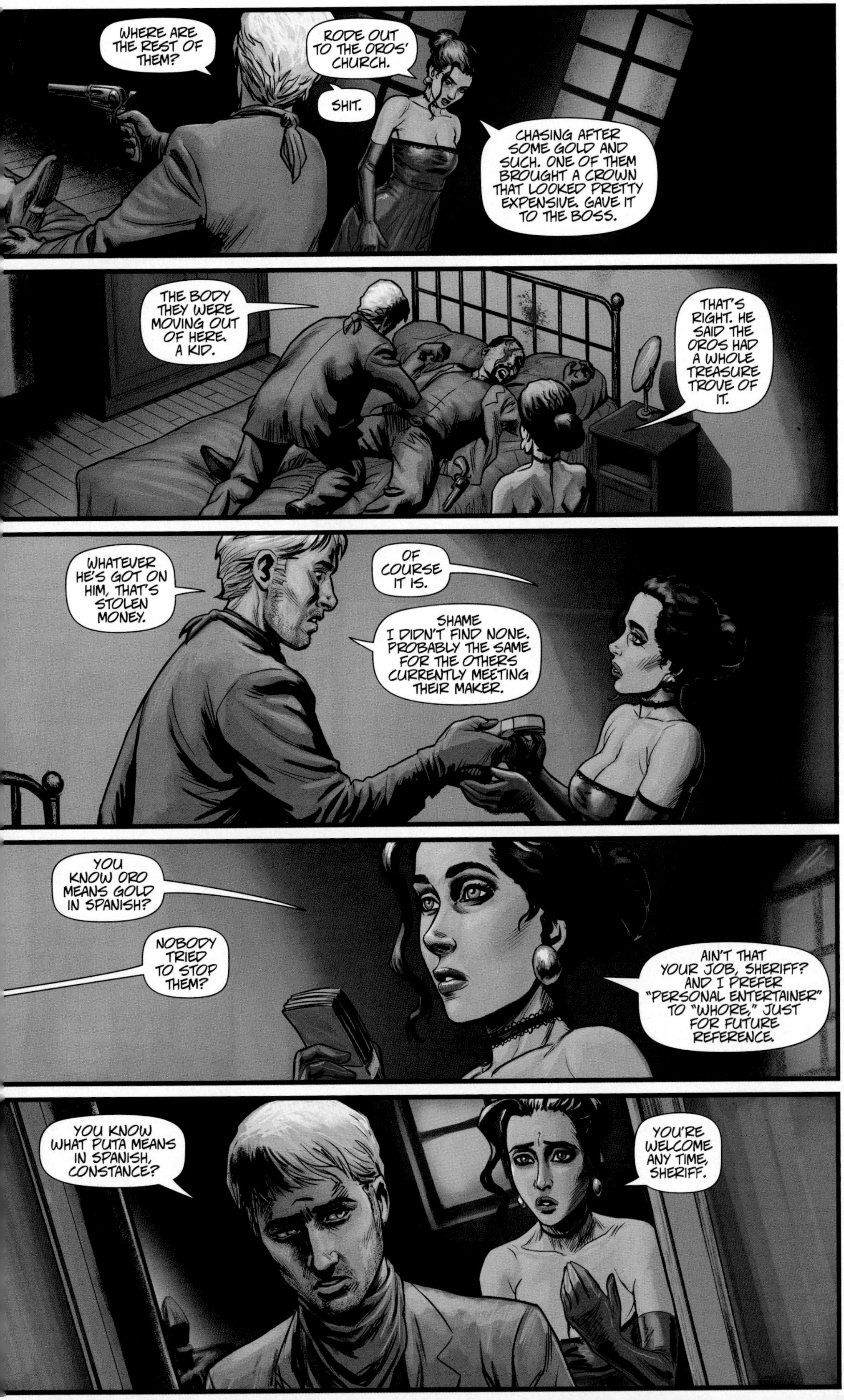
WHERE ARE THE REST OF THEM?
RODE OUT TO THE OROS' CHURCH.
SHIT.
CHASING AFTER SOME GOLD AND SUCH. ONE OF THEM BROUGHT A CROWN THAT LOOKED PRETTY EXPENSIVE. GAVE IT TO THE BOSS.
THE BODY THEY WERE MOVING OUT OF HERE. A KID.
THAT'S RIGHT. HE SAID THE OROS HAD A WHOLE TREASURE TROVE OF IT.
WHATEVER HE'S GOT ON HIM, THAT'S STOLEN MONEY.
OF COURSE IT IS.
SHAME I DIDN'T FIND NONE. PROBABLY THE SAME FOR THE OTHERS CURRENTLY MEETING THEIR MAKER.
YOU KNOW ORO MEANS GOLD IN SPANISH?
NOBODY TRIED TO STOP THEM?
AIN'T THAT YOUR JOB, SHERIFF? AND I PREFER "PERSONAL ENTERTAINER" TO "WHORE," JUST FOR FUTURE REFERENCE.
YOU KNOW WHAT PUTA MEANS IN SPANISH, CONSTANCE?
YOU'RE WELCOME ANY TIME, SHERIFF.

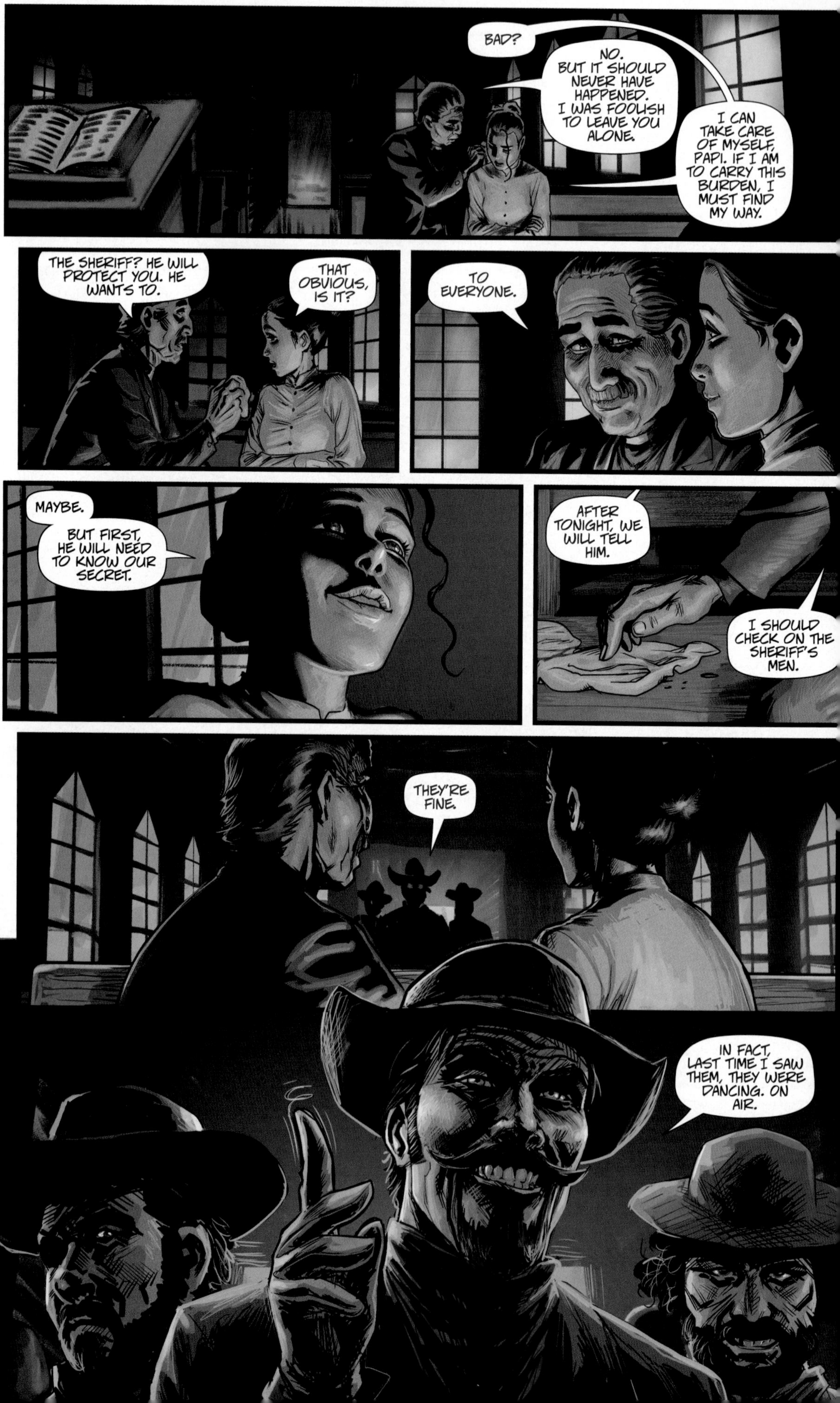
BAD?
NO. BUT IT SHOULD NEVER HAVE HAPPENED. I WAS FOOLISH TO LEAVE YOU ALONE.
I CAN TAKE CARE OF MYSELF, PAPI. IF I AM TO CARRY THIS BURDEN, I MUST FIND MY WAY.
THE SHERIFF? HE WILL PROTECT YOU. HE WANTS TO.
THAT OBVIOUS, IS IT?
TO EVERYONE.
MAYBE.
BUT FIRST, HE WILL NEED TO KNOW OUR SECRET.
AFTER TONIGHT, WE WILL TELL HIM.
I SHOULD CHECK ON THE SHERIFF'S MEN.
THEY'RE FINE.
IN FACT, LAST TIME I SAW THEM, THEY WERE DANCING. ON AIR.

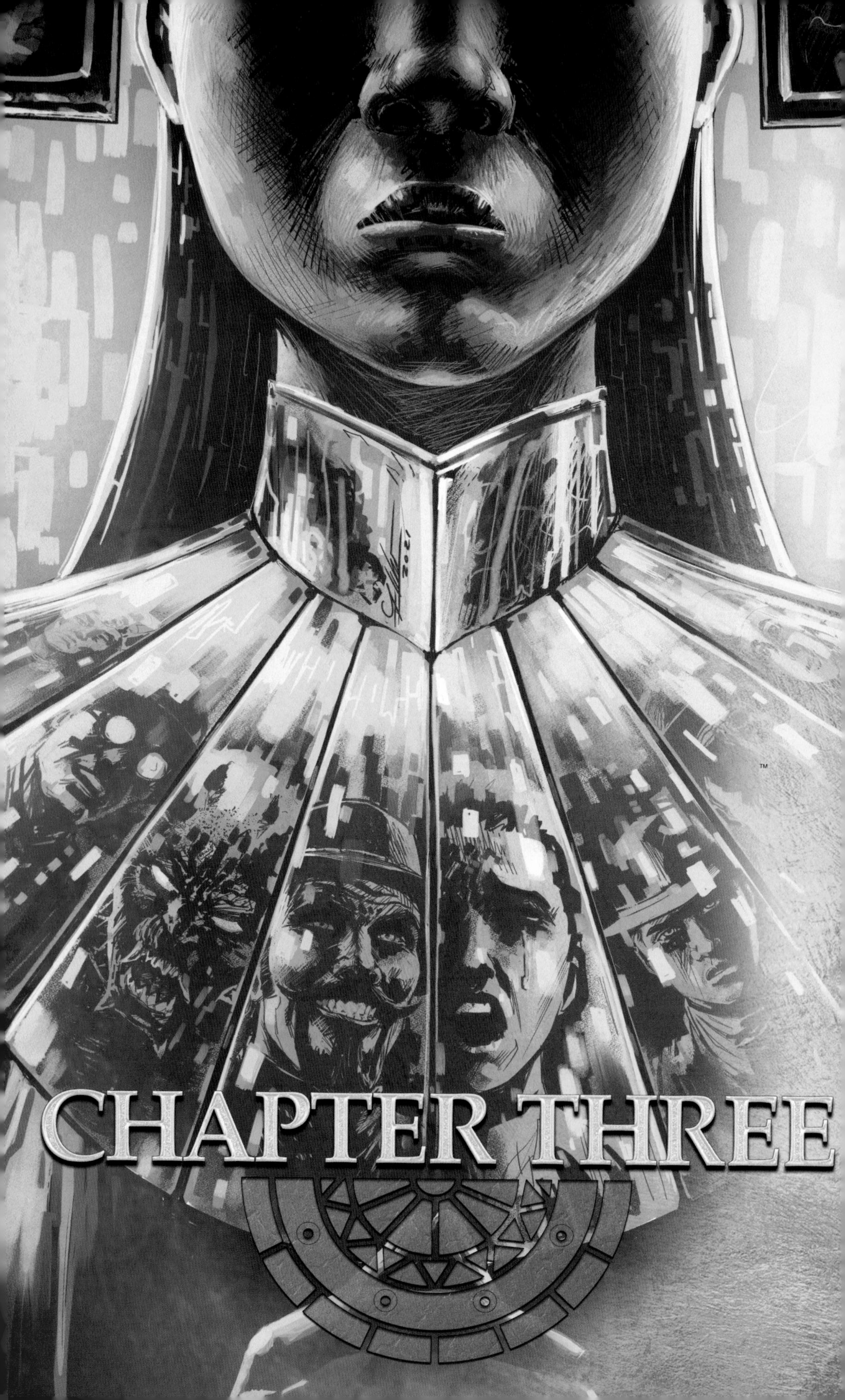

CHAPTER THREE

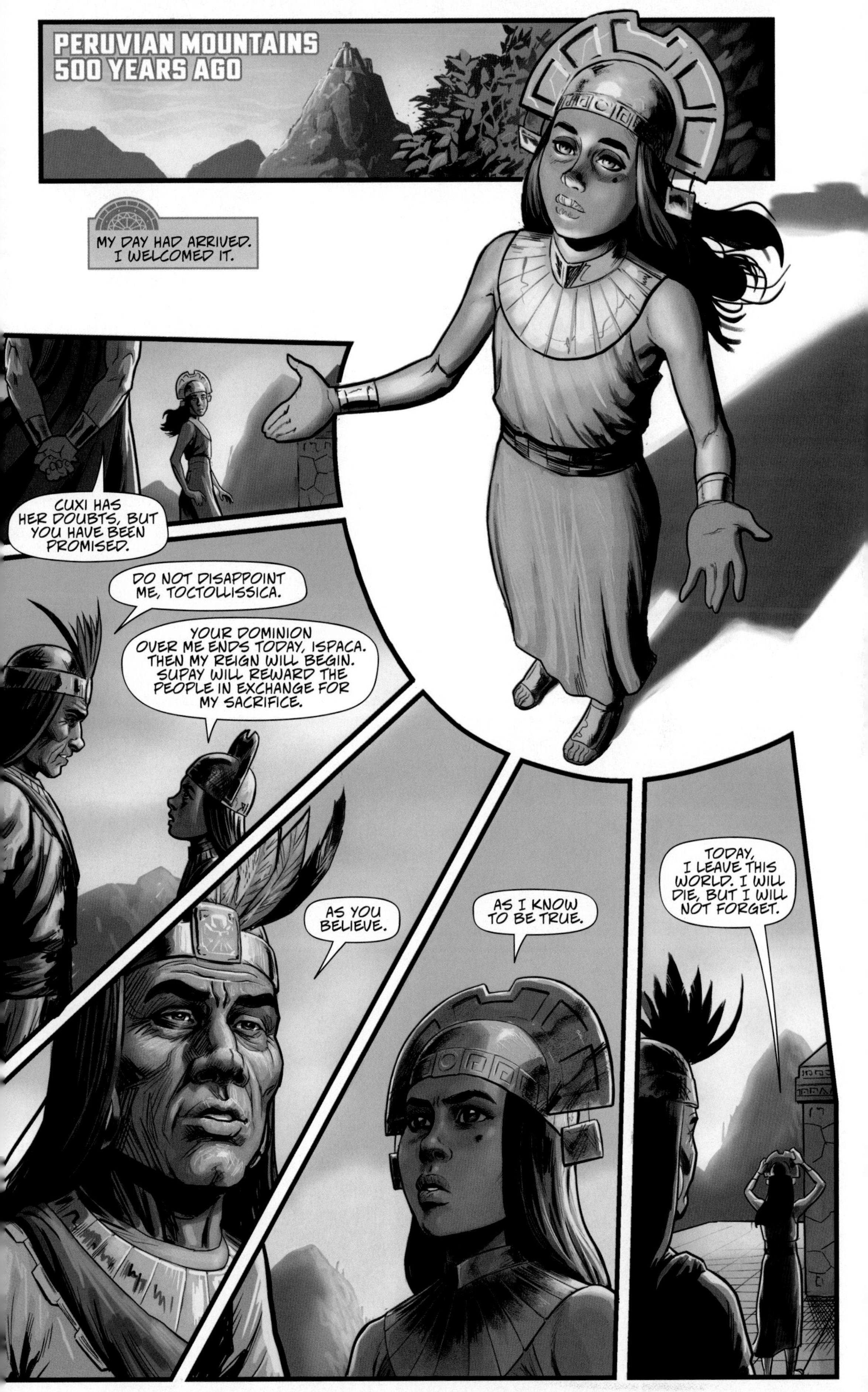

PERUVIAN MOUNTAINS
500 YEARS AGO
MY DAY HAD ARRIVED. I WELCOMED IT.
CUXI HAS HER DOUBTS, BUT YOU HAVE BEEN PROMISED.
DO NOT DISAPPOINT ME, TOCTOLLISSICA.
YOUR DOMINION OVER ME ENDS TODAY, ISPACA. THEN MY REIGN WILL BEGIN. SUPAY WILL REWARD THE PEOPLE IN EXCHANGE FOR MY SACRIFICE.
AS YOU BELIEVE.
AS I KNOW TO BE TRUE.
TODAY, I LEAVE THIS WORLD. I WILL DIE, BUT I WILL NOT FORGET.

THERE IS NO SANCTUARY OR SALVATION HERE THIS NIGHT. ANYTHING ELSE YOU SEEK CANNOT BE FOUND IN CHURCH.

WHOA, NOW.

I AIN'T BEEN RIGHT WITH GOD FOR LONGER THAN I CAN REMEMBER.

YOU MIGHT SAY WE HAD SOMETHING OF A FALLING OUT.

NOW, THERE'S NO NEED FOR ALARM OR CONCERN. MY NAME'S FRANK DANTON, AND I'VE JUST COME TO THANK YOU FOR THE KINDNESS YOU SHOWED TOWARD ONE OF MY BOYS.

HE WASN'T THE NICEST OF FELLOWS. HE DO THAT TO YOU, OUR ALEX?

SI.

BUT HOPEFULLY NO WORSE. BECAUSE HIS MIND WAS LIKE THE RAILROAD. TWO TRACKS. VIOLENCE AND WOMEN.

HE'S DEAD, NOW. IF THAT IS ANY SOLACE.

IT IS NOT, SIR.

HE'S A LIAR.

THAT HE WAS. SURELY.

BUT NO NEED TO SPEAK ILL O' THE RECENTL DEPARTED.

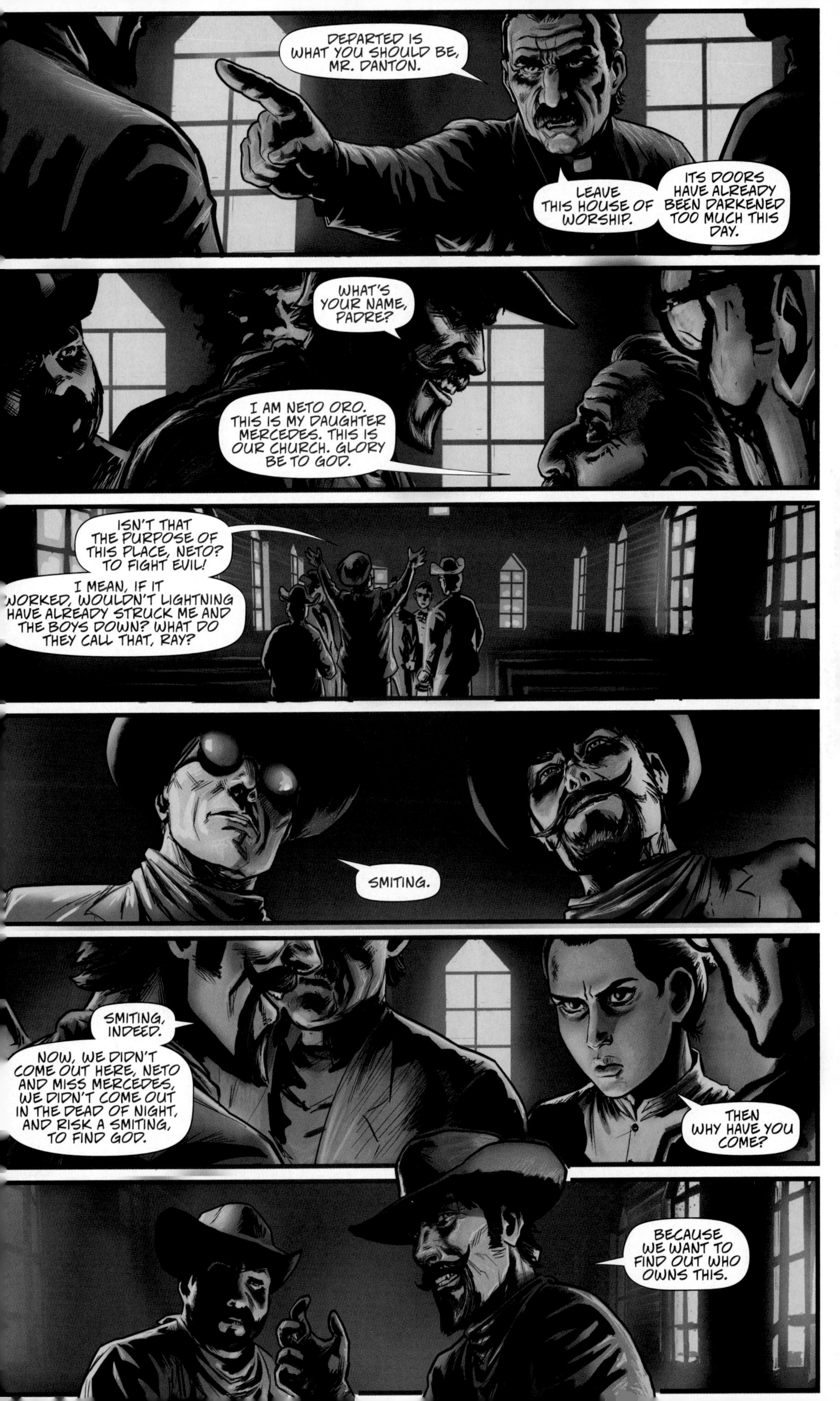
DEPARTED IS WHAT YOU SHOULD BE, MR. DANTON.
LEAVE THIS HOUSE OF WORSHIP.
ITS DOORS HAVE ALREADY BEEN DARKENED TOO MUCH THIS DAY.
WHAT'S YOUR NAME, PADRE?
I AM NETO ORO. THIS IS MY DAUGHTER MERCEDES. THIS IS OUR CHURCH. GLORY BE TO GOD.
ISN'T THAT THE PURPOSE OF THIS PLACE, NETO? TO FIGHT EVIL!
I MEAN, IF IT WORKED, WOULDN'T LIGHTNING HAVE ALREADY STRUCK ME AND THE BOYS DOWN? WHAT DO THEY CALL THAT, RAY?
SMITING.
SMITING, INDEED.
NOW, WE DIDN'T COME OUT HERE, NETO AND MISS MERCEDES, WE DIDN'T COME OUT IN THE DEAD OF NIGHT, AND RISK A SMITING, TO FIND GOD.
THEN WHY HAVE YOU COME?
BECAUSE WE WANT TO FIND OUT WHO OWNS THIS.

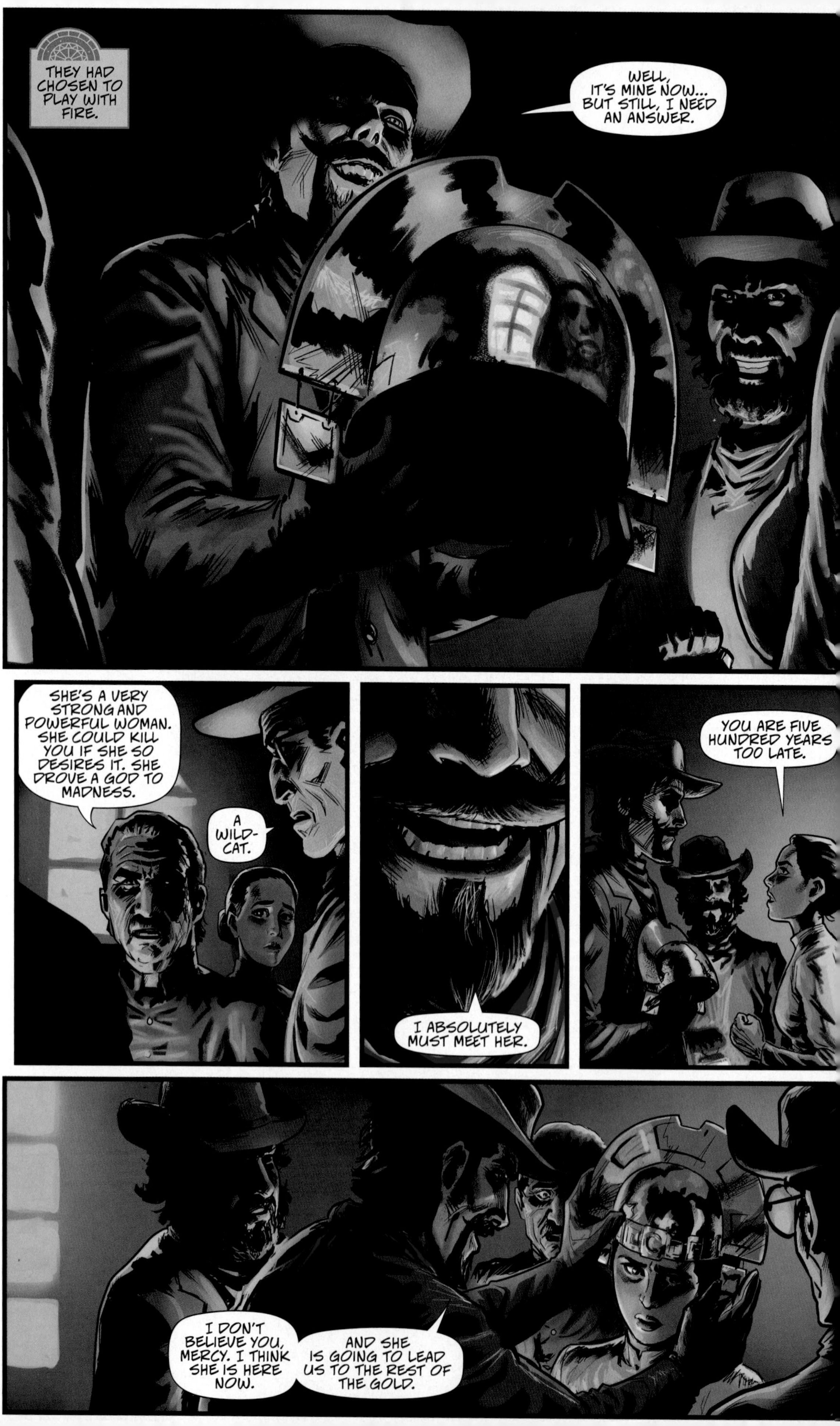
THEY HAD CHOSEN TO PLAY WITH FIRE.
WELL, IT'S MINE NOW... BUT STILL, I NEED AN ANSWER.
SHE'S A VERY STRONG AND POWERFUL WOMAN. SHE COULD KILL YOU IF SHE SO DESIRES IT. SHE DROVE A GOD TO MADNESS.
A WILD-CAT.
I ABSOLUTELY MUST MEET HER.
YOU ARE FIVE HUNDRED YEARS TOO LATE.
I DON'T BELIEVE YOU, MERCY. I THINK SHE IS HERE NOW.
AND SHE IS GOING TO LEAD US TO THE REST OF THE GOLD.

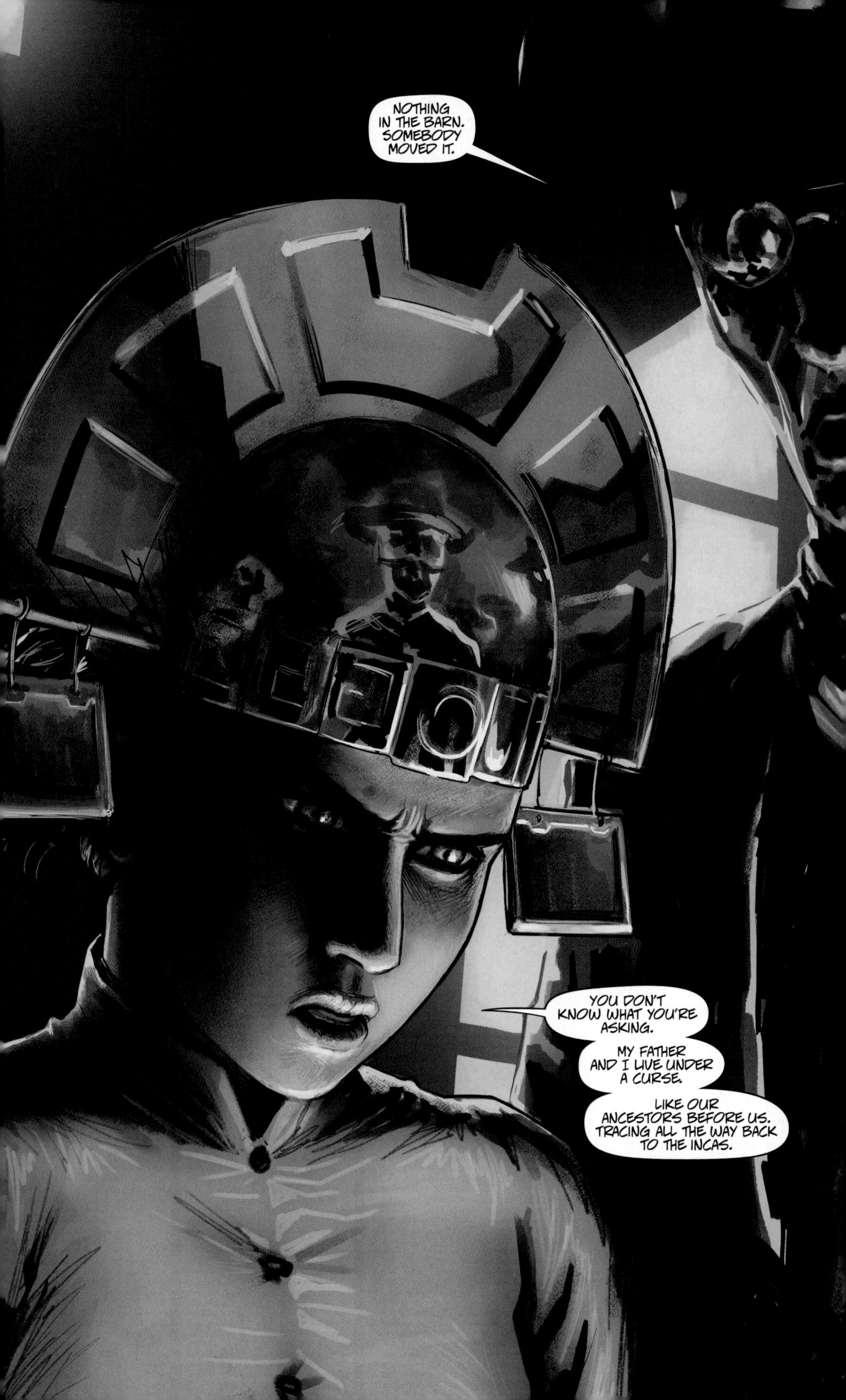
NOTHING IN THE BARN. SOMEBODY MOVED IT.
YOU DON'T KNOW WHAT YOU'RE ASKING.
MY FATHER AND I LIVE UNDER A CURSE.
LIKE OUR ANCESTORS BEFORE US. TRACING ALL THE WAY BACK TO THE INCAS.

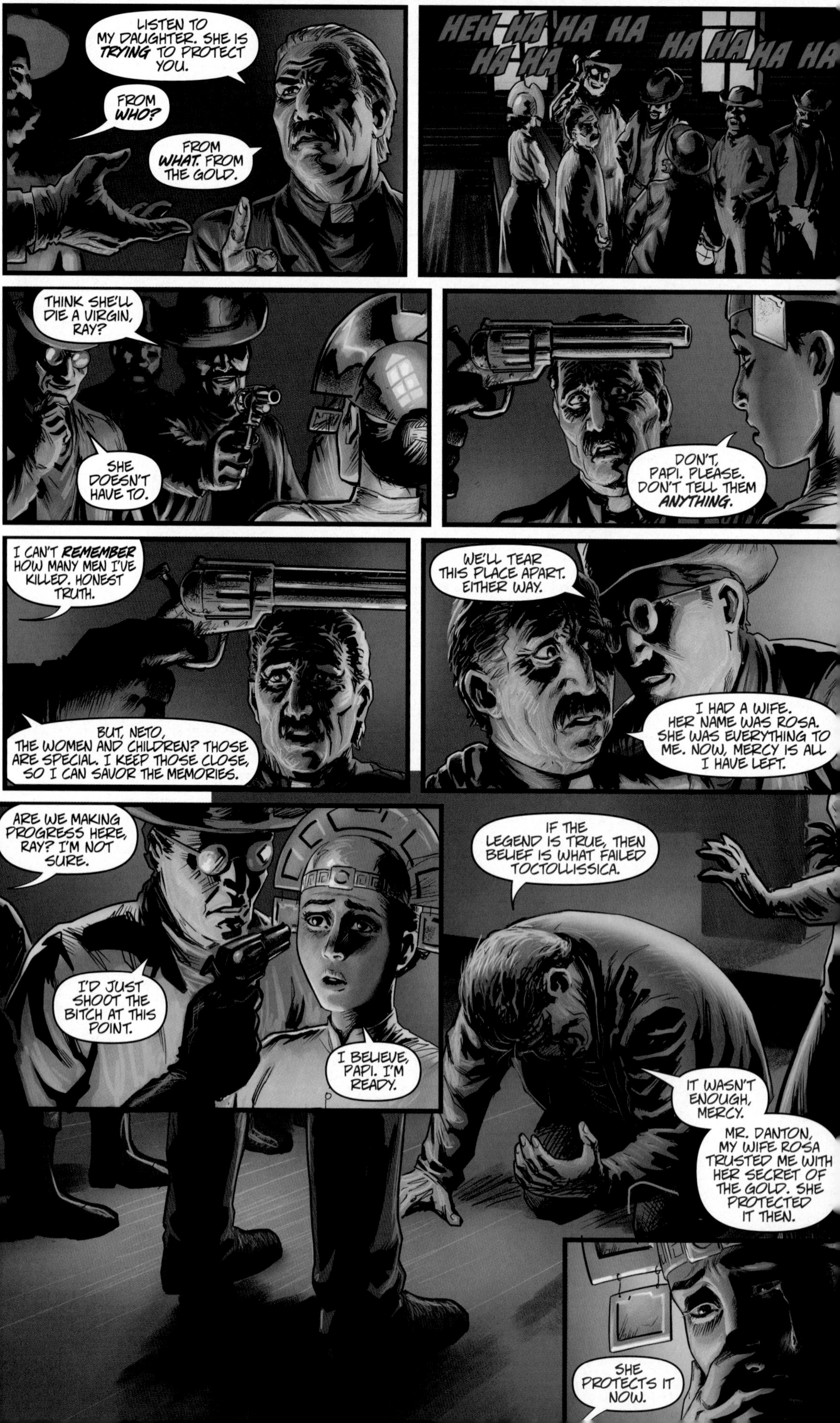

LISTEN TO MY DAUGHTER. SHE IS TRYING TO PROTECT YOU.
FROM WHO?
FROM WHAT. FROM THE GOLD.
HEH HA HA HA HA HA HA HA HA HA
THINK SHE'LL DIE A VIRGIN, RAY?
SHE DOESN'T HAVE TO.
DON'T, PAPI. PLEASE. DON'T TELL THEM ANYTHING.
I CAN'T REMEMBER HOW MANY MEN I'VE KILLED. HONEST TRUTH.
BUT, NETO, THE WOMEN AND CHILDREN? THOSE ARE SPECIAL. I KEEP THOSE CLOSE, SO I CAN SAVOR THE MEMORIES.
WE'LL TEAR THIS PLACE APART. EITHER WAY.
I HAD A WIFE. HER NAME WAS ROSA. SHE WAS EVERYTHING TO ME. NOW, MERCY IS ALL I HAVE LEFT.
ARE WE MAKING PROGRESS HERE, RAY? I'M NOT SURE.
I'D JUST SHOOT THE BITCH AT THIS POINT.
I BELIEVE, PAPI. I'M READY.
IF THE LEGEND IS TRUE, THEN BELIEF IS WHAT FAILED TOCTOLLISSICA.
IT WASN'T ENOUGH, MERCY.
MR. DANTON, MY WIFE ROSA TRUSTED ME WITH HER SECRET OF THE GOLD. SHE PROTECTED IT THEN.
SHE PROTECTS IT NOW.

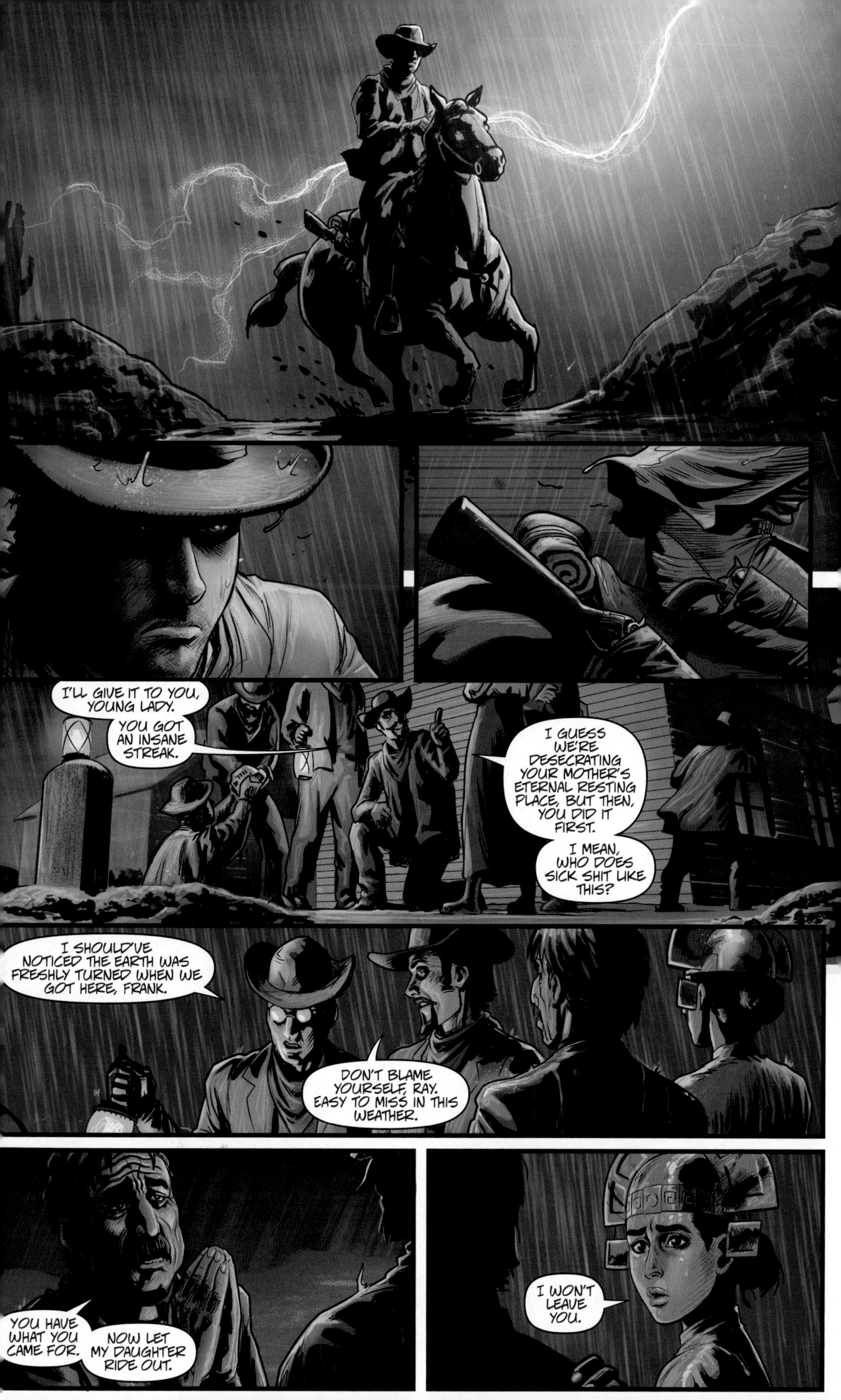
I'LL GIVE IT TO YOU, YOUNG LADY.
YOU GOT AN INSANE STREAK.
I GUESS WE'RE DESECRATING YOUR MOTHER'S ETERNAL RESTING PLACE, BUT THEN, YOU DID IT FIRST.
I MEAN, WHO DOES SICK SHIT LIKE THIS?
I SHOULD'VE NOTICED THE EARTH WAS FRESHLY TURNED WHEN WE GOT HERE, FRANK.
DON'T BLAME YOURSELF, RAY. EASY TO MISS IN THIS WEATHER.
YOU HAVE WHAT YOU CAME FOR.
NOW LET MY DAUGHTER RIDE OUT.
I WON'T LEAVE YOU.

FAMILY.

I KNOW. I KNOW.

NO. LET MY FATHER GO. THIS BURDEN IS MINE TO BEAR. IN THIS LIFE, AND IN THE NEXT.

CRAZY AND BRAVE. LETHAL COMBINATION.

I'M GETTING HARD.

THAT'S THE LAST OF IT, MR. DANTON.

LOOK AT THIS DAMN THING. WHAT'D THEY USE THIS FOR?

IT IS CALLED CAPACOCHA. THE RITUALISTIC SACRIFICE OF CHILDREN.

THIS IS A BLEEDING INSTRUMENT.

IT IS SACRED AND WORTH MORE TO THE INCANS THAN YOU CAN COMPREHEND.

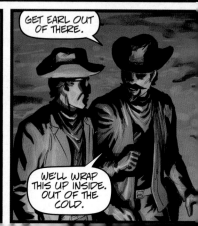

GET EARL OUT OF THERE.

WE'LL WRAP THIS UP INSIDE. OUT OF THE COLD.

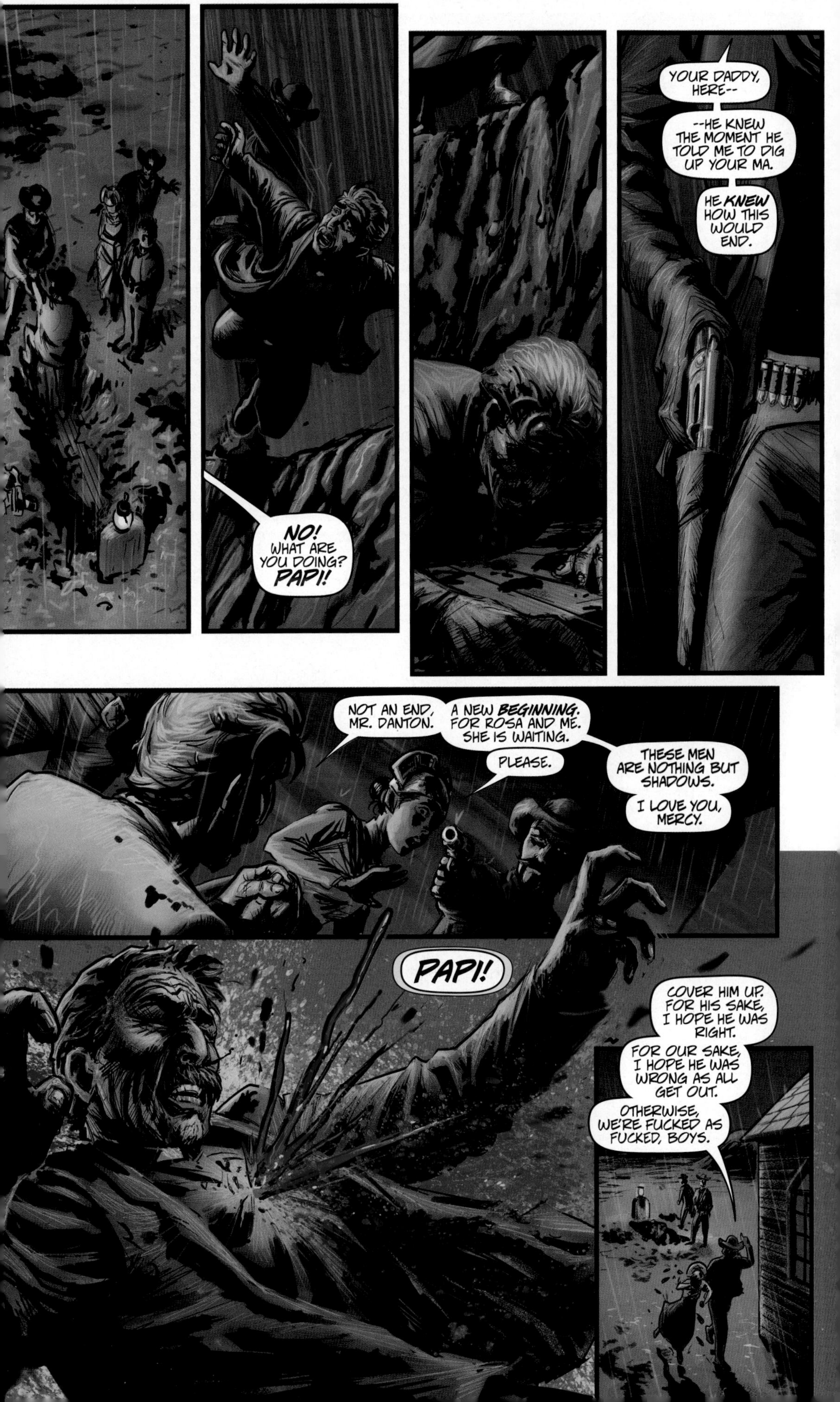

NO! WHAT ARE YOU DOING? PAPI!
YOUR DADDY, HERE--
--HE KNEW THE MOMENT HE TOLD ME TO DIG UP YOUR MA.
HE KNEW HOW THIS WOULD END.
NOT AN END, MR. DANTON.
A NEW BEGINNING. FOR ROSA AND ME. SHE IS WAITING.
PLEASE.
THESE MEN ARE NOTHING BUT SHADOWS.
I LOVE YOU, MERCY.
PAPI!
COVER HIM UP. FOR HIS SAKE, I HOPE HE WAS RIGHT.
FOR OUR SAKE, I HOPE HE WAS WRONG AS ALL GET OUT.
OTHERWISE, WE'RE FUCKED AS FUCKED, BOYS.

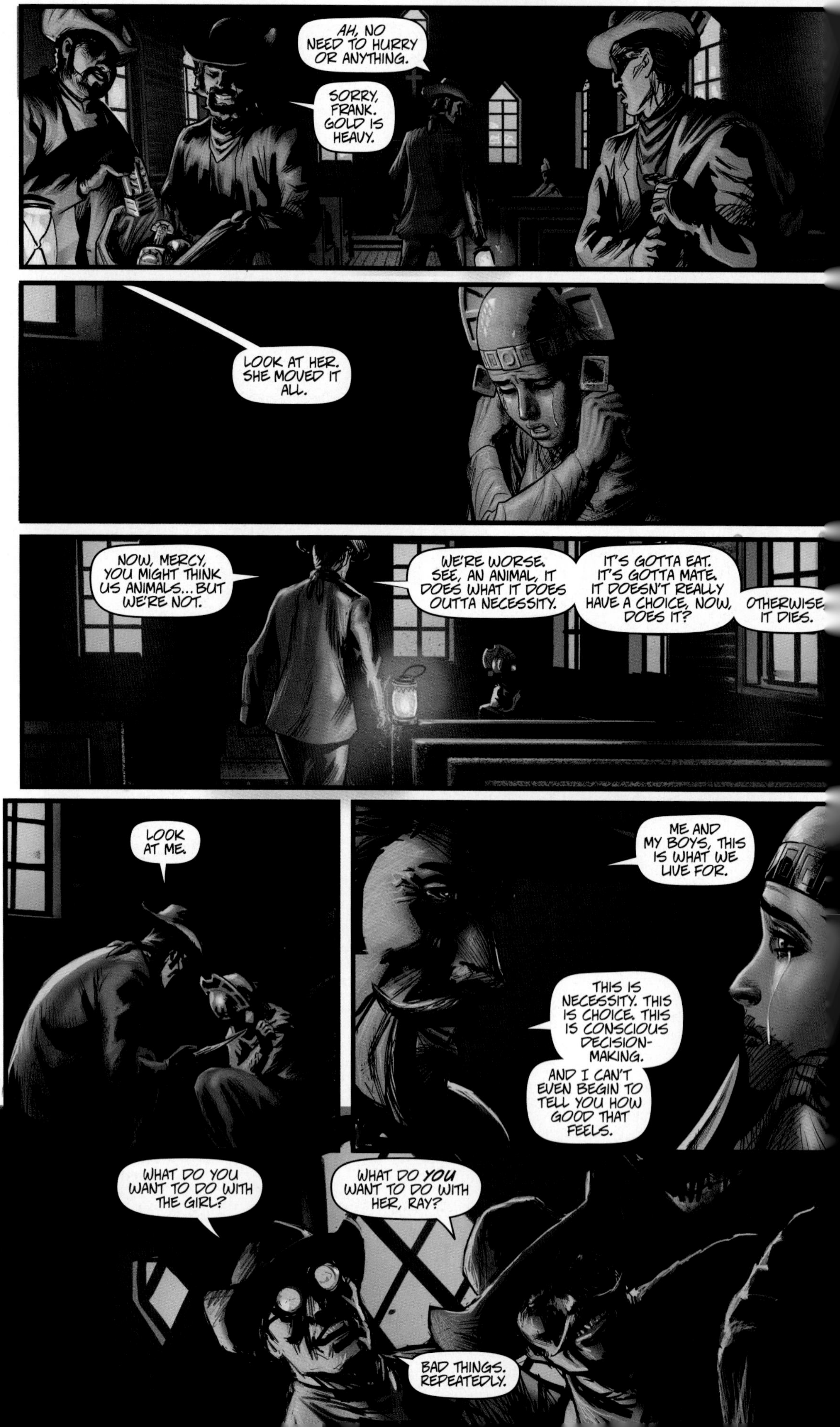
AH, NO NEED TO HURRY OR ANYTHING.
SORRY, FRANK. GOLD IS HEAVY.
LOOK AT HER. SHE MOVED IT ALL.
NOW, MERCY, YOU MIGHT THINK US ANIMALS... BUT WE'RE NOT.
WE'RE WORSE. SEE, AN ANIMAL, IT DOES WHAT IT DOES OUTTA NECESSITY.
IT'S GOTTA EAT. IT'S GOTTA MATE. IT DOESN'T REALLY HAVE A CHOICE, NOW, DOES IT?
OTHERWISE, IT DIES.
LOOK AT ME.
ME AND MY BOYS, THIS IS WHAT WE LIVE FOR.
THIS IS NECESSITY. THIS IS CHOICE. THIS IS CONSCIOUS DECISION-MAKING.
AND I CAN'T EVEN BEGIN TO TELL YOU HOW GOOD THAT FEELS.
WHAT DO YOU WANT TO DO WITH THE GIRL?
WHAT DO *YOU* WANT TO DO WITH HER, RAY?
BAD THINGS. REPEATEDLY.

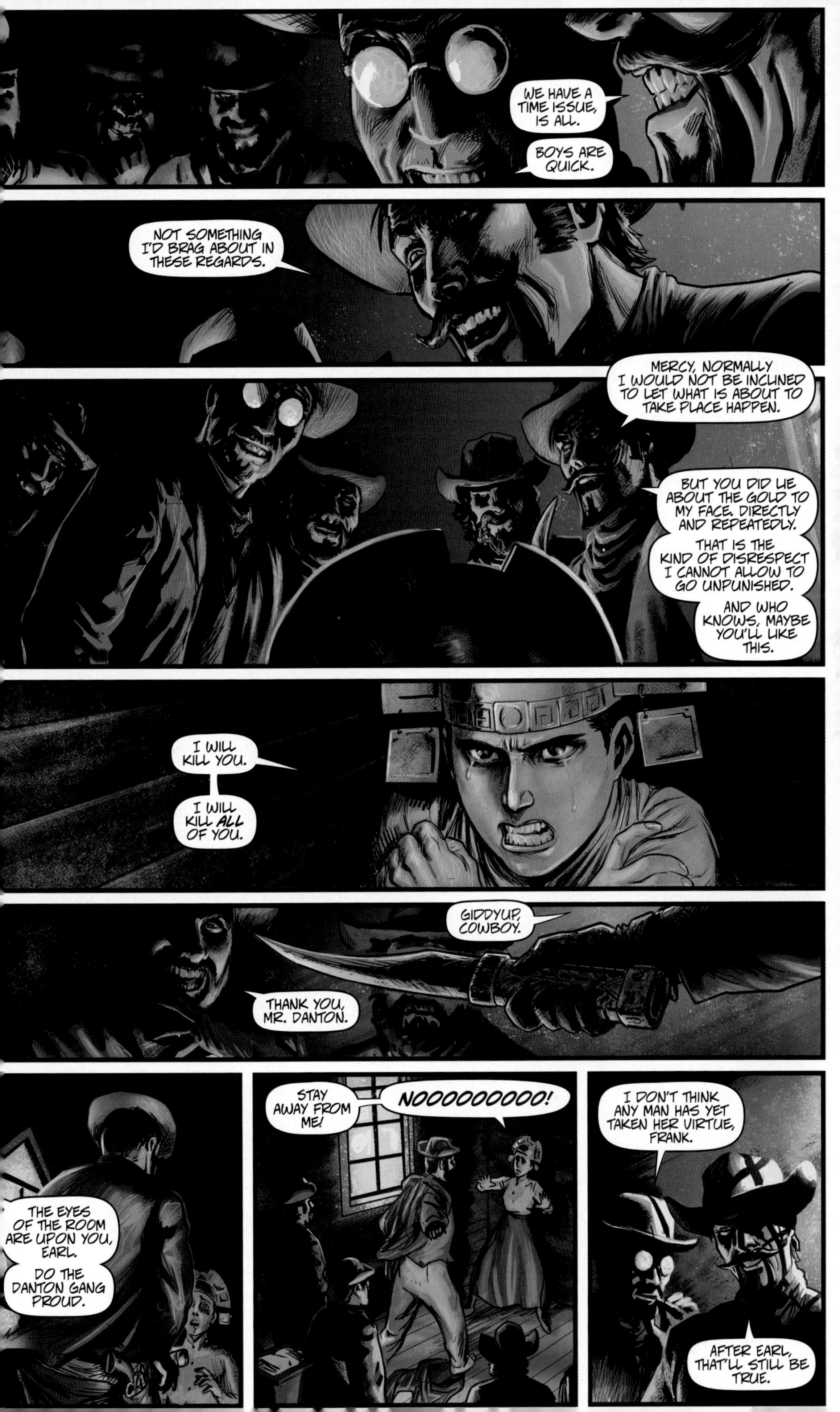
WE HAVE A TIME ISSUE, IS ALL.
BOYS ARE QUICK.
NOT SOMETHING I'D BRAG ABOUT IN THESE REGARDS.
MERCY, NORMALLY I WOULD NOT BE INCLINED TO LET WHAT IS ABOUT TO TAKE PLACE HAPPEN.
BUT YOU DID LIE ABOUT THE GOLD TO MY FACE. DIRECTLY AND REPEATEDLY.
THAT IS THE KIND OF DISRESPECT I CANNOT ALLOW TO GO UNPUNISHED.
AND WHO KNOWS, MAYBE YOU'LL LIKE THIS.
I WILL KILL YOU.
I WILL KILL *ALL* OF YOU.
GIDDYUP, COWBOY.
THANK YOU, MR. DANTON.
THE EYES OF THE ROOM ARE UPON YOU, EARL.
DO THE DANTON GANG PROUD.
STAY AWAY FROM ME!
NOOOOOOOOO!
I DON'T THINK ANY MAN HAS YET TAKEN HER VIRTUE, FRANK.
AFTER EARL, THAT'LL STILL BE TRUE.

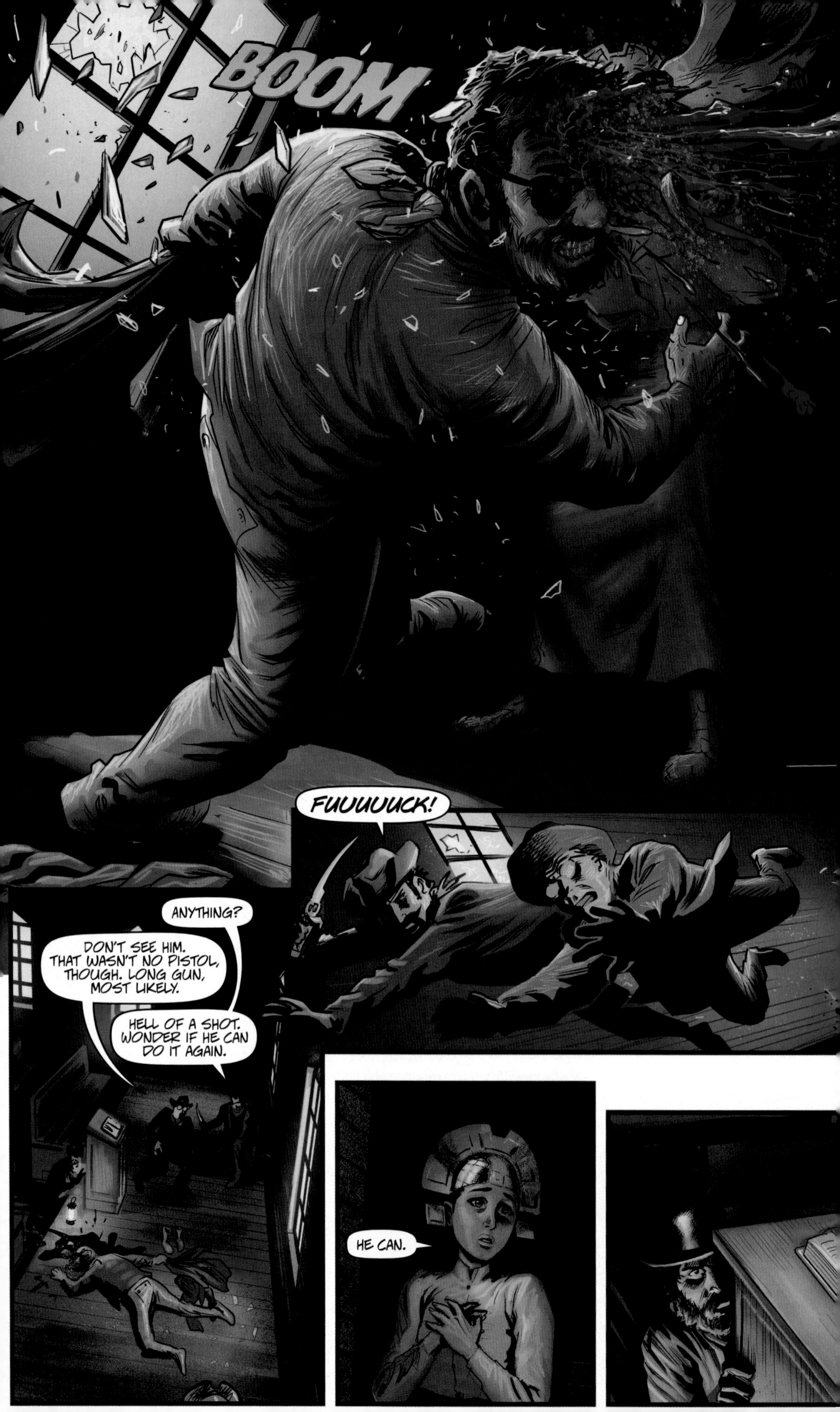
BOOM
FUUUUUCK!
ANYTHING?
DON'T SEE HIM. THAT WASN'T NO PISTOL, THOUGH. LONG GUN, MOST LIKELY.
HELL OF A SHOT. WONDER IF HE CAN DO IT AGAIN.
HE CAN.

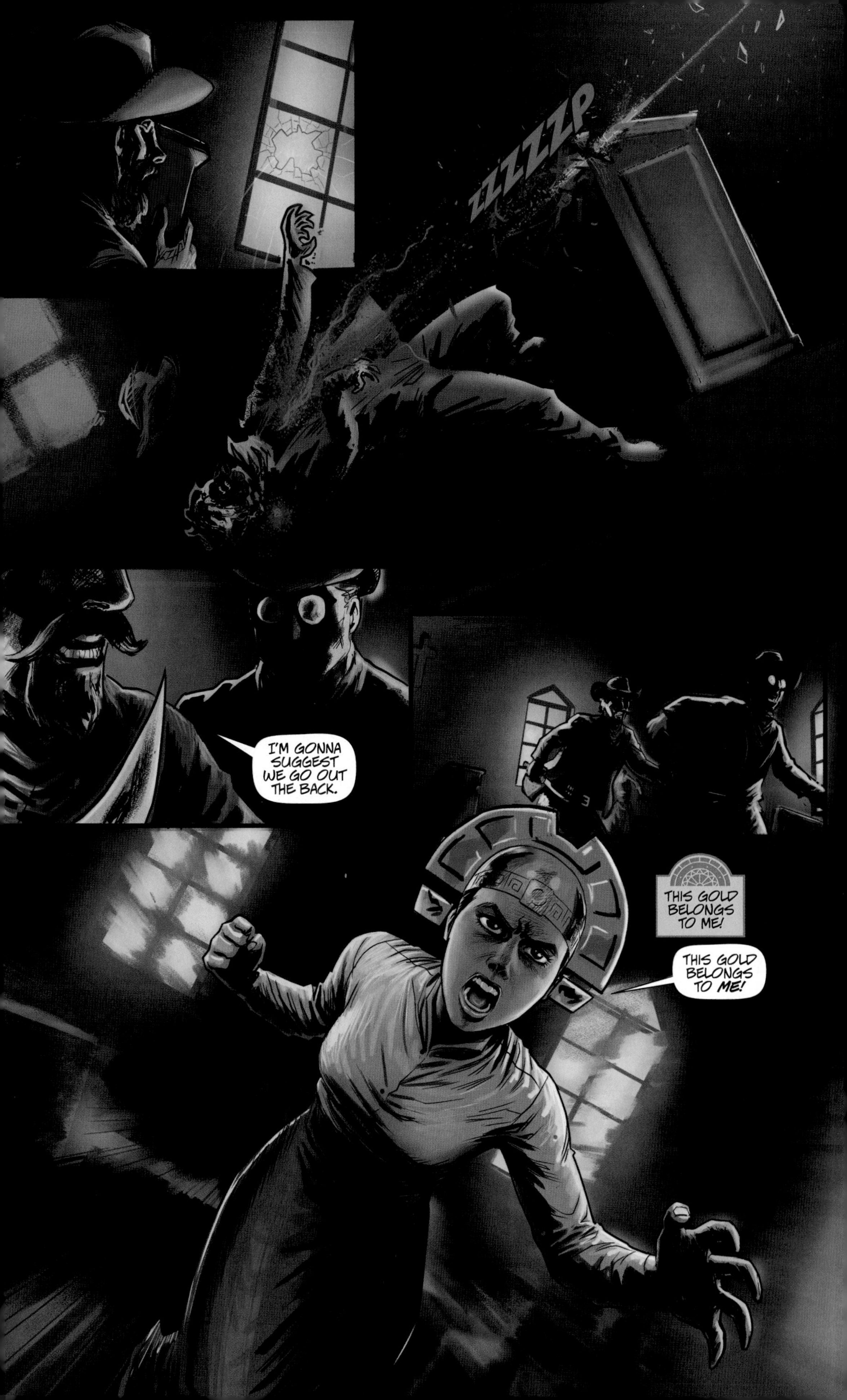
ZZZZZP
I'M GONNA SUGGEST WE GO OUT THE BACK.
THIS GOLD BELONGS TO ME!
THIS GOLD BELONGS TO ME!

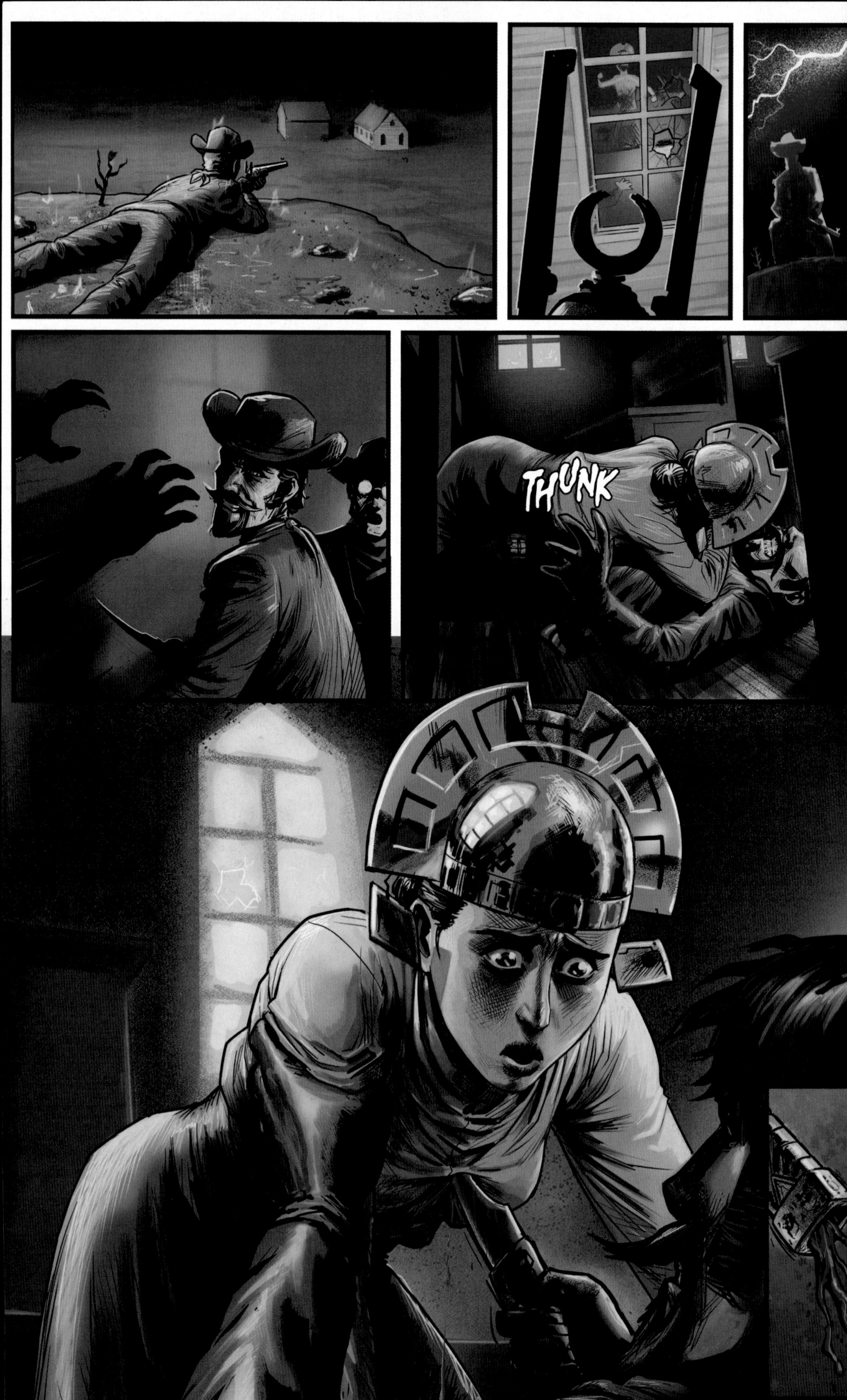
THUNK

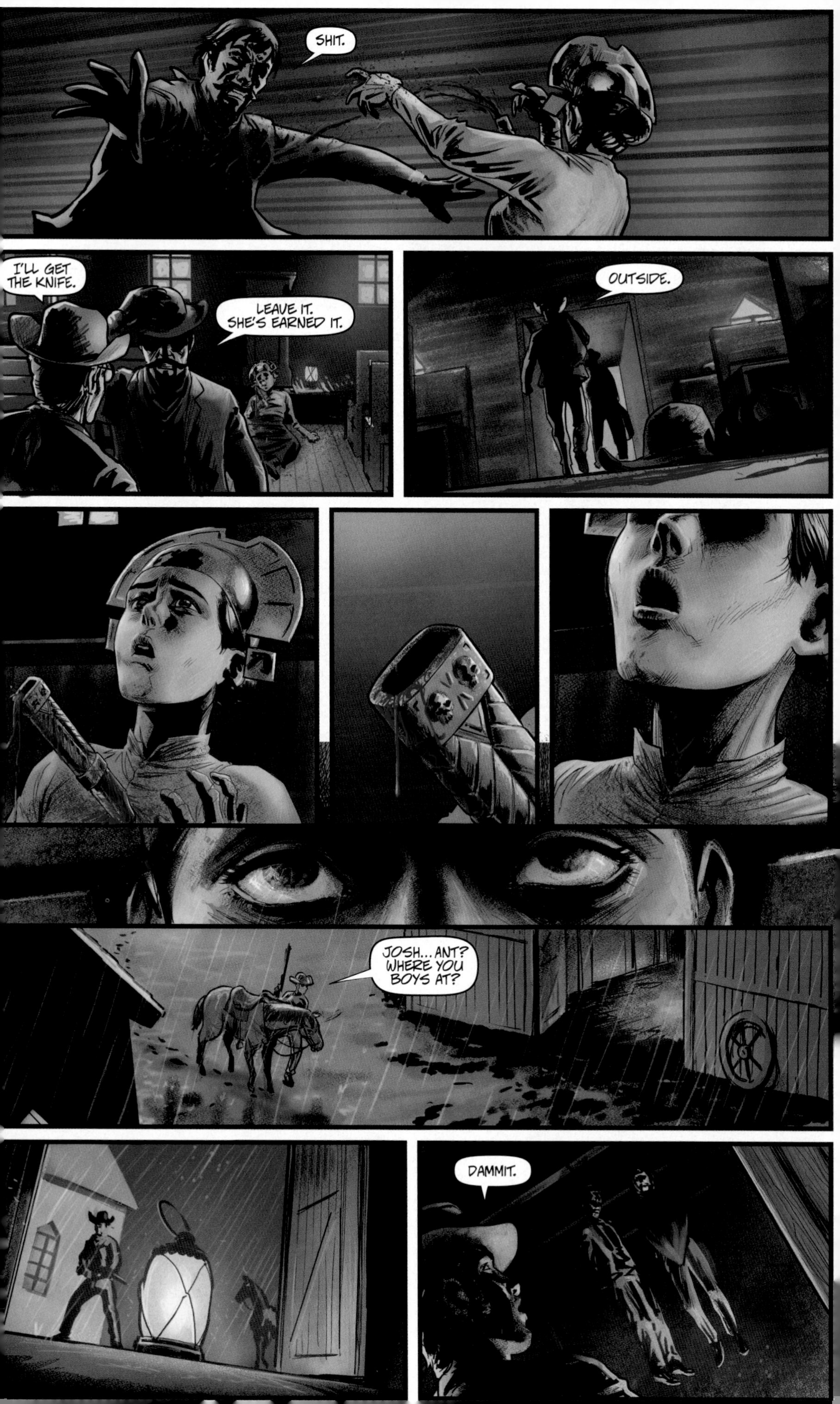
SHIT.
I'LL GET THE KNIFE.
LEAVE IT. SHE'S EARNED IT.
OUTSIDE.
JOSH... ANT? WHERE YOU BOYS AT?
DAMMIT.

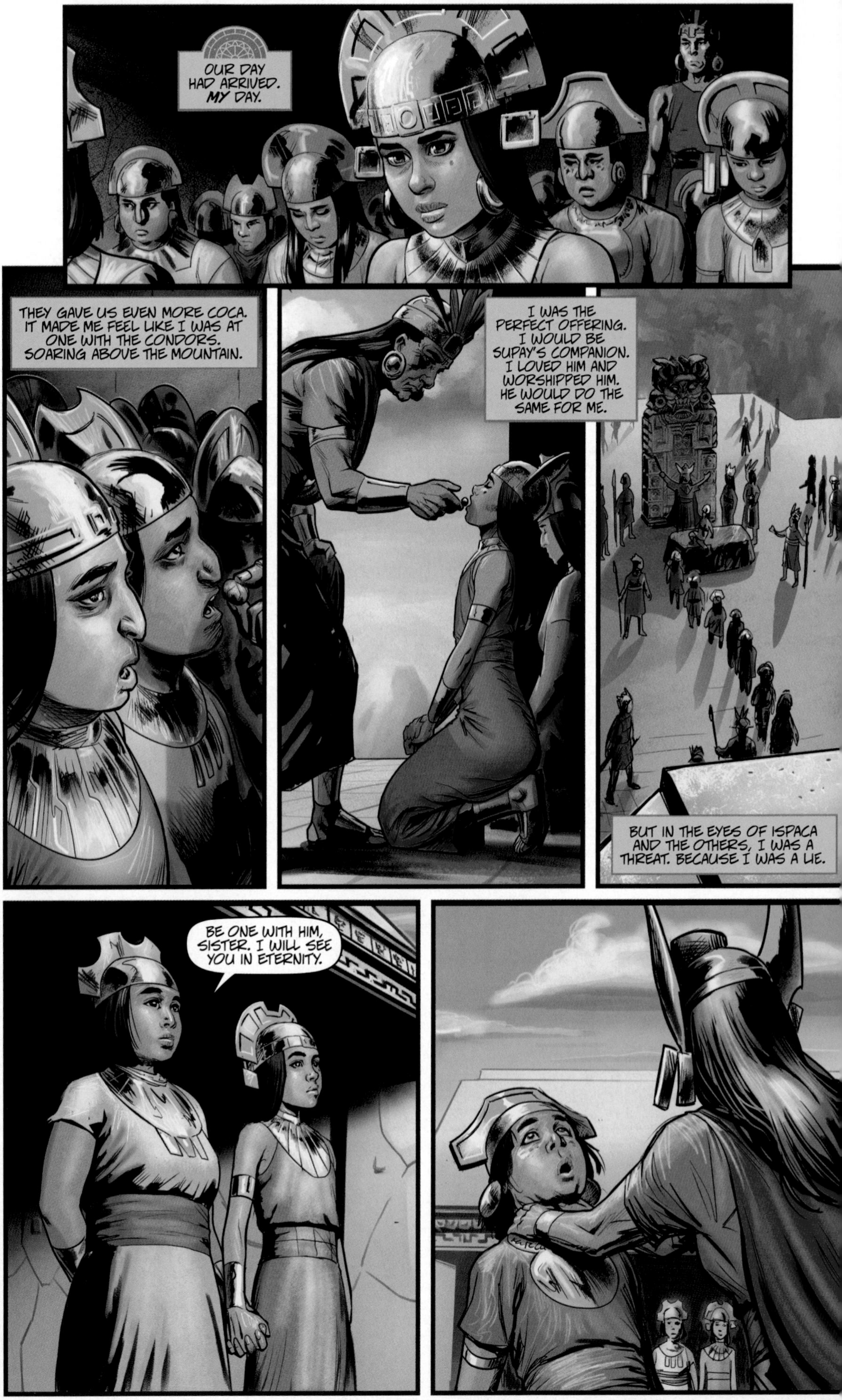
OUR DAY HAD ARRIVED. MY DAY.
THEY GAVE US EVEN MORE COCA. IT MADE ME FEEL LIKE I WAS AT ONE WITH THE CONDORS. SOARING ABOVE THE MOUNTAIN.
I WAS THE PERFECT OFFERING. I WOULD BE SUPAY'S COMPANION. I LOVED HIM AND WORSHIPPED HIM. HE WOULD DO THE SAME FOR ME.
BUT IN THE EYES OF ISPACA AND THE OTHERS, I WAS A THREAT. BECAUSE I WAS A LIE.
BE ONE WITH HIM, SISTER. I WILL SEE YOU IN ETERNITY.

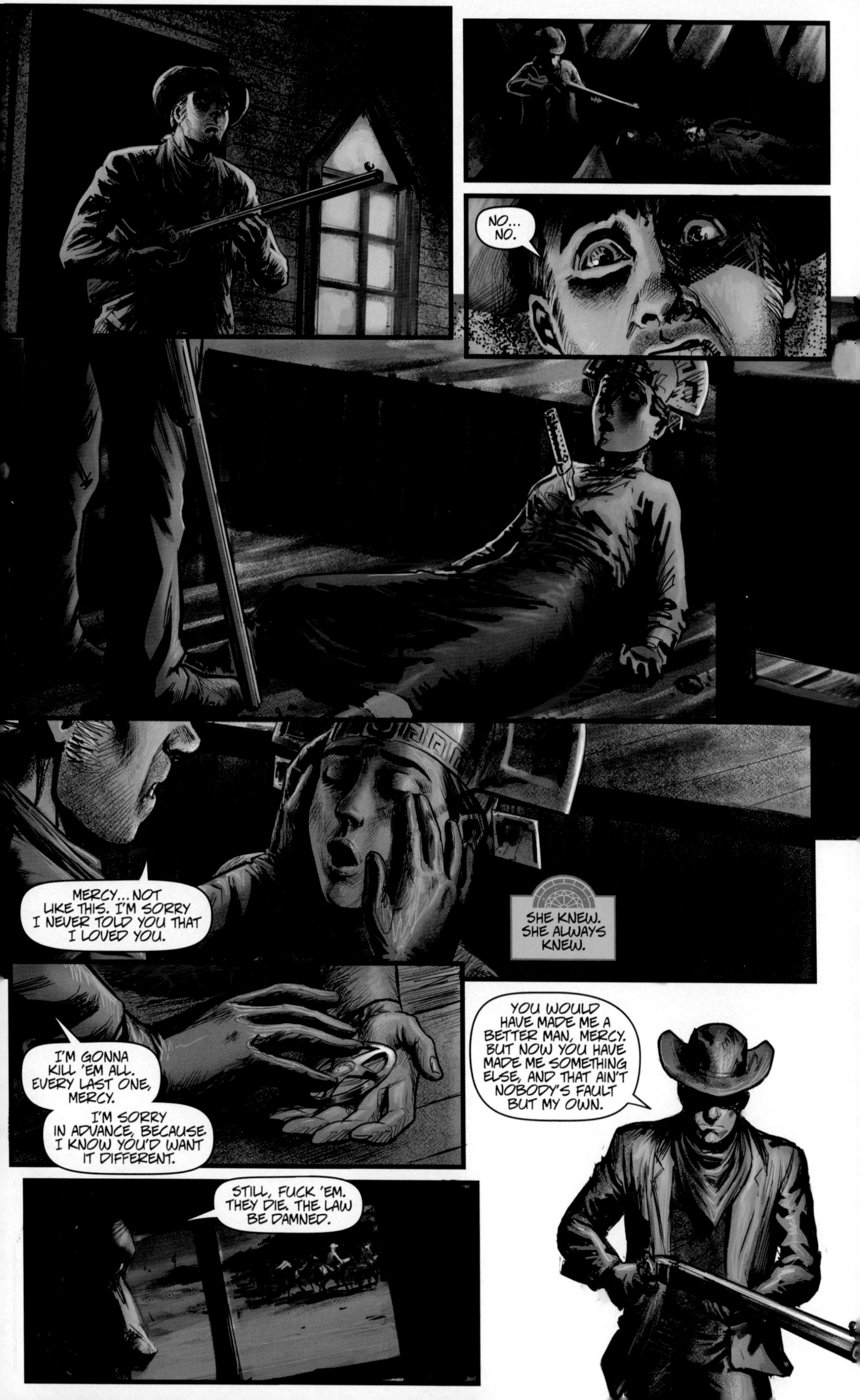
NO... NO.
MERCY... NOT LIKE THIS. I'M SORRY I NEVER TOLD YOU THAT I LOVED YOU.
SHE KNEW. SHE ALWAYS KNEW.
I'M GONNA KILL 'EM ALL. EVERY LAST ONE, MERCY.
I'M SORRY IN ADVANCE, BECAUSE I KNOW YOU'D WANT IT DIFFERENT.
STILL, FUCK 'EM. THEY DIE. THE LAW BE DAMNED.
YOU WOULD HAVE MADE ME A BETTER MAN, MERCY. BUT NOW YOU HAVE MADE ME SOMETHING ELSE, AND THAT AIN'T NOBODY'S FAULT BUT MY OWN.

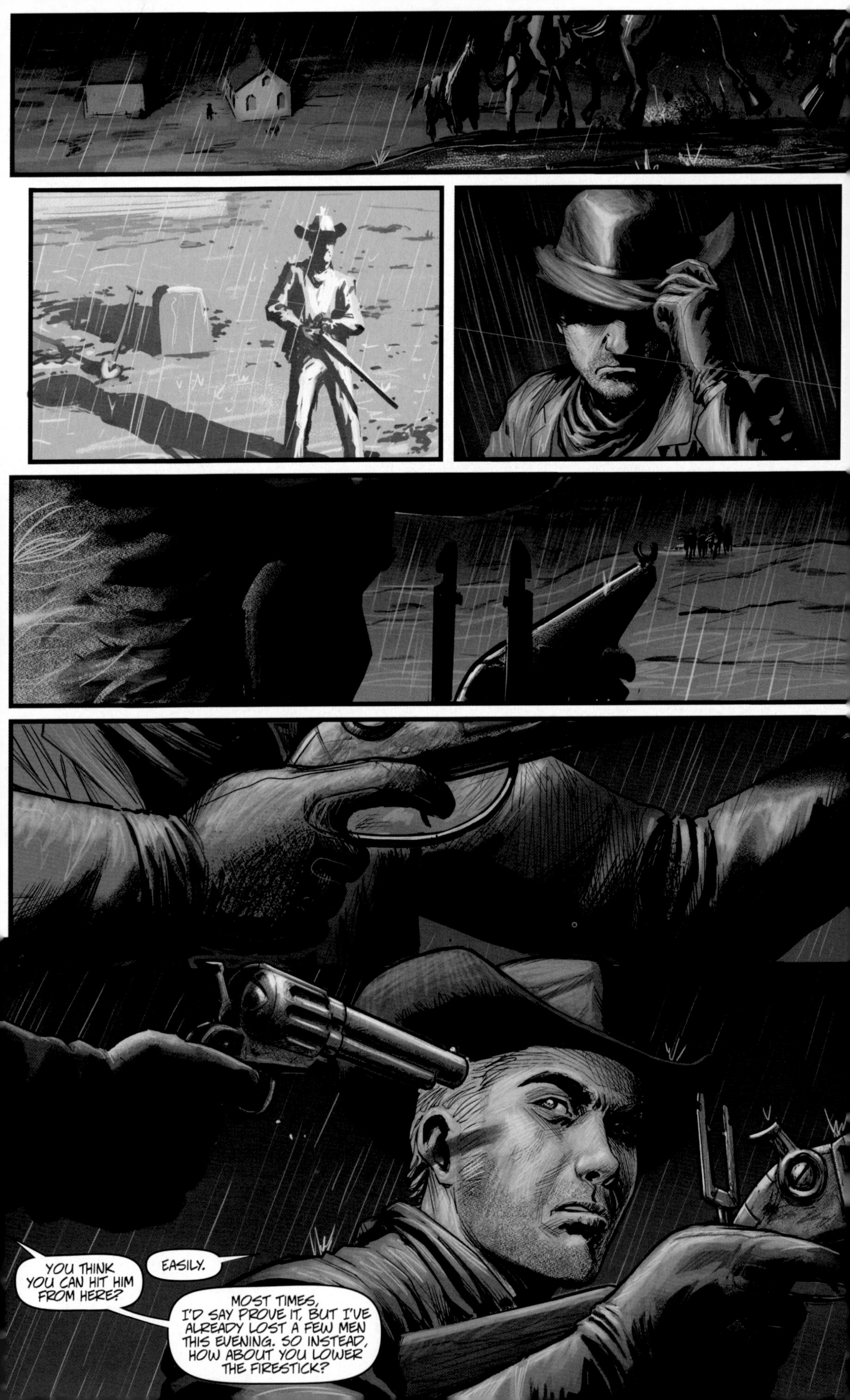
YOU THINK YOU CAN HIT HIM FROM HERE?
EASILY.
MOST TIMES, I'D SAY PROVE IT, BUT I'VE ALREADY LOST A FEW MEN THIS EVENING. SO INSTEAD, HOW ABOUT YOU LOWER THE FIRESTICK?

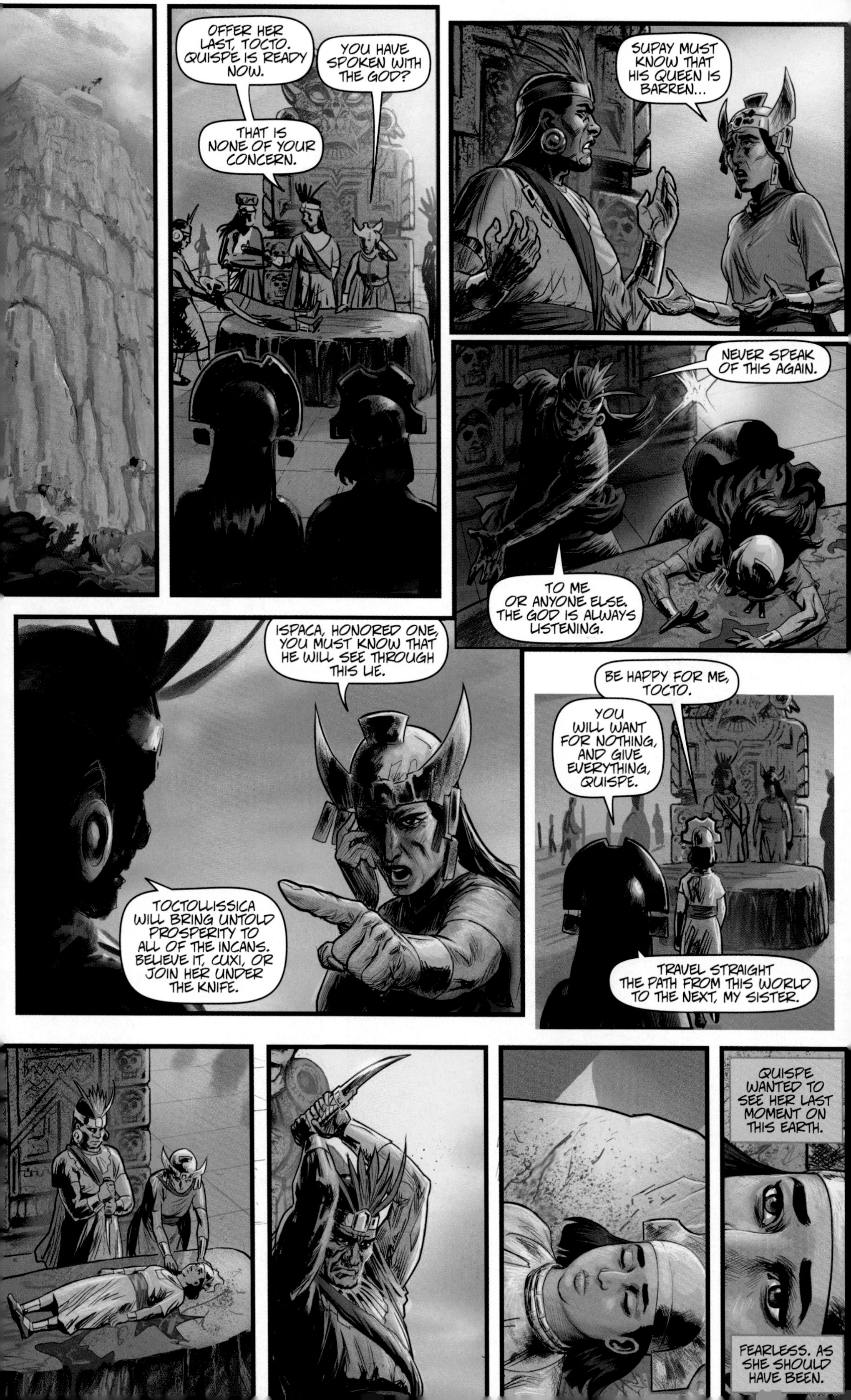
OFFER HER LAST, TOCTO. QUISPE IS READY NOW.
YOU HAVE SPOKEN WITH THE GOD?
THAT IS NONE OF YOUR CONCERN.
SUPAY MUST KNOW THAT HIS QUEEN IS BARREN...
NEVER SPEAK OF THIS AGAIN.
TO ME OR ANYONE ELSE. THE GOD IS ALWAYS LISTENING.
ISPACA, HONORED ONE, YOU MUST KNOW THAT HE WILL SEE THROUGH THIS LIE.
TOCTOLLISSICA WILL BRING UNTOLD PROSPERITY TO ALL OF THE INCANS. BELIEVE IT, CUXI, OR JOIN HER UNDER THE KNIFE.
BE HAPPY FOR ME, TOCTO.
YOU WILL WANT FOR NOTHING, AND GIVE EVERYTHING, QUISPE.
TRAVEL STRAIGHT THE PATH FROM THIS WORLD TO THE NEXT, MY SISTER.
QUISPE WANTED TO SEE HER LAST MOMENT ON THIS EARTH.
FEARLESS. AS SHE SHOULD HAVE BEEN.

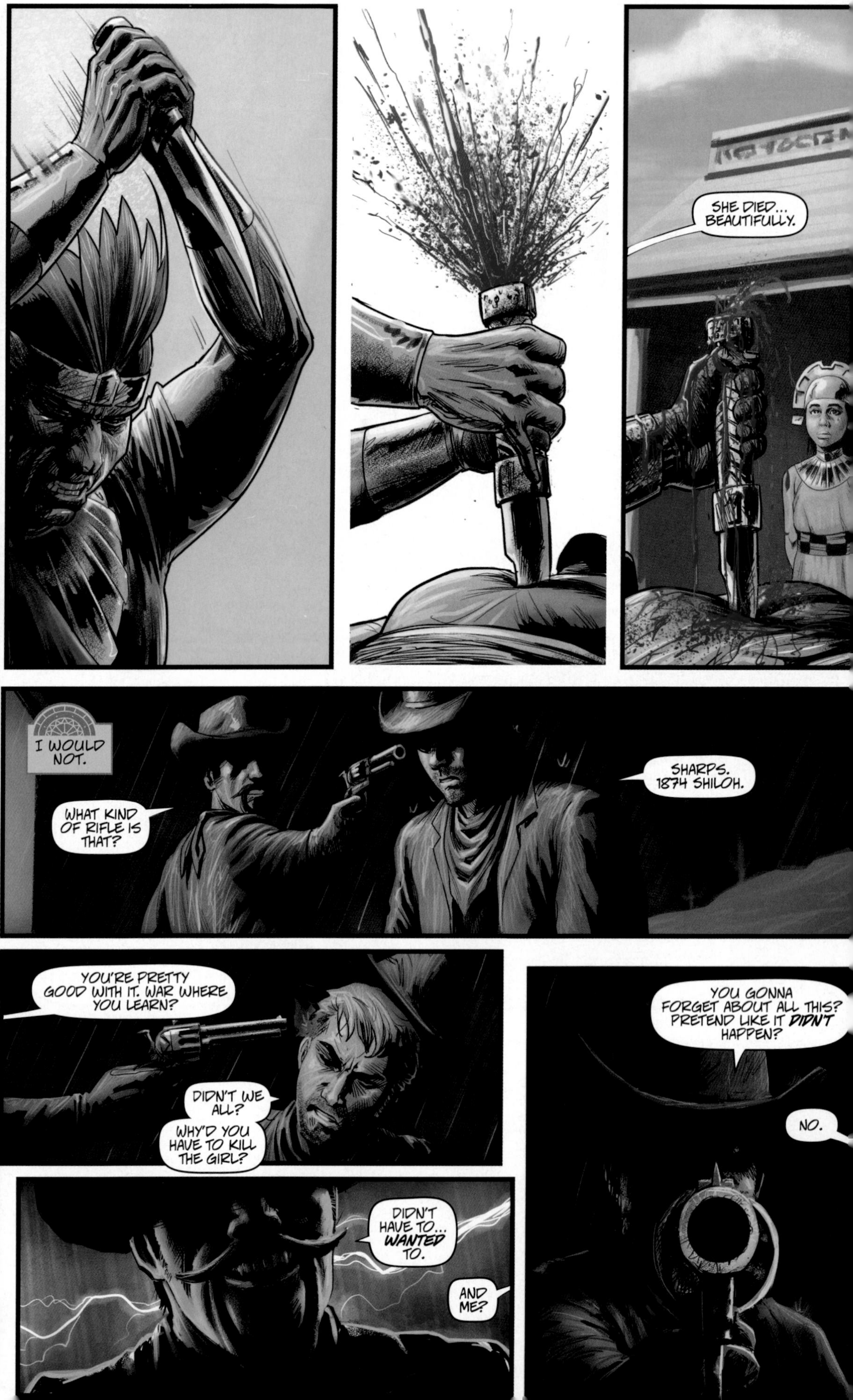
SHE DIED... BEAUTIFULLY.
I WOULD NOT.
WHAT KIND OF RIFLE IS THAT?
SHARPS. 1874 SHILOH.
YOU'RE PRETTY GOOD WITH IT. WAR WHERE YOU LEARN?
DIDN'T WE ALL?
WHY'D YOU HAVE TO KILL THE GIRL?
DIDN'T HAVE TO... **WANTED** TO.
AND ME?
YOU GONNA FORGET ABOUT ALL THIS? PRETEND LIKE IT **DIDN'T** HAPPEN?
NO.

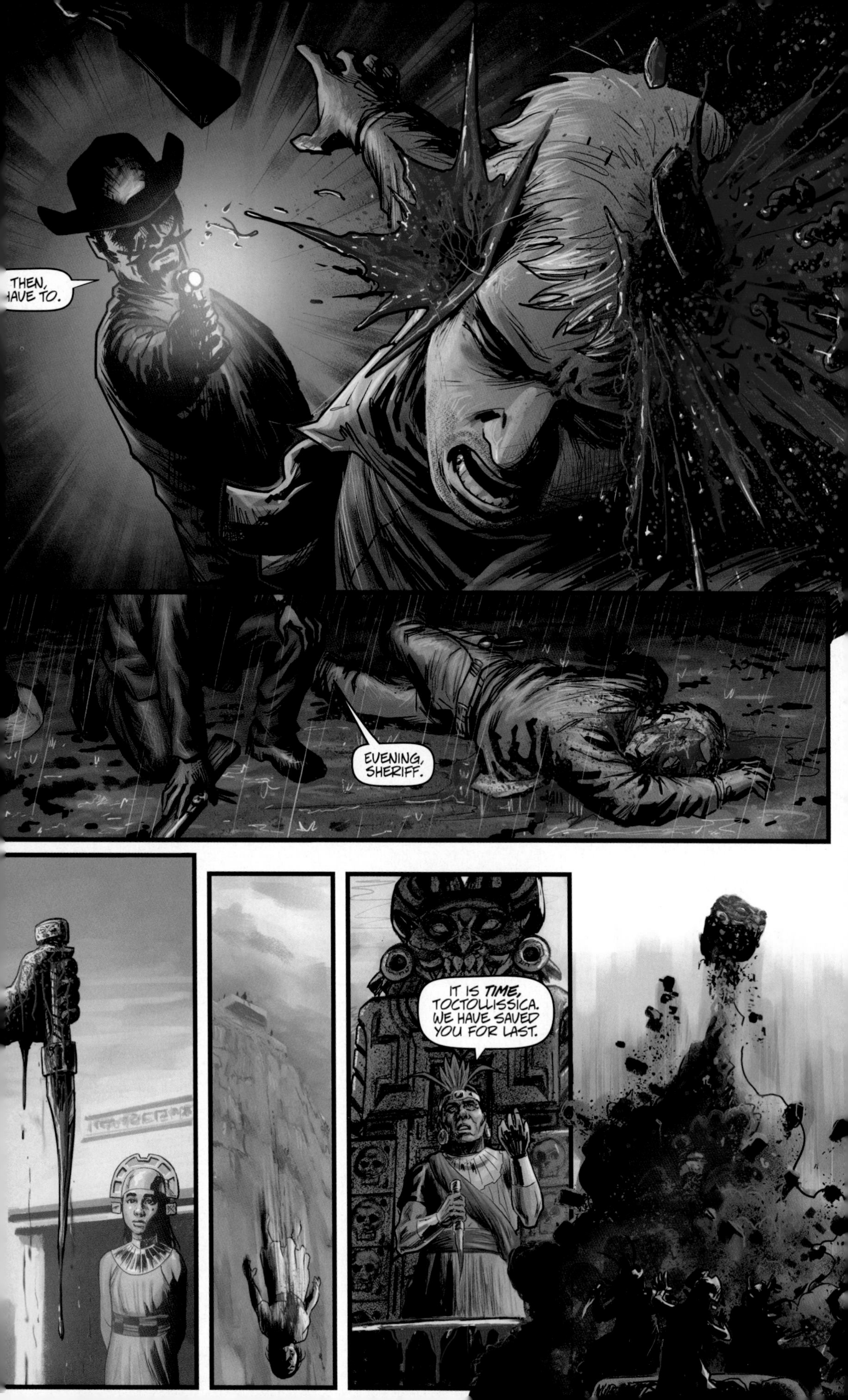
THEN,
HAVE TO.
EVENING,
SHERIFF.
IT IS *TIME*,
TOCTOLLISSICA.
WE HAVE SAVED
YOU FOR LAST.

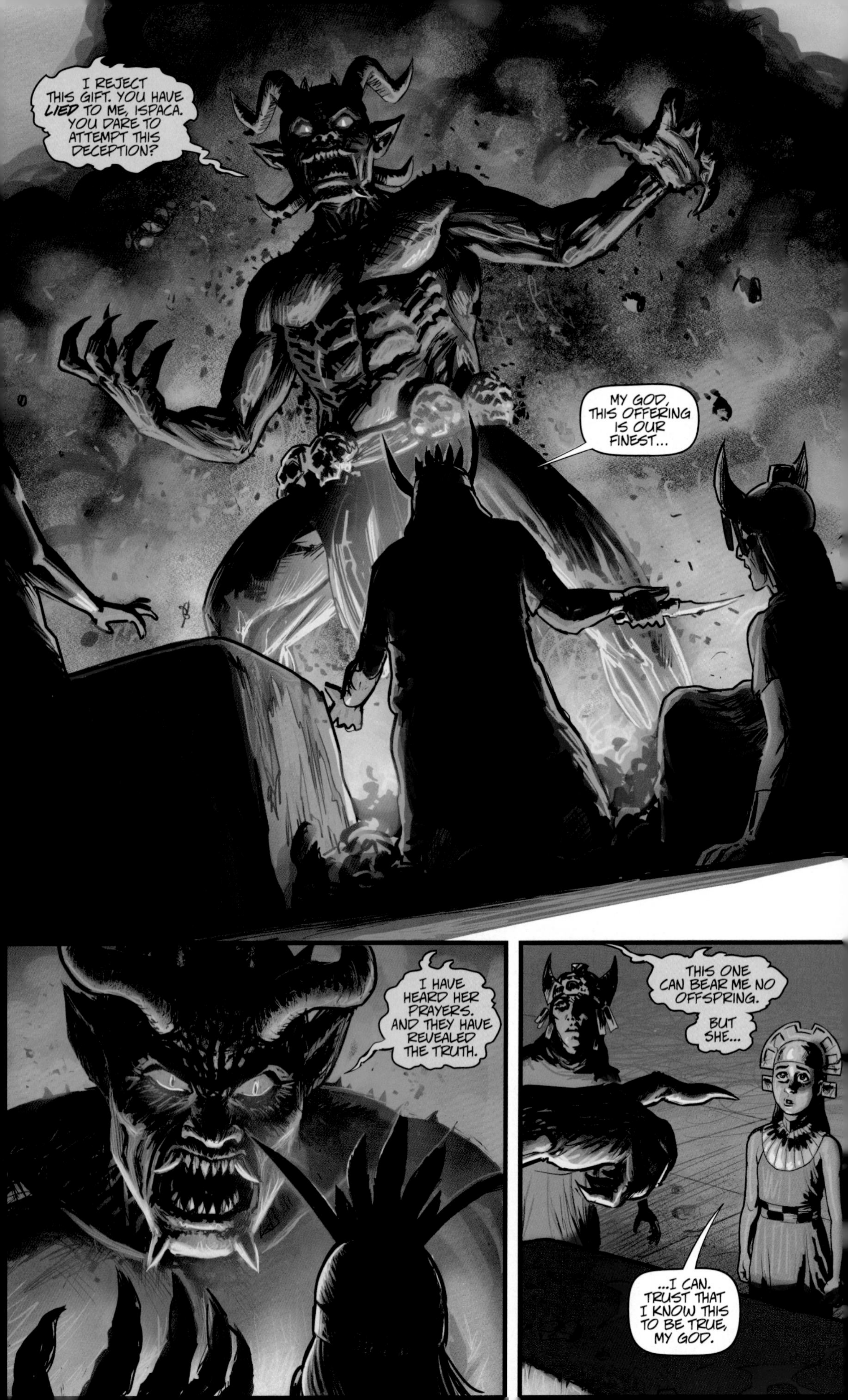
I REJECT THIS GIFT. YOU HAVE LIED TO ME, ISPACA. YOU DARE TO ATTEMPT THIS DECEPTION?
MY GOD, THIS OFFERING IS OUR FINEST...
I HAVE HEARD HER PRAYERS. AND THEY HAVE REVEALED THE TRUTH.
THIS ONE CAN BEAR ME NO OFFSPRING.
BUT SHE...
...I CAN. TRUST THAT I KNOW THIS TO BE TRUE, MY GOD.

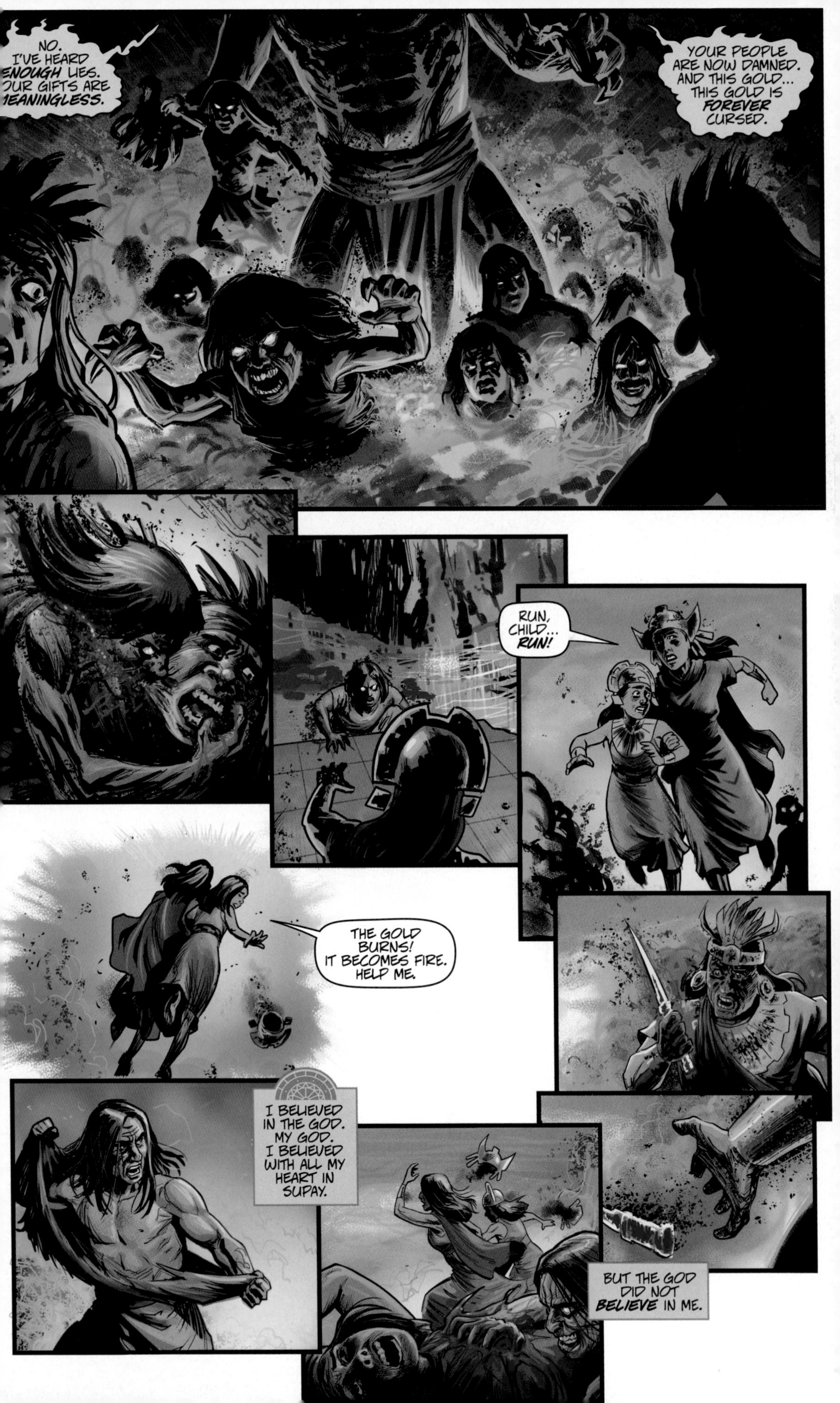

NO. I'VE HEARD ENOUGH LIES. YOUR GIFTS ARE MEANINGLESS.
YOUR PEOPLE ARE NOW DAMNED. AND THIS GOLD... THIS GOLD IS FOREVER CURSED.
RUN, CHILD... RUN!
THE GOLD BURNS! IT BECOMES FIRE. HELP ME.
I BELIEVED IN THE GOD. MY GOD. I BELIEVED WITH ALL MY HEART IN SUPAY.
BUT THE GOD DID NOT BELIEVE IN ME.

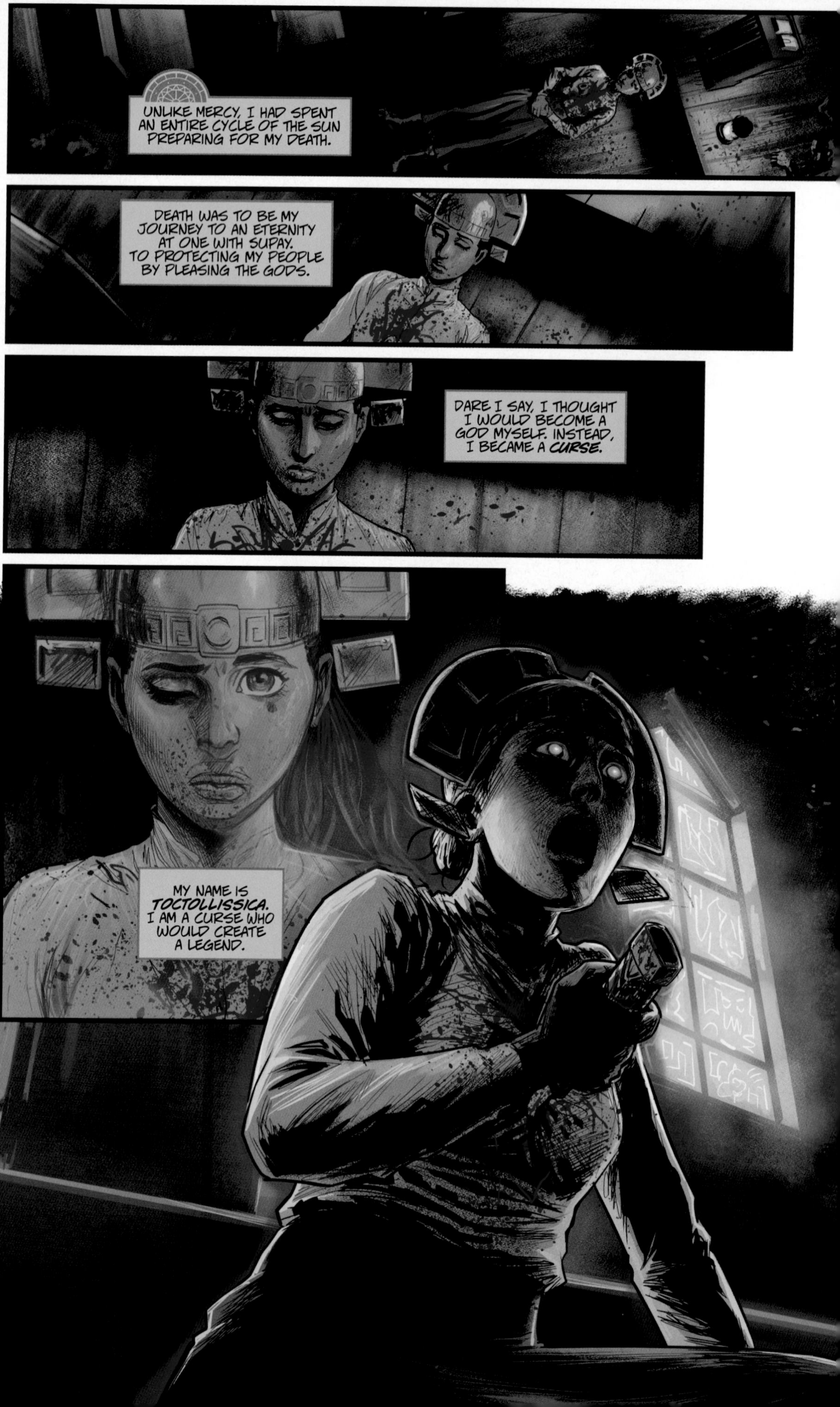
UNLIKE MERCY, I HAD SPENT AN ENTIRE CYCLE OF THE SUN PREPARING FOR MY DEATH.
DEATH WAS TO BE MY JOURNEY TO AN ETERNITY AT ONE WITH SUPAY. TO PROTECTING MY PEOPLE BY PLEASING THE GODS.
DARE I SAY, I THOUGHT I WOULD BECOME A GOD MYSELF. INSTEAD, I BECAME A CURSE.
MY NAME IS TOCTOLLISSICA. I AM A CURSE WHO WOULD CREATE A LEGEND.

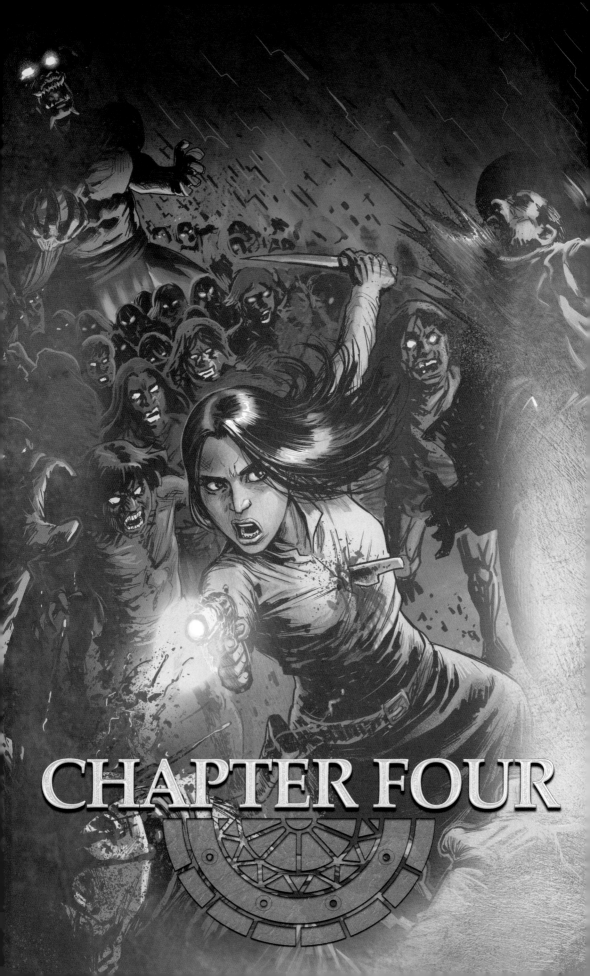

CHAPTER FOUR

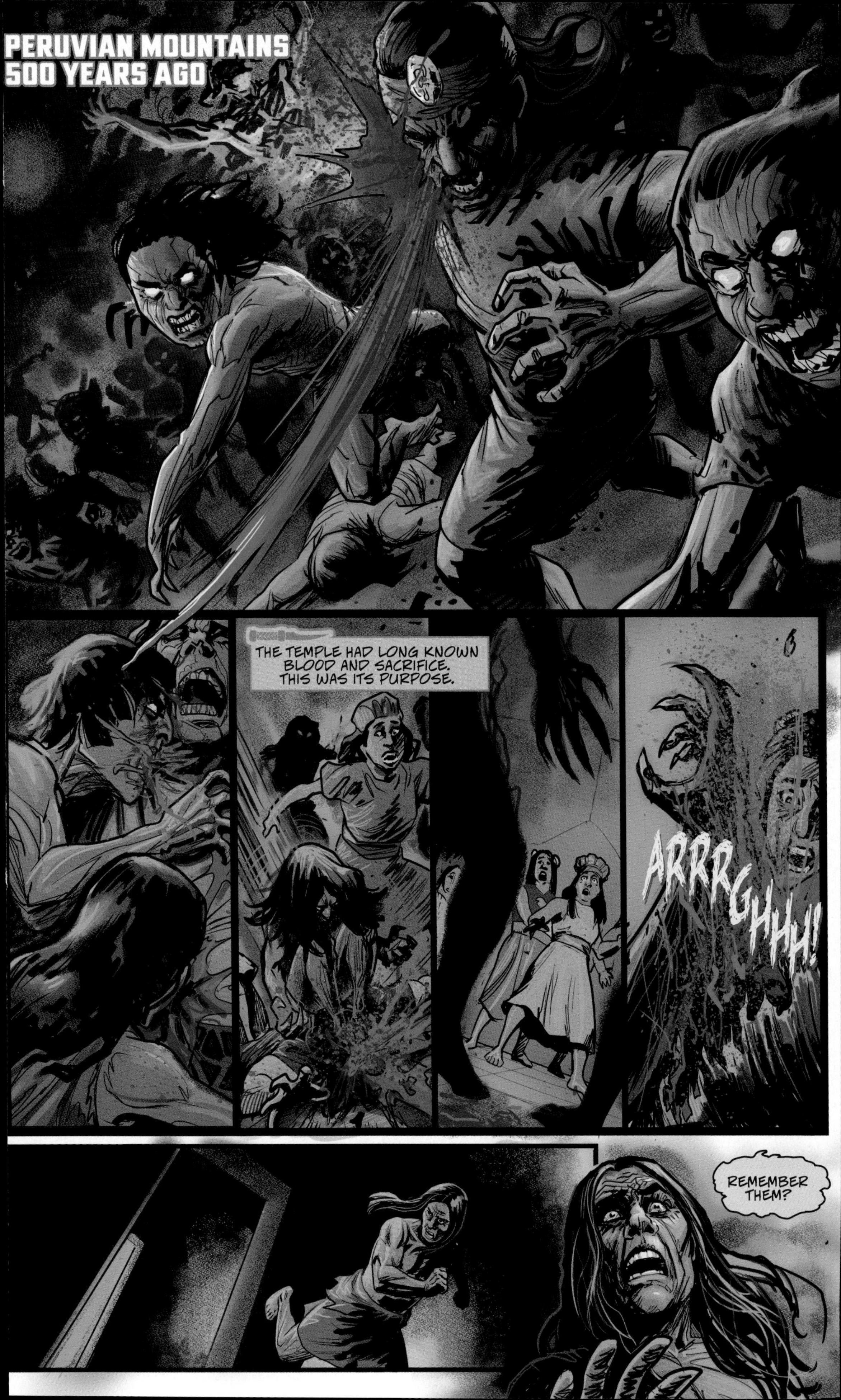
PERUVIAN MOUNTAINS
500 YEARS AGO
THE TEMPLE HAD LONG KNOWN BLOOD AND SACRIFICE. THIS WAS ITS PURPOSE.
ARRRGHHH!
REMEMBER THEM?

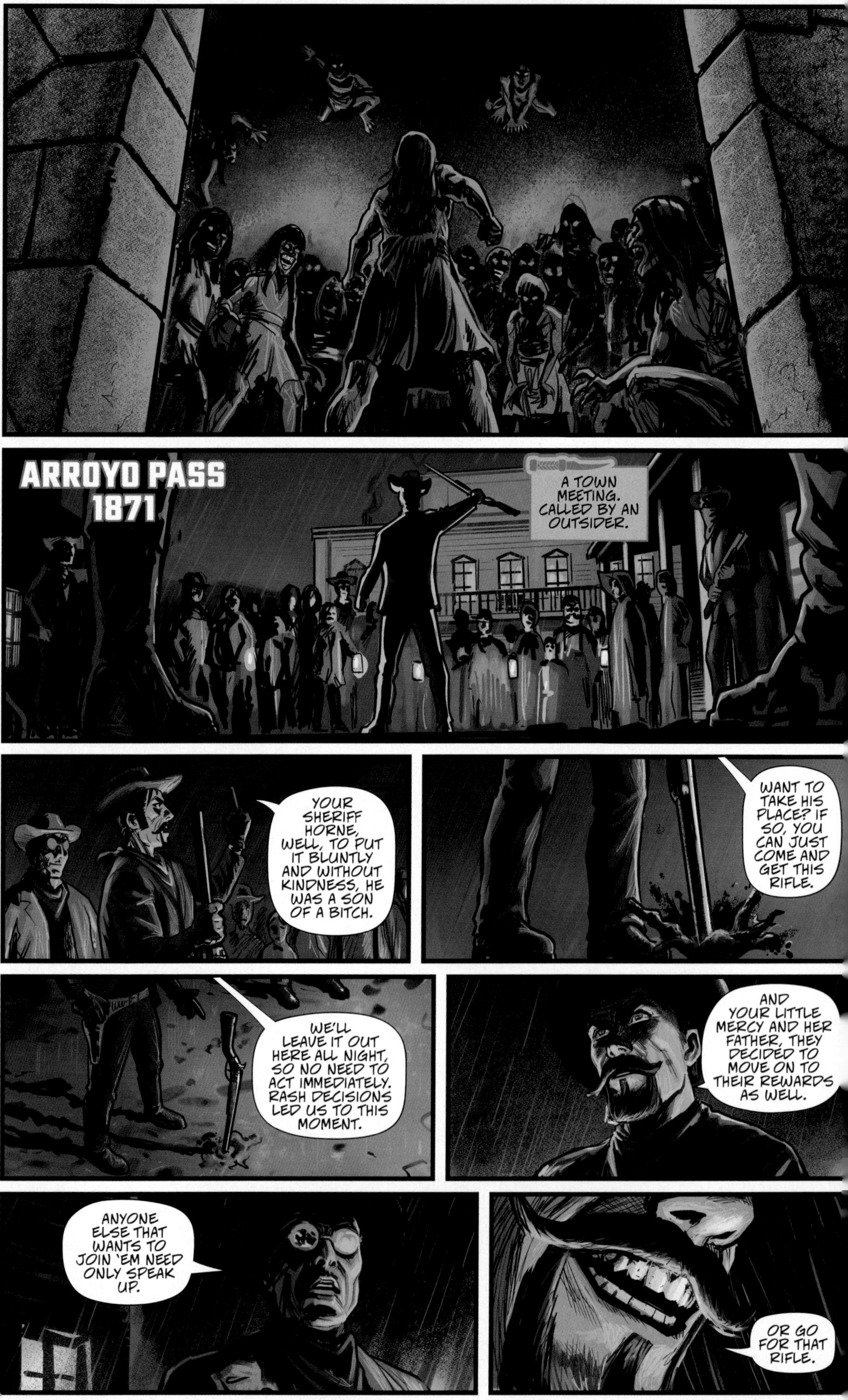
ARROYO PASS 1871
A TOWN MEETING. CALLED BY AN OUTSIDER.
YOUR SHERIFF HORNE, WELL, TO PUT IT BLUNTLY AND WITHOUT KINDNESS, HE WAS A SON OF A BITCH.
WANT TO TAKE HIS PLACE? IF SO, YOU CAN JUST COME AND GET THIS RIFLE.
WE'LL LEAVE IT OUT HERE ALL NIGHT, SO NO NEED TO ACT IMMEDIATELY. RASH DECISIONS LED US TO THIS MOMENT.
AND YOUR LITTLE MERCY AND HER FATHER, THEY DECIDED TO MOVE ON TO THEIR REWARDS AS WELL.
ANYONE ELSE THAT WANTS TO JOIN 'EM NEED ONLY SPEAK UP.
OR GO FOR THAT RIFLE.

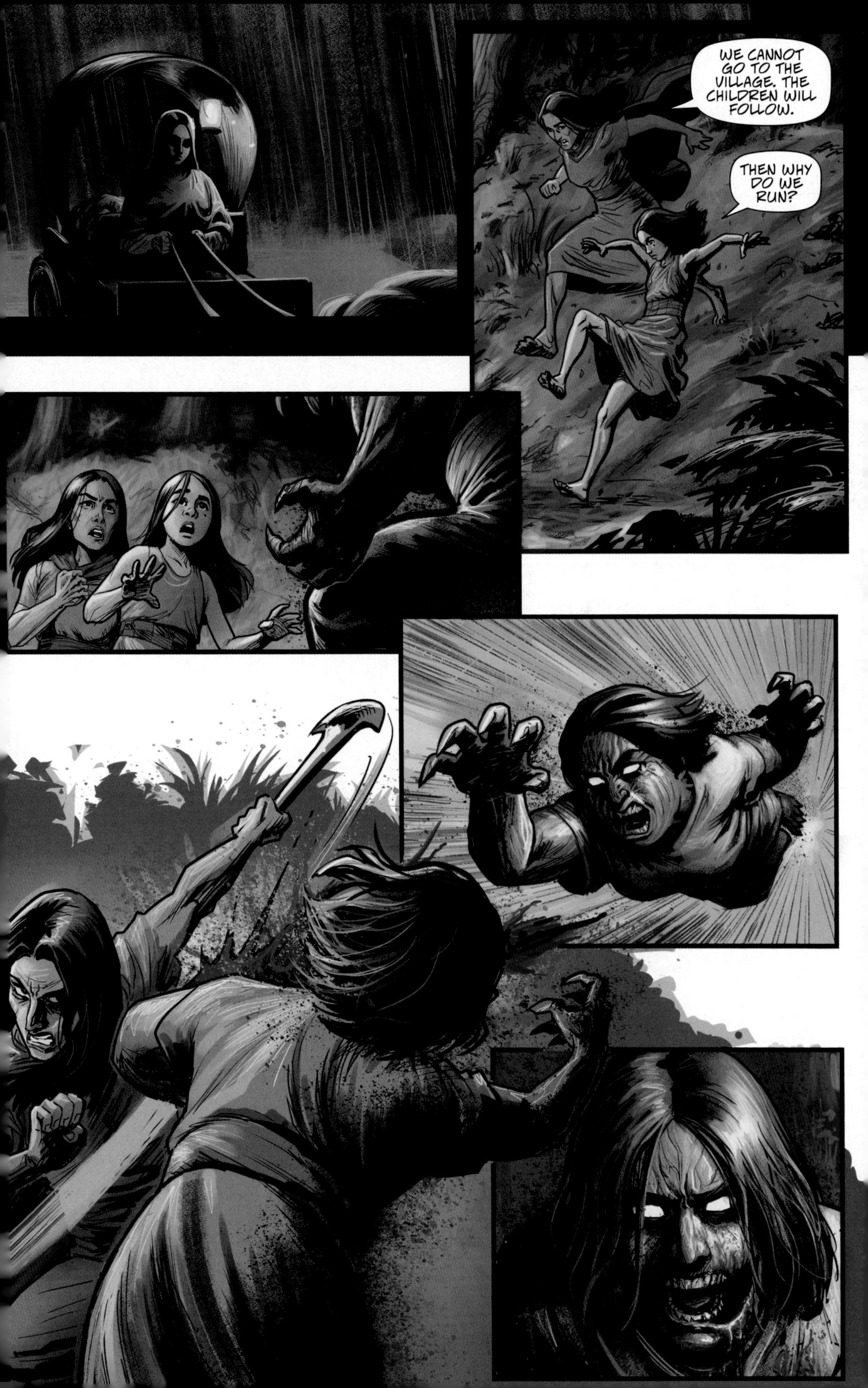
WE CANNOT GO TO THE VILLAGE. THE CHILDREN WILL FOLLOW.
THEN WHY DO WE RUN?

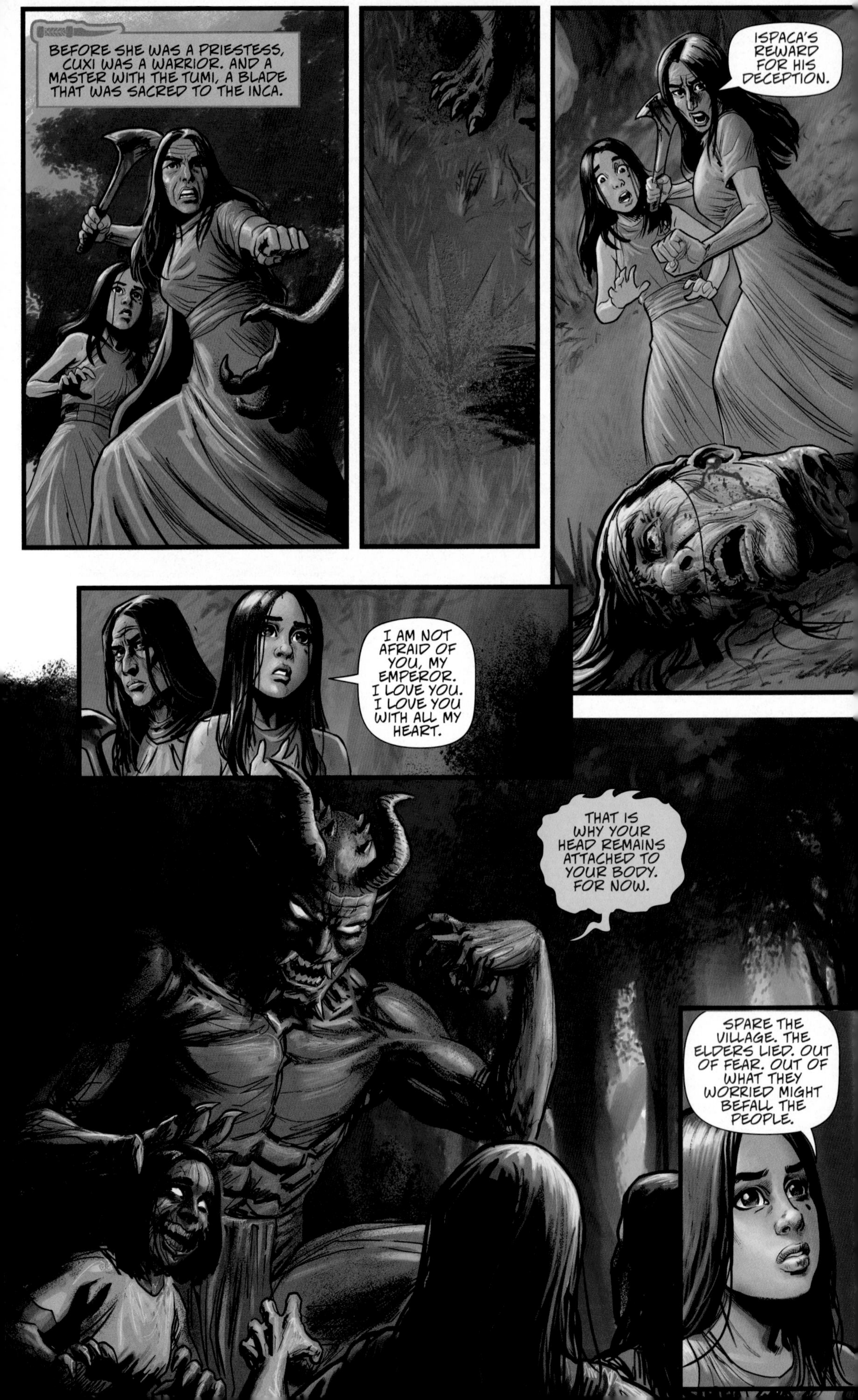
BEFORE SHE WAS A PRIESTESS, CUXI WAS A WARRIOR. AND A MASTER WITH THE TUMI, A BLADE THAT WAS SACRED TO THE INCA.
ISPACA'S REWARD FOR HIS DECEPTION.
I AM NOT AFRAID OF YOU, MY EMPEROR. I LOVE YOU. I LOVE YOU WITH ALL MY HEART.
THAT IS WHY YOUR HEAD REMAINS ATTACHED TO YOUR BODY. FOR NOW.
SPARE THE VILLAGE. THE ELDERS LIED. OUT OF FEAR. OUT OF WHAT THEY WORRIED MIGHT BEFALL THE PEOPLE.

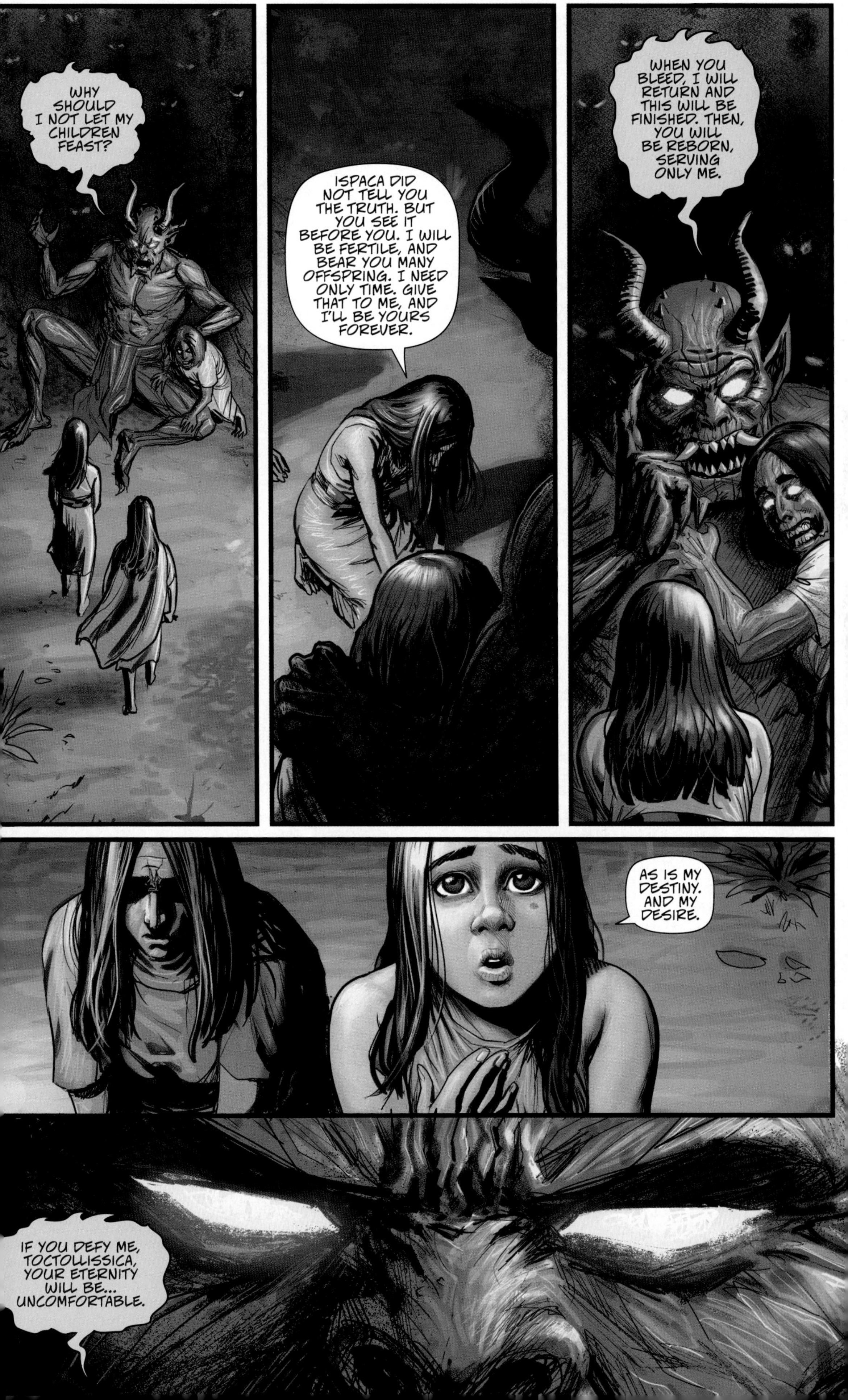
WHY SHOULD I NOT LET MY CHILDREN FEAST?
ISPACA DID NOT TELL YOU THE TRUTH. BUT YOU SEE IT BEFORE YOU. I WILL BE FERTILE, AND BEAR YOU MANY OFFSPRING. I NEED ONLY TIME. GIVE THAT TO ME, AND I'LL BE YOURS FOREVER.
WHEN YOU BLEED, I WILL RETURN AND THIS WILL BE FINISHED. THEN, YOU WILL BE REBORN, SERVING ONLY ME.
AS IS MY DESTINY. AND MY DESIRE.
IF YOU DEFY ME, TOCTOLLISSICA, YOUR ETERNITY WILL BE... UNCOMFORTABLE.

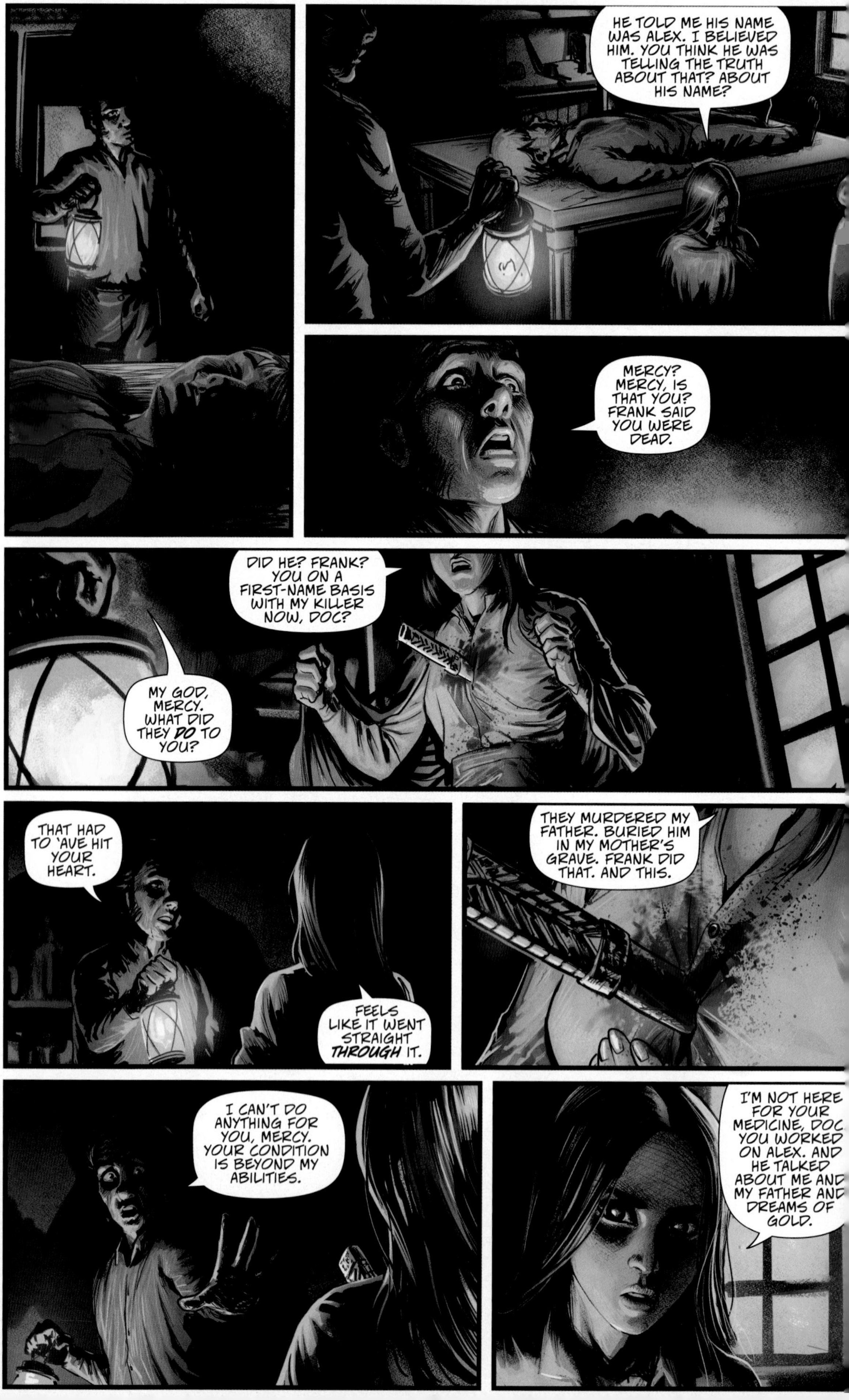
HE TOLD ME HIS NAME WAS ALEX. I BELIEVED HIM. YOU THINK HE WAS TELLING THE TRUTH ABOUT THAT? ABOUT HIS NAME?
MERCY? MERCY, IS THAT YOU? FRANK SAID YOU WERE DEAD.
DID HE? FRANK? YOU ON A FIRST-NAME BASIS WITH MY KILLER NOW, DOC?
MY GOD, MERCY. WHAT DID THEY DO TO YOU?
THAT HAD TO 'AVE HIT YOUR HEART.
FEELS LIKE IT WENT STRAIGHT THROUGH IT.
THEY MURDERED MY FATHER. BURIED HIM IN MY MOTHER'S GRAVE. FRANK DID THAT. AND THIS.
I CAN'T DO ANYTHING FOR YOU, MERCY. YOUR CONDITION IS BEYOND MY ABILITIES.
I'M NOT HERE FOR YOUR MEDICINE, DOC. YOU WORKED ON ALEX. AND HE TALKED ABOUT ME AND MY FATHER AND DREAMS OF GOLD.

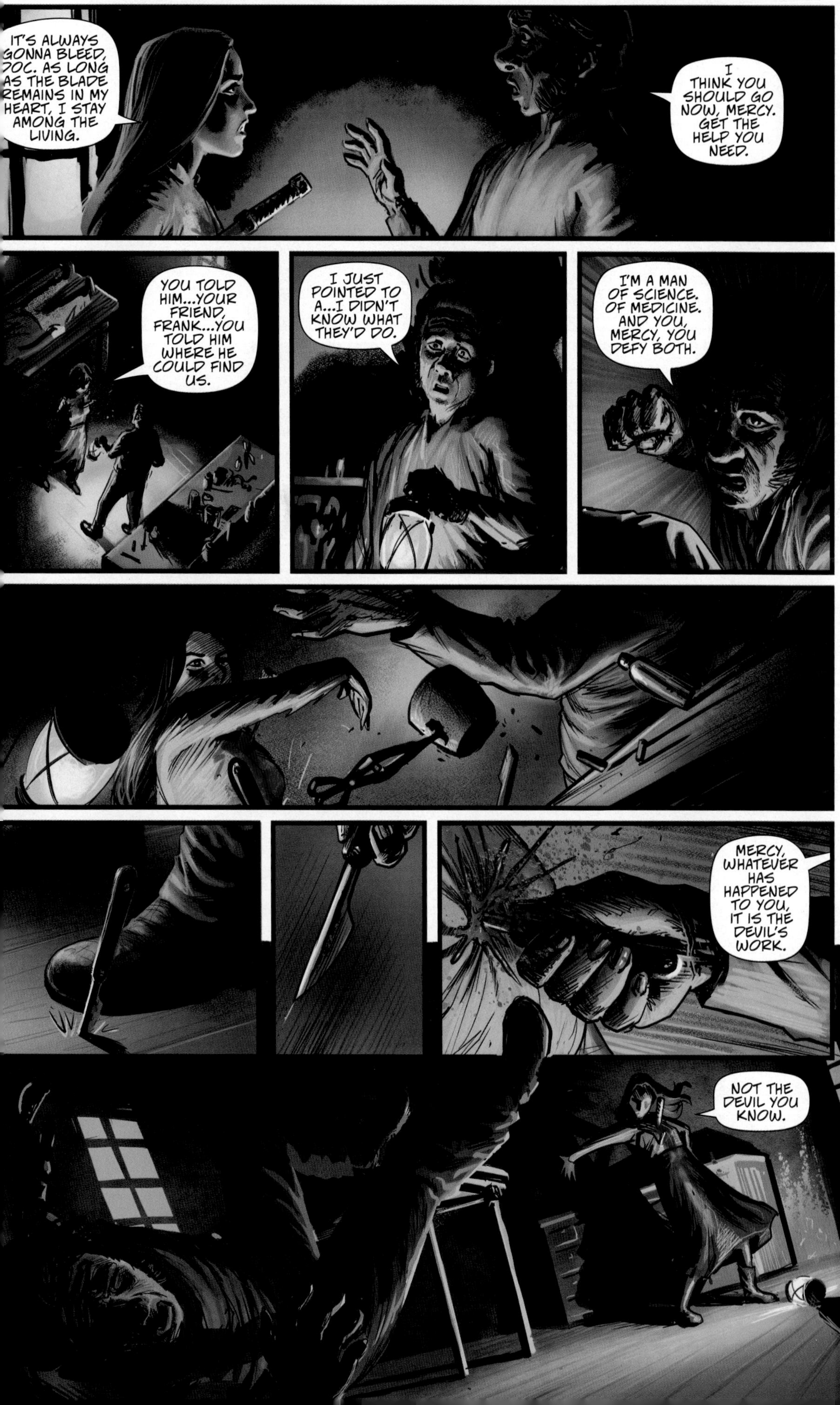

IT'S ALWAYS GONNA BLEED, DOC. AS LONG AS THE BLADE REMAINS IN MY HEART, I STAY AMONG THE LIVING.
I THINK YOU SHOULD GO NOW, MERCY. GET THE HELP YOU NEED.
YOU TOLD HIM...YOUR FRIEND, FRANK...YOU TOLD HIM WHERE HE COULD FIND US.
I JUST POINTED TO A...I DIDN'T KNOW WHAT THEY'D DO.
I'M A MAN OF SCIENCE. OF MEDICINE. AND YOU, MERCY, YOU DEFY BOTH.
MERCY, WHATEVER HAS HAPPENED TO YOU, IT IS THE DEVIL'S WORK.
NOT THE DEVIL YOU KNOW.

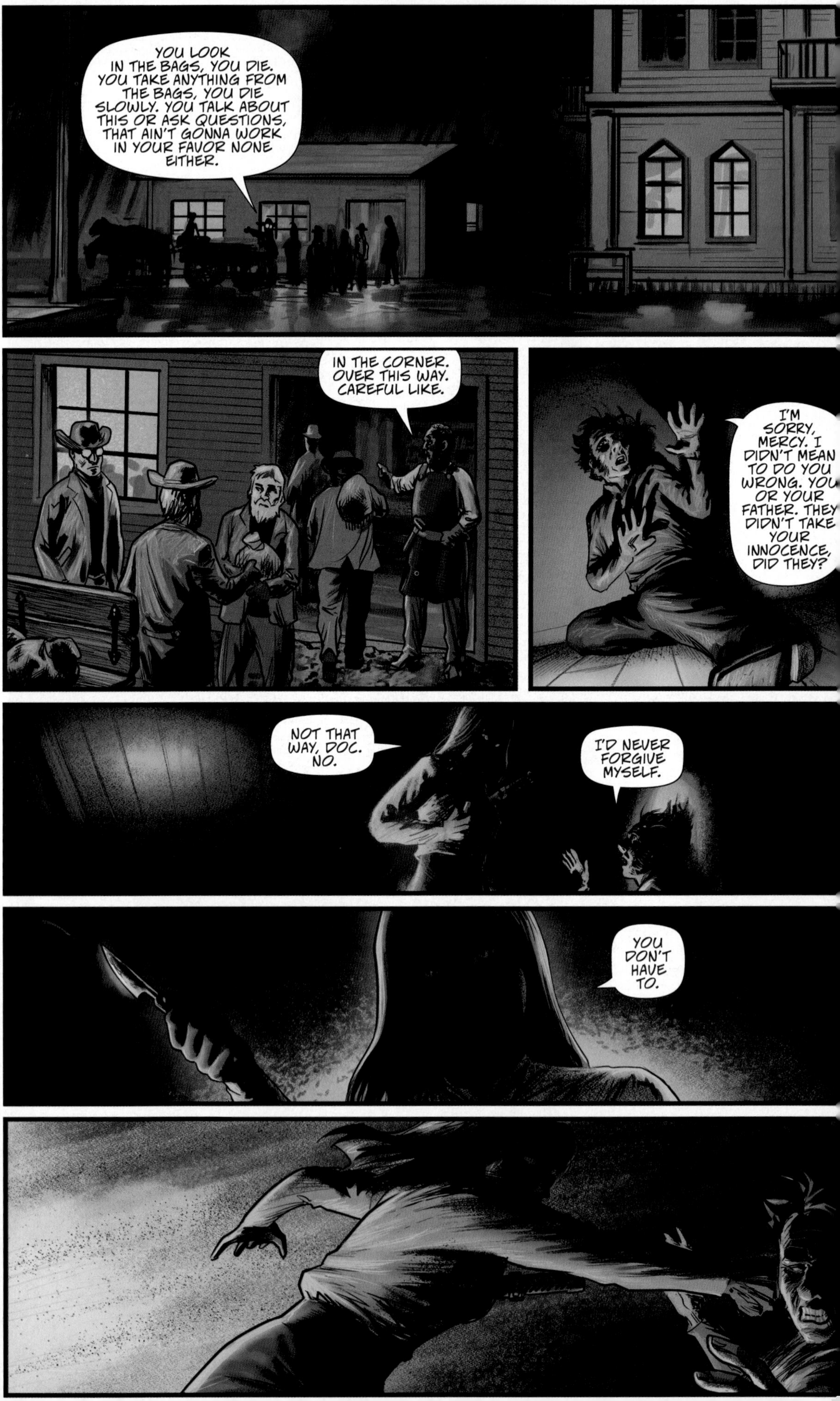
YOU LOOK IN THE BAGS, YOU DIE. YOU TAKE ANYTHING FROM THE BAGS, YOU DIE SLOWLY. YOU TALK ABOUT THIS OR ASK QUESTIONS, THAT AIN'T GONNA WORK IN YOUR FAVOR NONE EITHER.
IN THE CORNER. OVER THIS WAY. CAREFUL LIKE.
I'M SORRY, MERCY. I DIDN'T MEAN TO DO YOU WRONG. YOU OR YOUR FATHER. THEY DIDN'T TAKE YOUR INNOCENCE, DID THEY?
NOT THAT WAY, DOC. NO.
I'D NEVER FORGIVE MYSELF.
YOU DON'T HAVE TO.

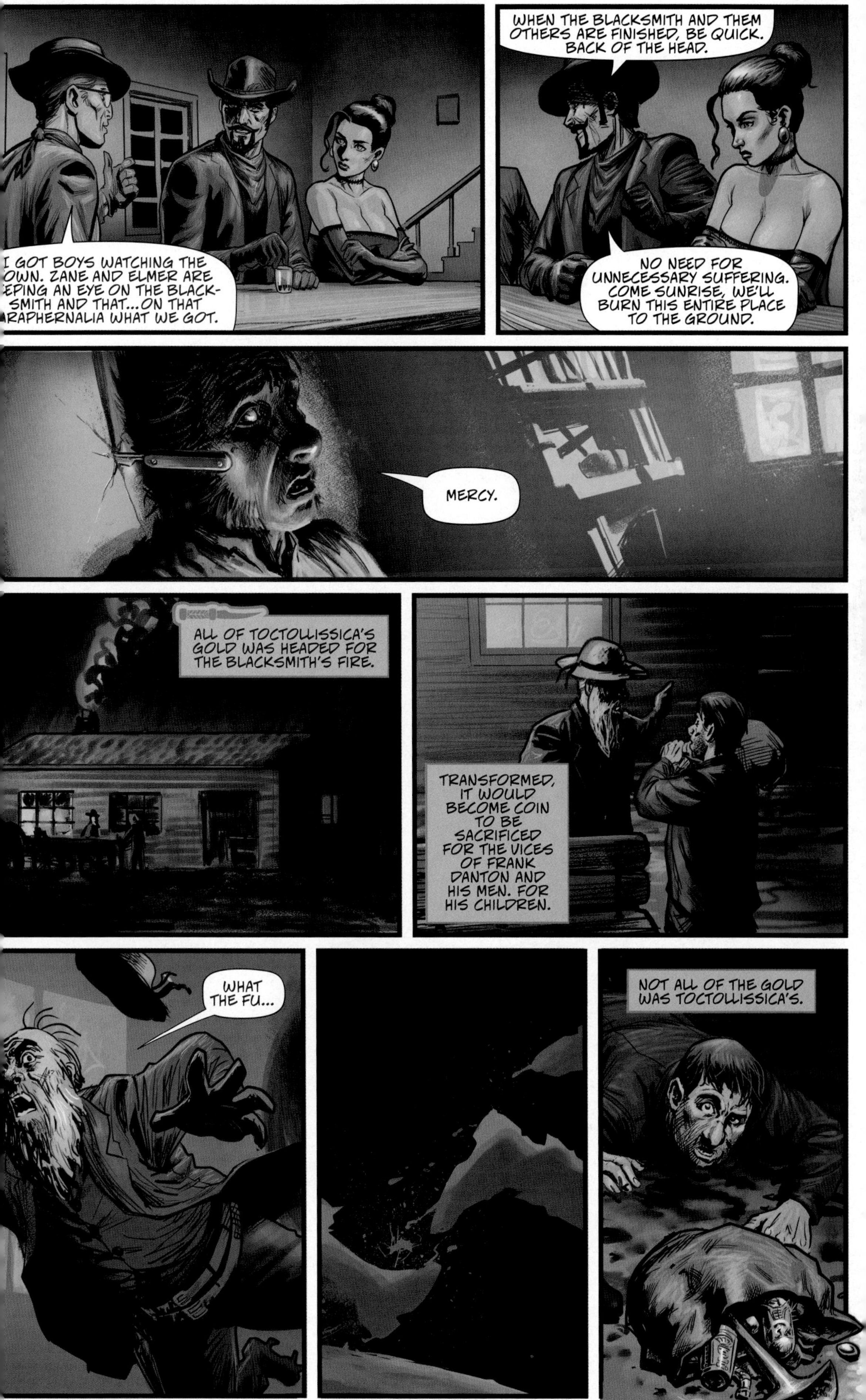
I GOT BOYS WATCHING THE
OWN. ZANE AND ELMER ARE
EPING AN EYE ON THE BLACK-
SMITH AND THAT...ON THAT
ARAPHERNALIA WHAT WE GOT.
WHEN THE BLACKSMITH AND THEM OTHERS ARE FINISHED, BE QUICK. BACK OF THE HEAD.
NO NEED FOR UNNECESSARY SUFFERING. COME SUNRISE, WE'LL BURN THIS ENTIRE PLACE TO THE GROUND.
MERCY.
ALL OF TOCTOLLISSICA'S GOLD WAS HEADED FOR THE BLACKSMITH'S FIRE.
TRANSFORMED, IT WOULD BECOME COIN TO BE SACRIFICED FOR THE VICES OF FRANK DANTON AND HIS MEN. FOR HIS CHILDREN.
WHAT THE FU...
NOT ALL OF THE GOLD WAS TOCTOLLISSICA'S.

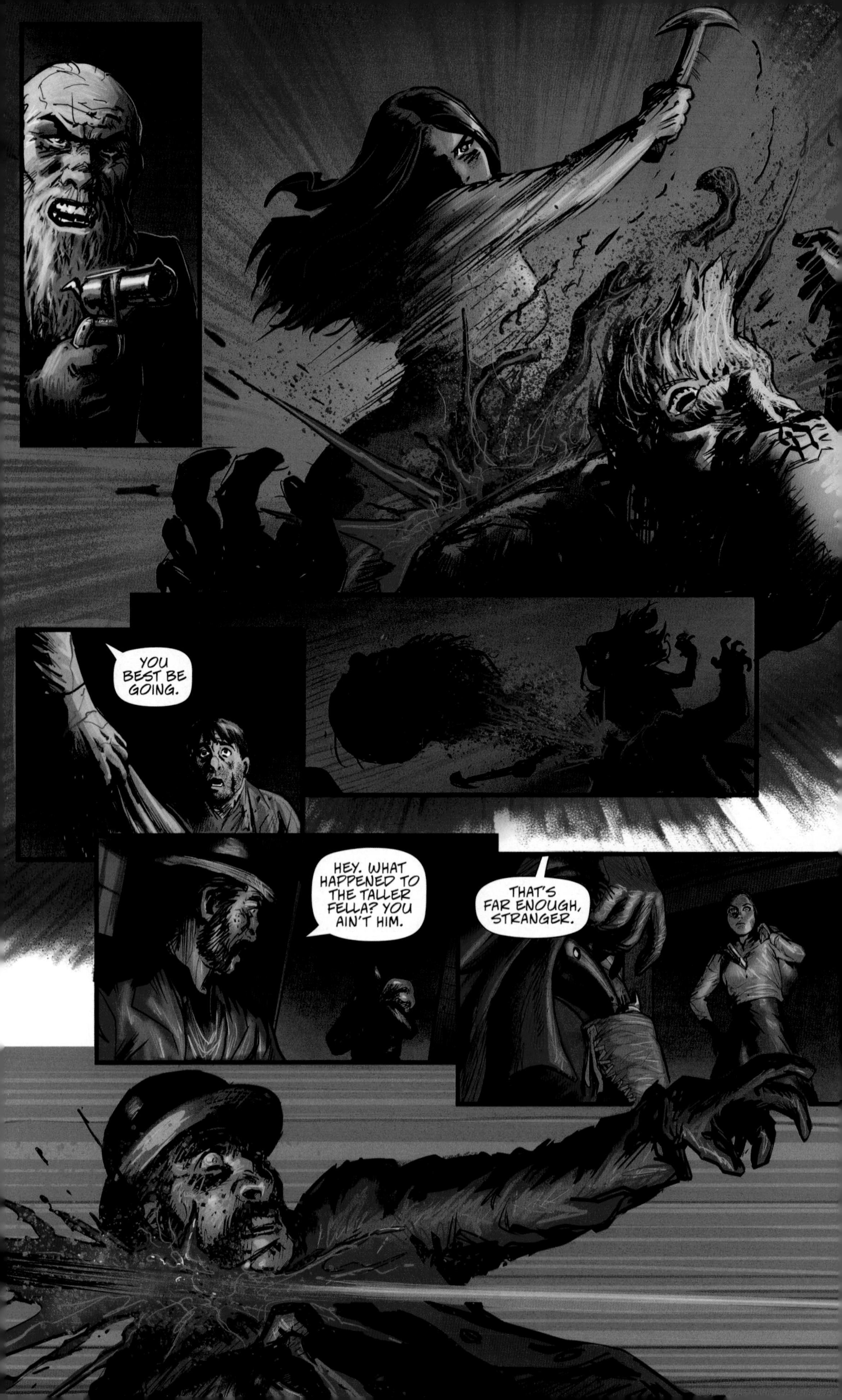
YOU BEST BE GOING.
HEY. WHAT HAPPENED TO THE TALLER FELLA? YOU AIN'T HIM.
THAT'S FAR ENOUGH, STRANGER.

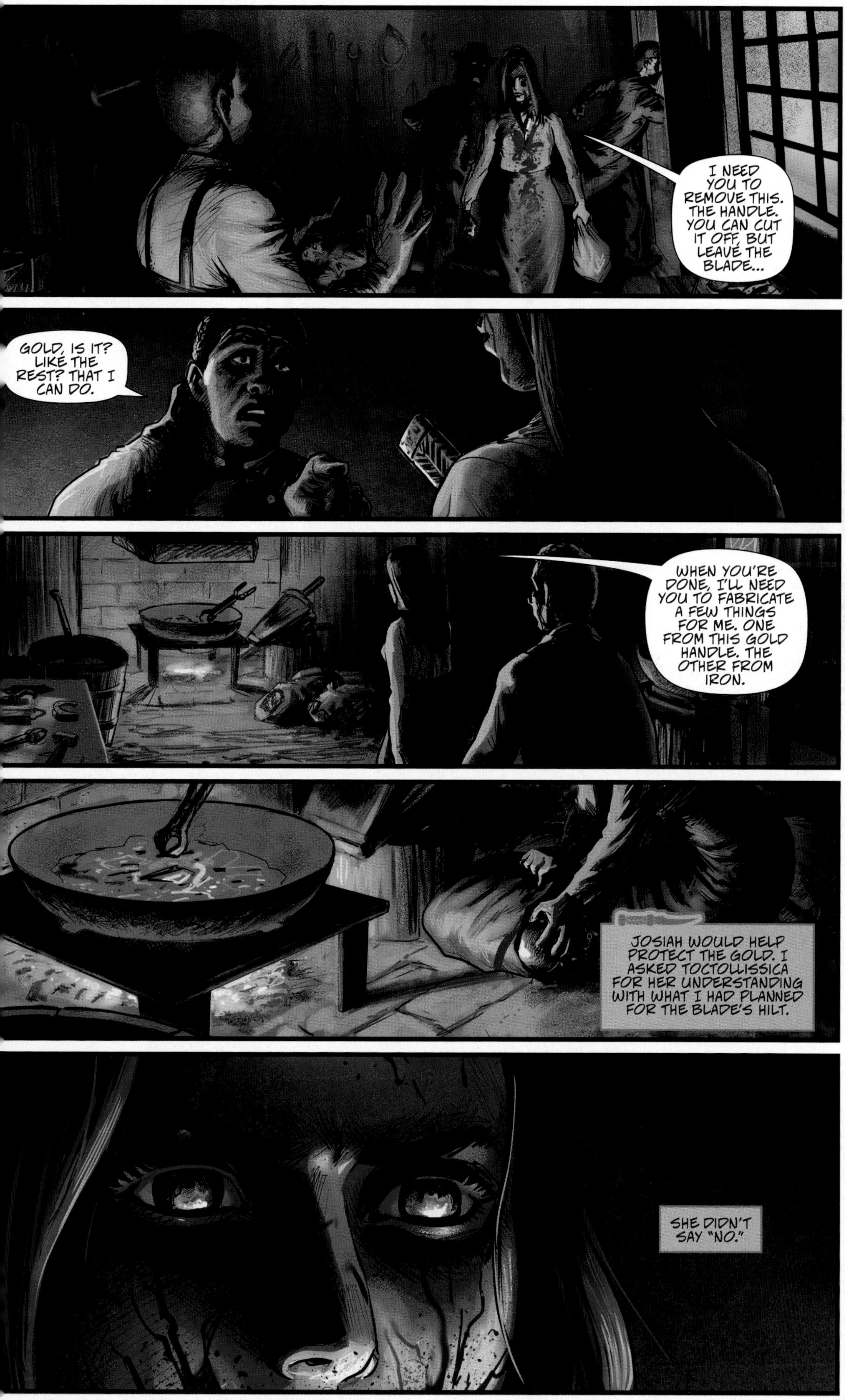
I NEED YOU TO REMOVE THIS. THE HANDLE. YOU CAN CUT IT OFF, BUT LEAVE THE BLADE...
GOLD, IS IT? LIKE THE REST? THAT I CAN DO.
WHEN YOU'RE DONE, I'LL NEED YOU TO FABRICATE A FEW THINGS FOR ME. ONE FROM THIS GOLD HANDLE. THE OTHER FROM IRON.
JOSIAH WOULD HELP PROTECT THE GOLD. I ASKED TOCTOLLISSICA FOR HER UNDERSTANDING WITH WHAT I HAD PLANNED FOR THE BLADE'S HILT.
SHE DIDN'T SAY "NO."

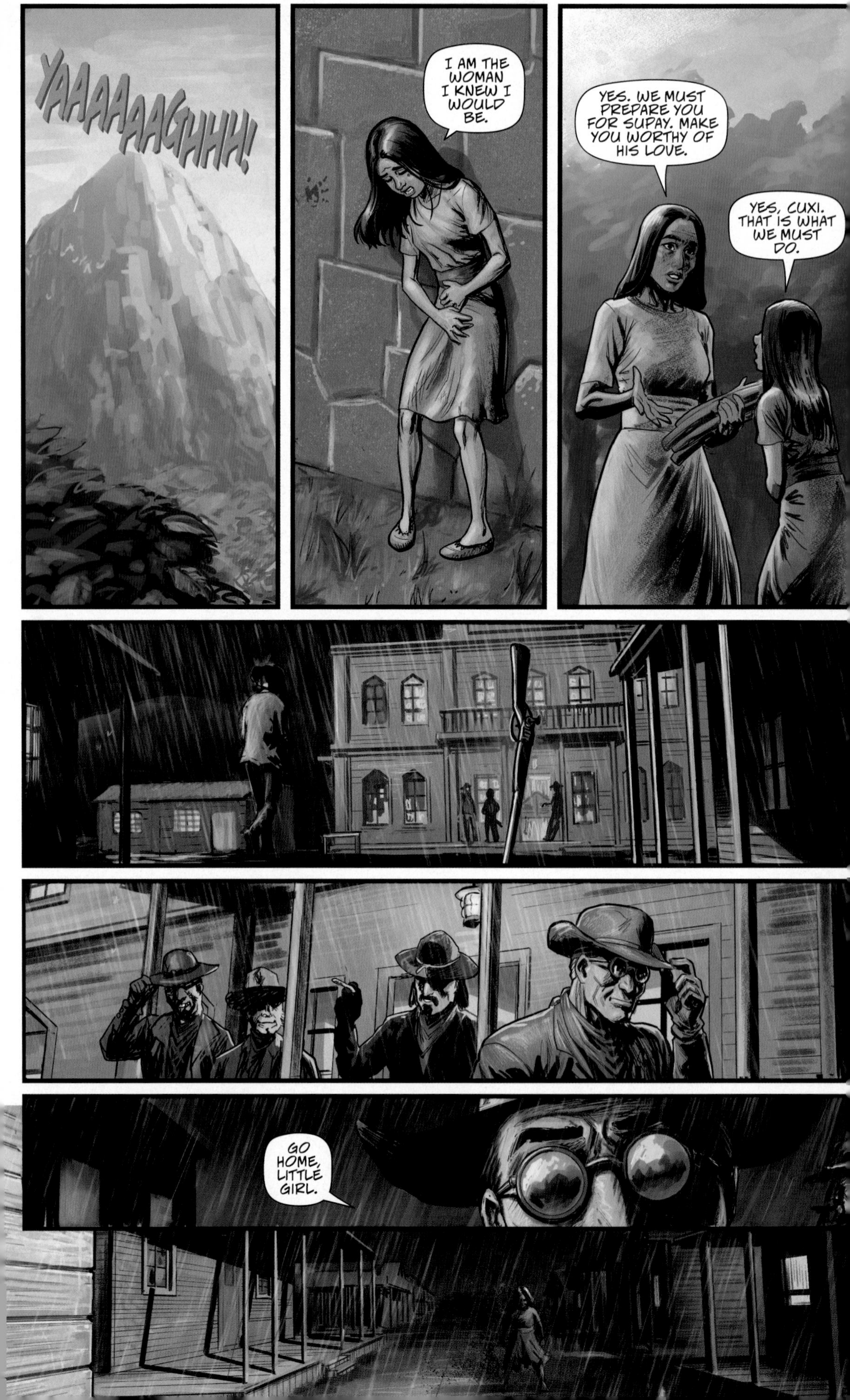
YAAAAAAGHHH!
I AM THE WOMAN I KNEW I WOULD BE.
YES. WE MUST PREPARE YOU FOR SUPAY. MAKE YOU WORTHY OF HIS LOVE.
YES, CUXI. THAT IS WHAT WE MUST DO.
GO HOME, LITTLE GIRL.

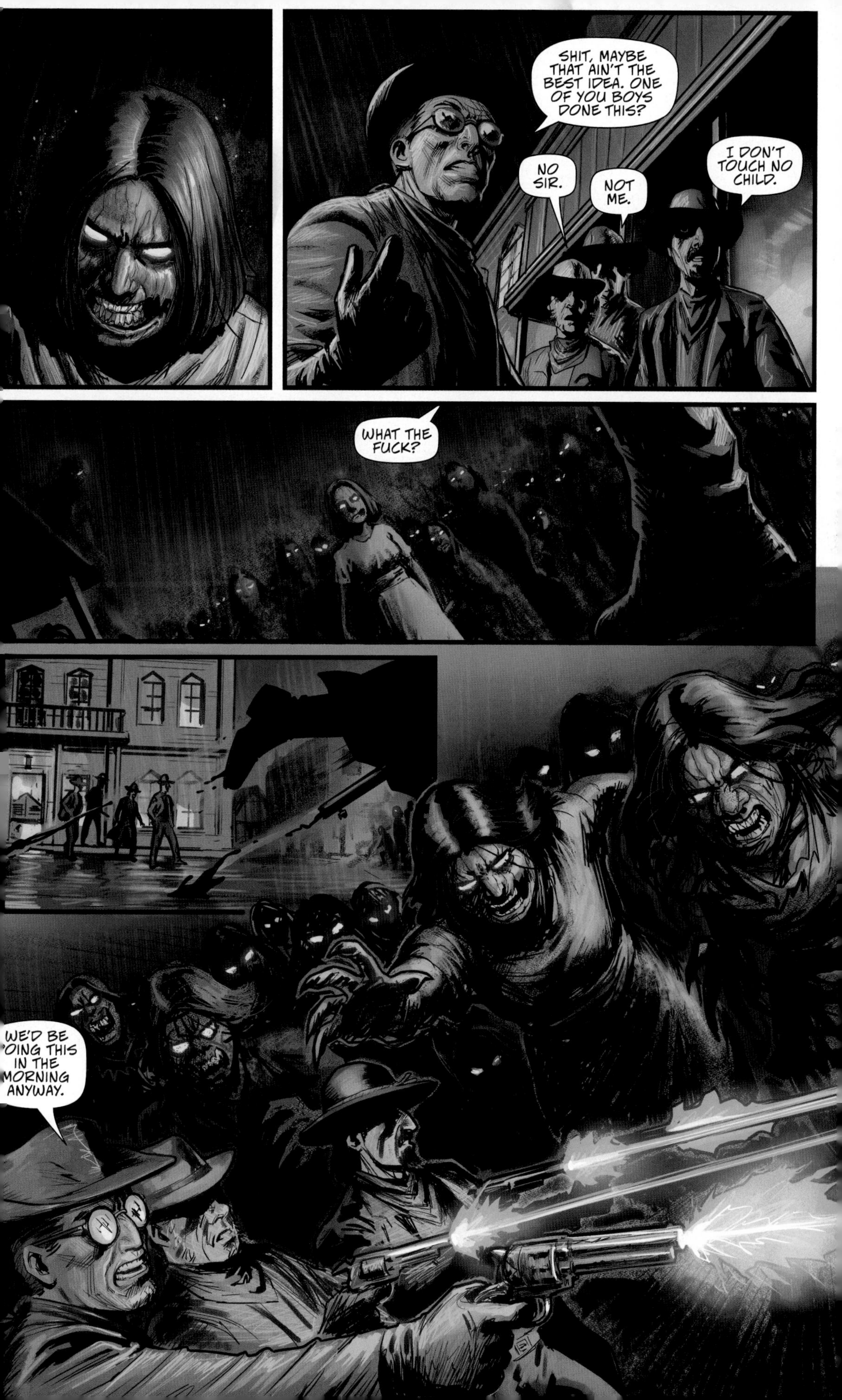
SHIT, MAYBE THAT AIN'T THE BEST IDEA. ONE OF YOU BOYS DONE THIS?
NO SIR.
NOT ME.
I DON'T TOUCH NO CHILD.
WHAT THE FUCK?
WE'D BE 'OING THIS IN THE MORNING ANYWAY.

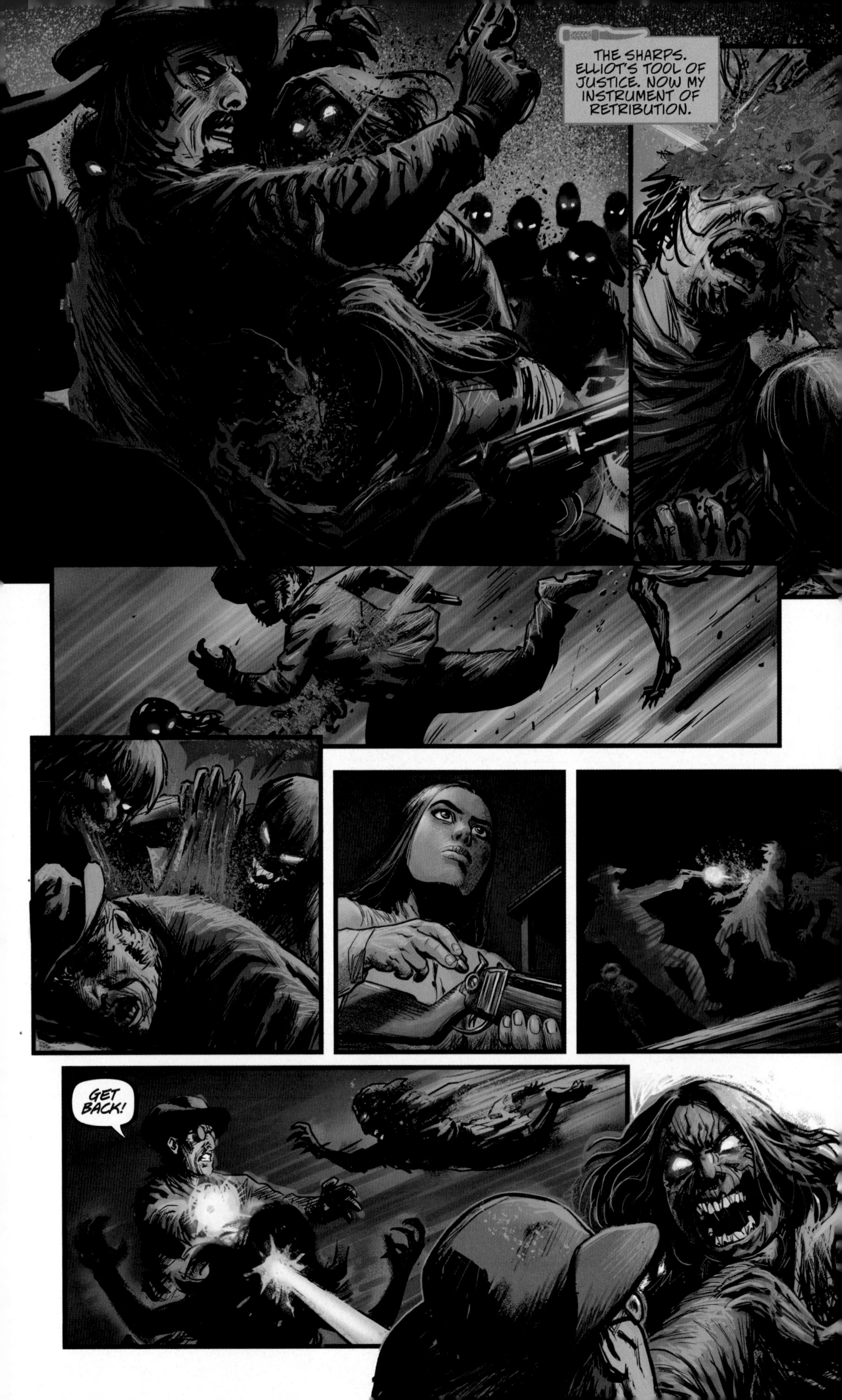
THE SHARPS. ELLIOT'S TOOL OF JUSTICE. NOW MY INSTRUMENT OF RETRIBUTION.
GET BACK!

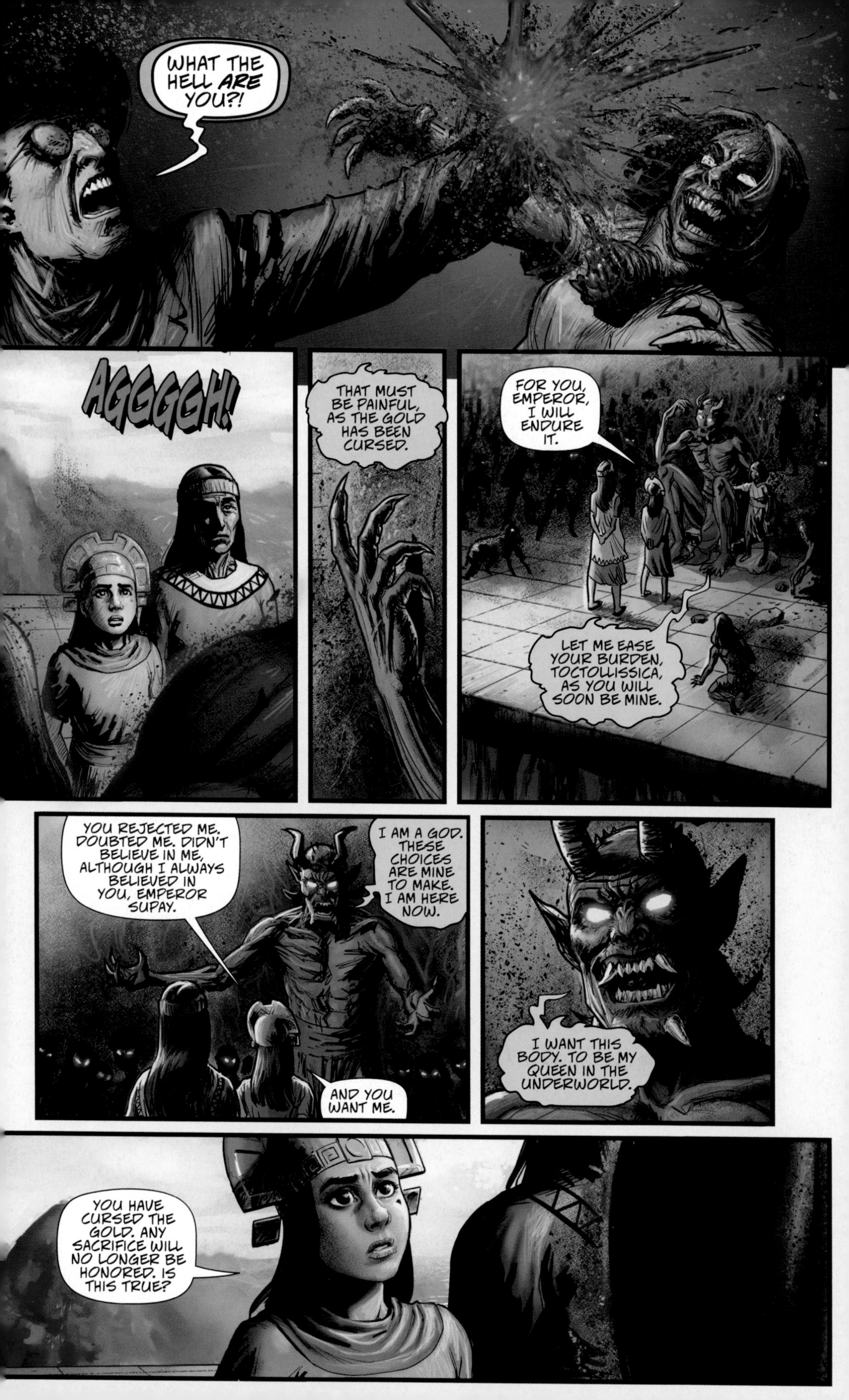
WHAT THE HELL *ARE* YOU?!
AGGGGH!
THAT MUST BE PAINFUL, AS THE GOLD HAS BEEN CURSED.
FOR YOU, EMPEROR, I WILL ENDURE IT.
LET ME EASE YOUR BURDEN, TOCTOLLISSICA, AS YOU WILL SOON BE MINE.
YOU REJECTED ME. DOUBTED ME. DIDN'T BELIEVE IN ME, ALTHOUGH I ALWAYS BELIEVED IN YOU, EMPEROR SUPAY.
I AM A GOD. THESE CHOICES ARE MINE TO MAKE. I AM HERE NOW.
AND YOU WANT ME.
I WANT THIS BODY. TO BE MY QUEEN IN THE UNDERWORLD.
YOU HAVE CURSED THE GOLD. ANY SACRIFICE WILL NO LONGER BE HONORED. IS THIS TRUE?

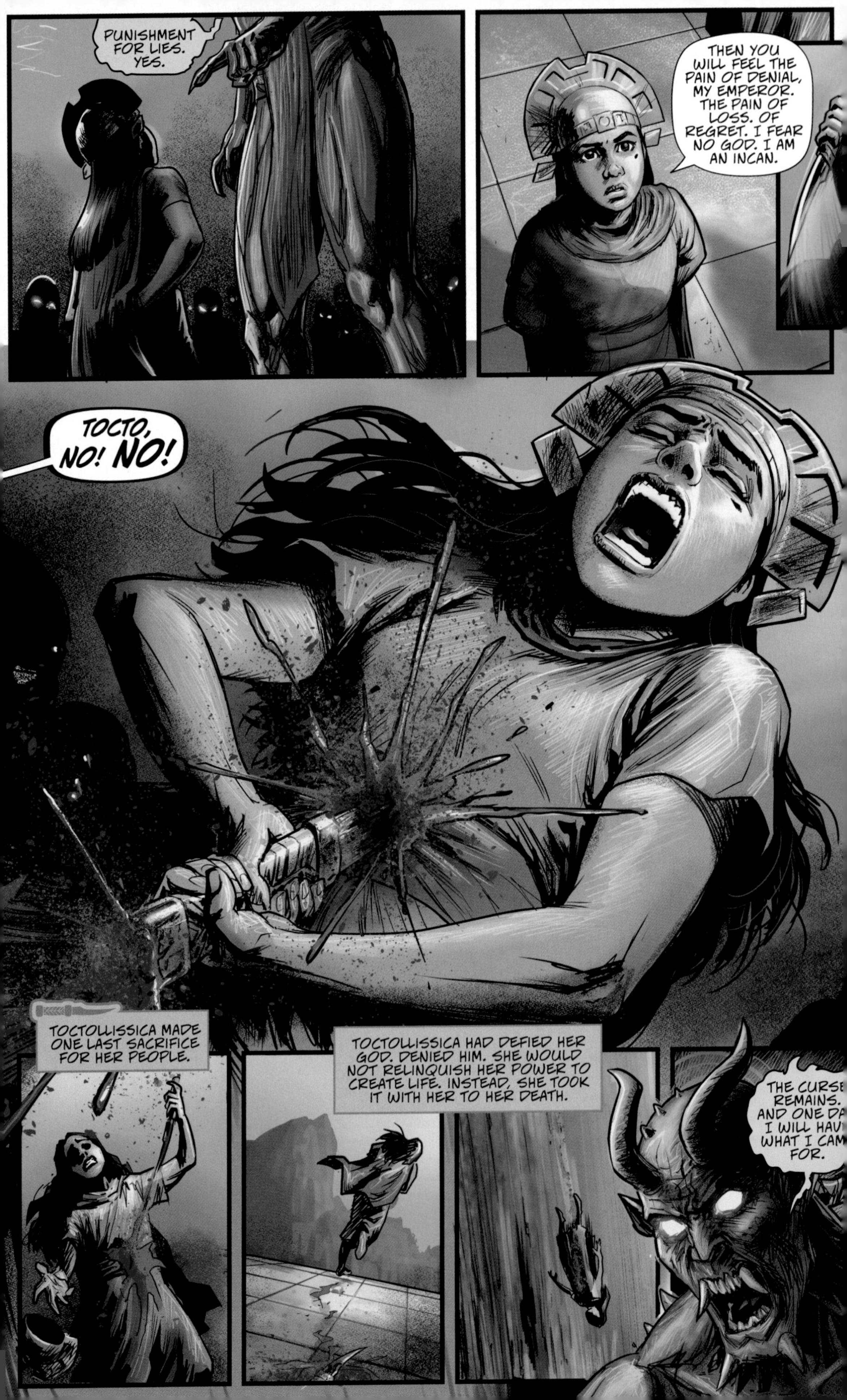
PUNISHMENT FOR LIES. YES.
THEN YOU WILL FEEL THE PAIN OF DENIAL, MY EMPEROR. THE PAIN OF LOSS. OF REGRET. I FEAR NO GOD. I AM AN INCAN.
TOCTO, NO! NO!
TOCTOLLISSICA MADE ONE LAST SACRIFICE FOR HER PEOPLE.
TOCTOLLISSICA HAD DEFIED HER GOD. DENIED HIM. SHE WOULD NOT RELINQUISH HER POWER TO CREATE LIFE. INSTEAD, SHE TOOK IT WITH HER TO HER DEATH.
THE CURSE REMAINS. AND ONE DA I WILL HAV WHAT I CAM FOR.

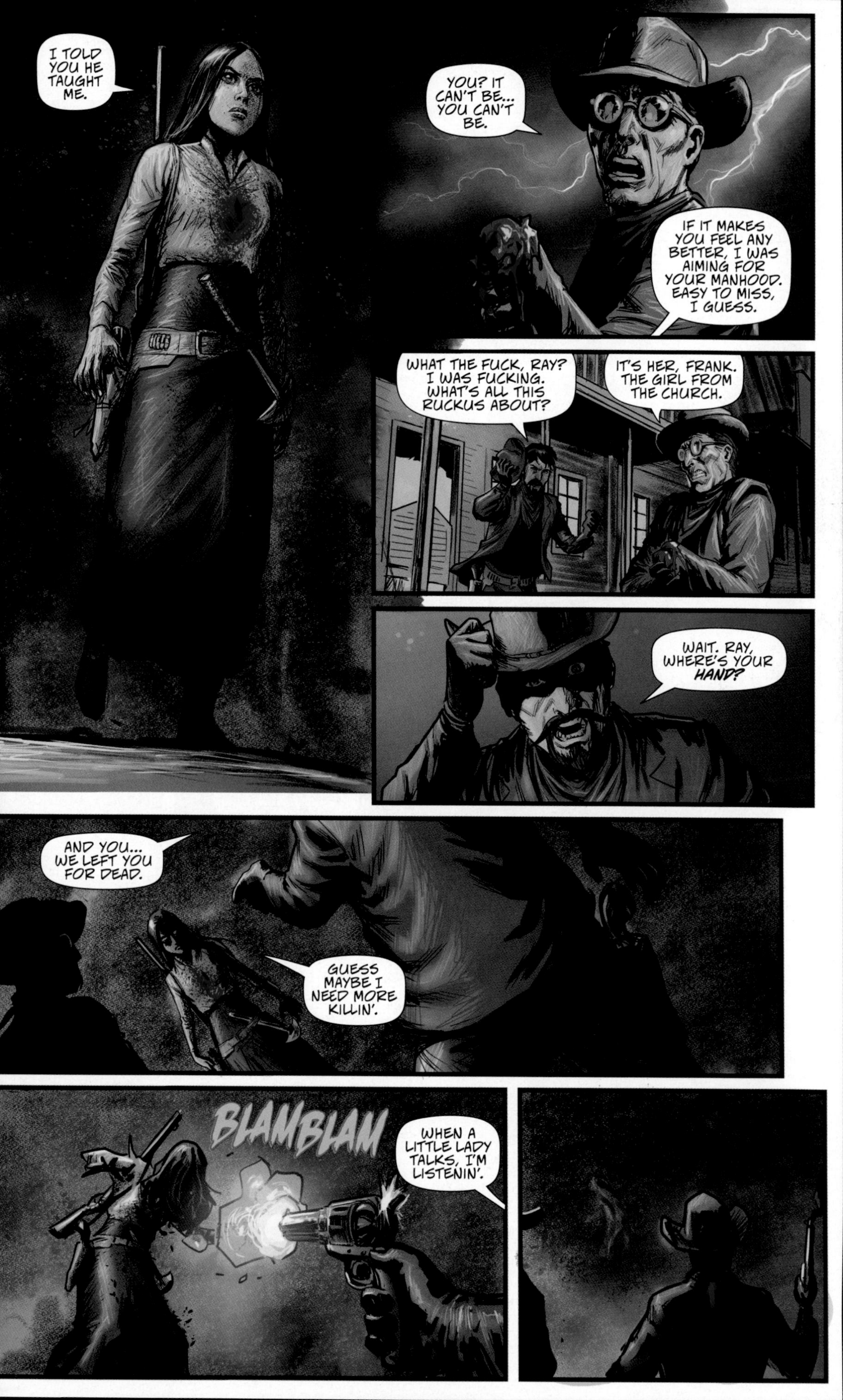
I TOLD YOU HE TAUGHT ME.
YOU? IT CAN'T BE... YOU CAN'T BE.
IF IT MAKES YOU FEEL ANY BETTER, I WAS AIMING FOR YOUR MANHOOD. EASY TO MISS, I GUESS.
WHAT THE FUCK, RAY? I WAS FUCKING. WHAT'S ALL THIS RUCKUS ABOUT?
IT'S HER, FRANK. THE GIRL FROM THE CHURCH.
WAIT. RAY, WHERE'S YOUR ***HAND?***
AND YOU... WE LEFT YOU FOR DEAD.
GUESS MAYBE I NEED MORE KILLIN'.
BLAMBLAM
WHEN A LITTLE LADY TALKS, I'M LISTENIN'.

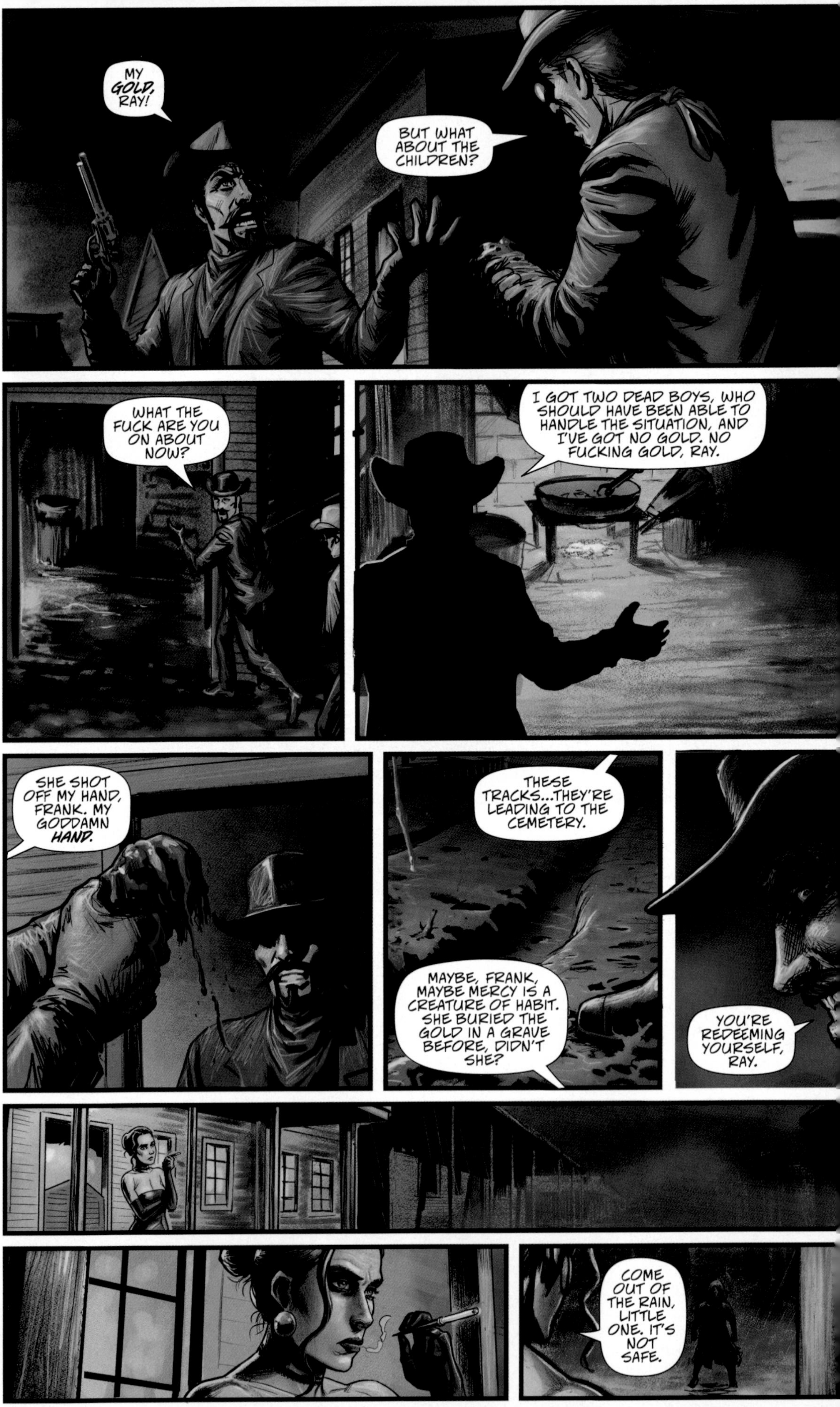

MY GOLD, RAY!
BUT WHAT ABOUT THE CHILDREN?
WHAT THE FUCK ARE YOU ON ABOUT NOW?
I GOT TWO DEAD BOYS, WHO SHOULD HAVE BEEN ABLE TO HANDLE THE SITUATION, AND I'VE GOT NO GOLD. NO FUCKING GOLD, RAY.
SHE SHOT OFF MY HAND, FRANK. MY GODDAMN HAND.
THESE TRACKS...THEY'RE LEADING TO THE CEMETERY.
MAYBE, FRANK, MAYBE MERCY IS A CREATURE OF HABIT. SHE BURIED THE GOLD IN A GRAVE BEFORE, DIDN'T SHE?
YOU'RE REDEEMING YOURSELF, RAY.
COME OUT OF THE RAIN, LITTLE ONE. IT'S NOT SAFE.

MY CHILDREN ARE COLD. AND HUNGRY.

I... I CAN FEED THEM.

YES. YES, YOU CAN.

MIGHT JUST BE THE TWO OF US REMAINING, FRANK.

WE'LL MANAGE. LIKE OLD TIMES.

NOTHIN'.

DON'T BELIEVE IT, RAY. THIS IS THE PLACE.

FUCK THE GOLD, FRANK. WE DID GOOD WITH THEM BANKNOTES. THOSE'LL SUSTAIN US FOR A LONG WHILE. MORE NOW THAT IT'S JUST ME AND YOU.

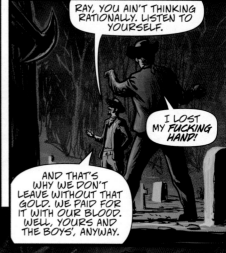

RAY, YOU AIN'T THINKING RATIONALLY. LISTEN TO YOURSELF.

I LOST MY FUCKING HAND!

AND THAT'S WHY WE DON'T LEAVE WITHOUT THAT GOLD. WE PAID FOR IT WITH OUR BLOOD. WELL, YOURS AND THE BOYS', ANYWAY.

SHIIIIT!

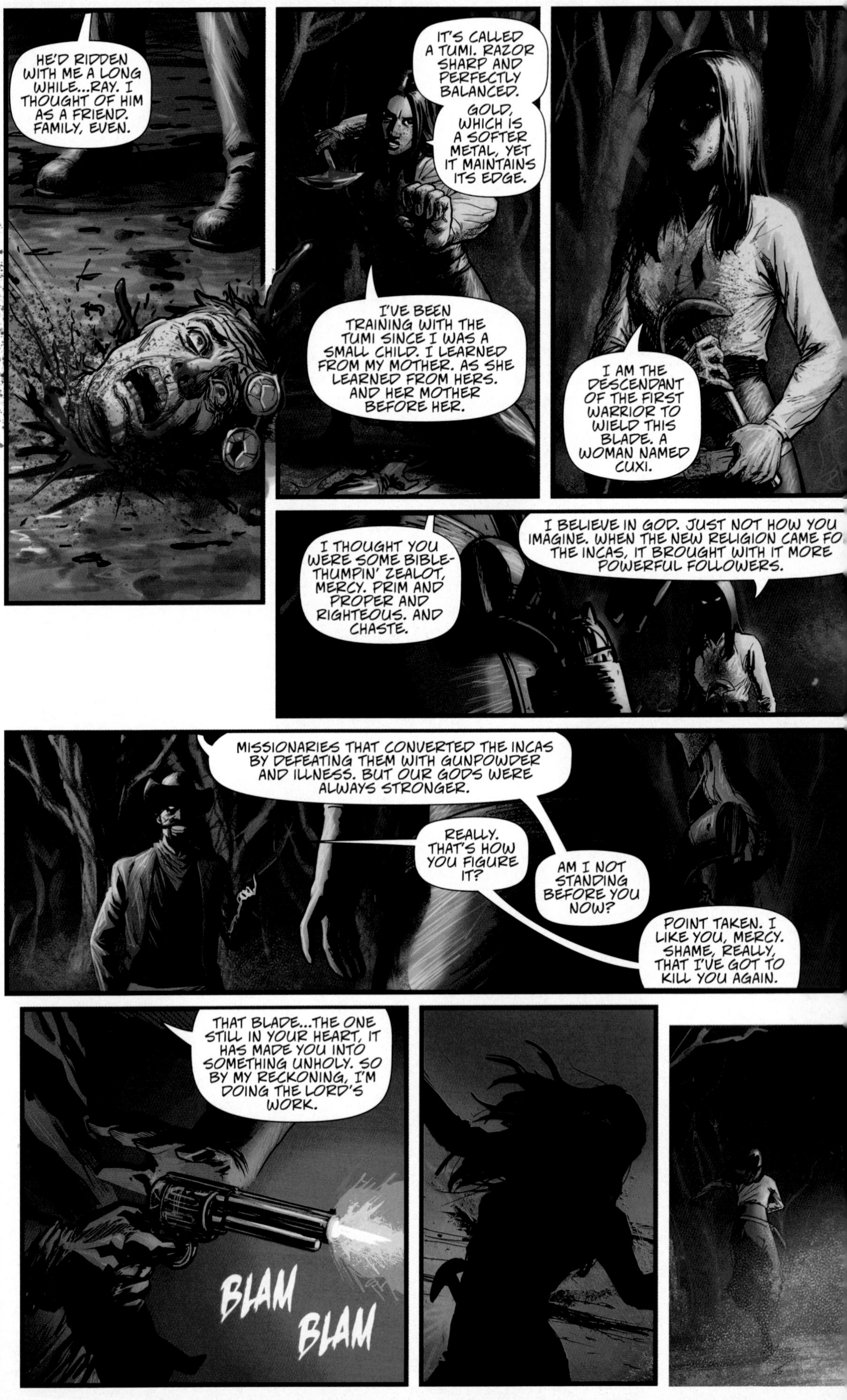
HE'D RIDDEN WITH ME A LONG WHILE...RAY. I THOUGHT OF HIM AS A FRIEND. FAMILY, EVEN.
IT'S CALLED A TUMI. RAZOR SHARP AND PERFECTLY BALANCED.
GOLD, WHICH IS A SOFTER METAL, YET IT MAINTAINS ITS EDGE.
I'VE BEEN TRAINING WITH THE TUMI SINCE I WAS A SMALL CHILD. I LEARNED FROM MY MOTHER. AS SHE LEARNED FROM HERS. AND HER MOTHER BEFORE HER.
I AM THE DESCENDANT OF THE FIRST WARRIOR TO WIELD THIS BLADE. A WOMAN NAMED CUXI.
I THOUGHT YOU WERE SOME BIBLE-THUMPIN' ZEALOT, MERCY. PRIM AND PROPER AND RIGHTEOUS. AND CHASTE.
I BELIEVE IN GOD. JUST NOT HOW YOU IMAGINE. WHEN THE NEW RELIGION CAME FO THE INCAS, IT BROUGHT WITH IT MORE POWERFUL FOLLOWERS.
MISSIONARIES THAT CONVERTED THE INCAS BY DEFEATING THEM WITH GUNPOWDER AND ILLNESS. BUT OUR GODS WERE ALWAYS STRONGER.
REALLY. THAT'S HOW YOU FIGURE IT?
AM I NOT STANDING BEFORE YOU NOW?
POINT TAKEN. I LIKE YOU, MERCY. SHAME, REALLY, THAT I'VE GOT TO KILL YOU AGAIN.
THAT BLADE...THE ONE STILL IN YOUR HEART, IT HAS MADE YOU INTO SOMETHING UNHOLY. SO BY MY RECKONING, I'M DOING THE LORD'S WORK.
BLAM
BLAM

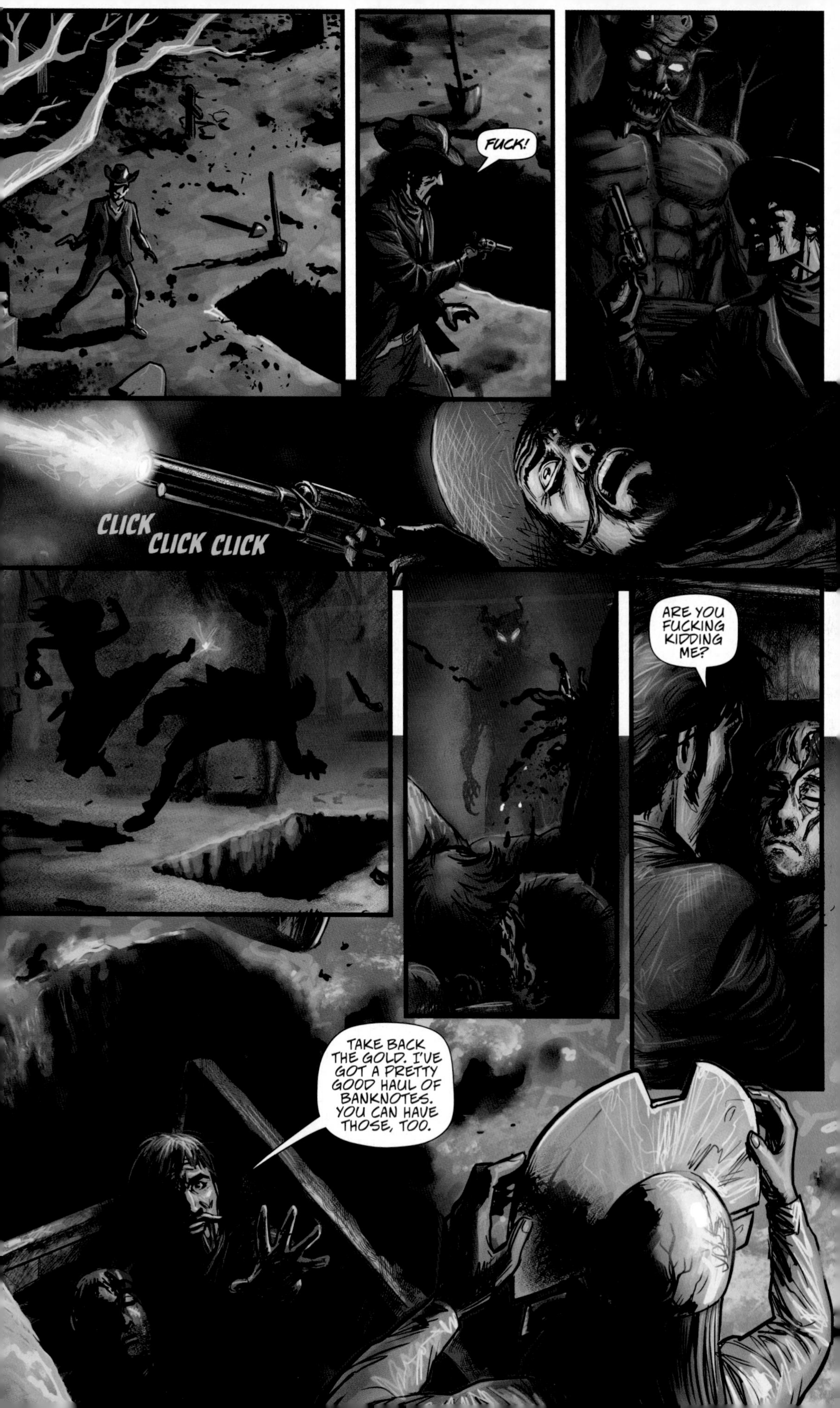
FUCK!
CLICK
CLICK CLICK
ARE YOU FUCKING KIDDING ME?
TAKE BACK THE GOLD. I'VE GOT A PRETTY GOOD HAUL OF BANKNOTES. YOU CAN HAVE THOSE, TOO.

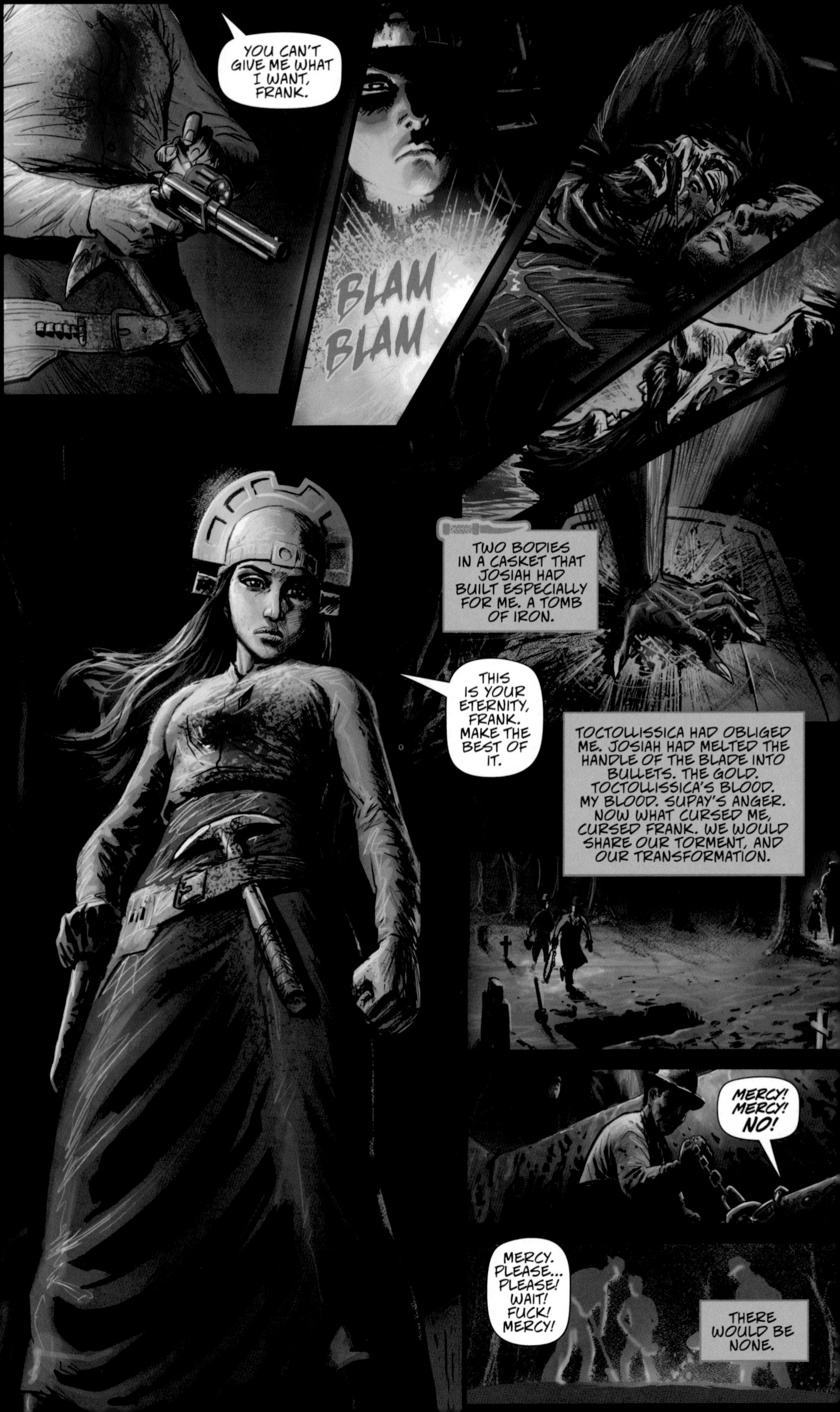
YOU CAN'T GIVE ME WHAT I WANT, FRANK.
BLAM BLAM
TWO BODIES IN A CASKET THAT JOSIAH HAD BUILT ESPECIALLY FOR ME. A TOMB OF IRON.
THIS IS YOUR ETERNITY, FRANK. MAKE THE BEST OF IT.
TOCTOLLISSICA HAD OBLIGED ME. JOSIAH HAD MELTED THE HANDLE OF THE BLADE INTO BULLETS. THE GOLD. TOCTOLLISSICA'S BLOOD. MY BLOOD. SUPAY'S ANGER. NOW WHAT CURSED ME, CURSED FRANK. WE WOULD SHARE OUR TORMENT, AND OUR TRANSFORMATION.
MERCY! MERCY! NO!
MERCY. PLEASE... PLEASE! WAIT! FUCK! MERCY!
THERE WOULD BE NONE.

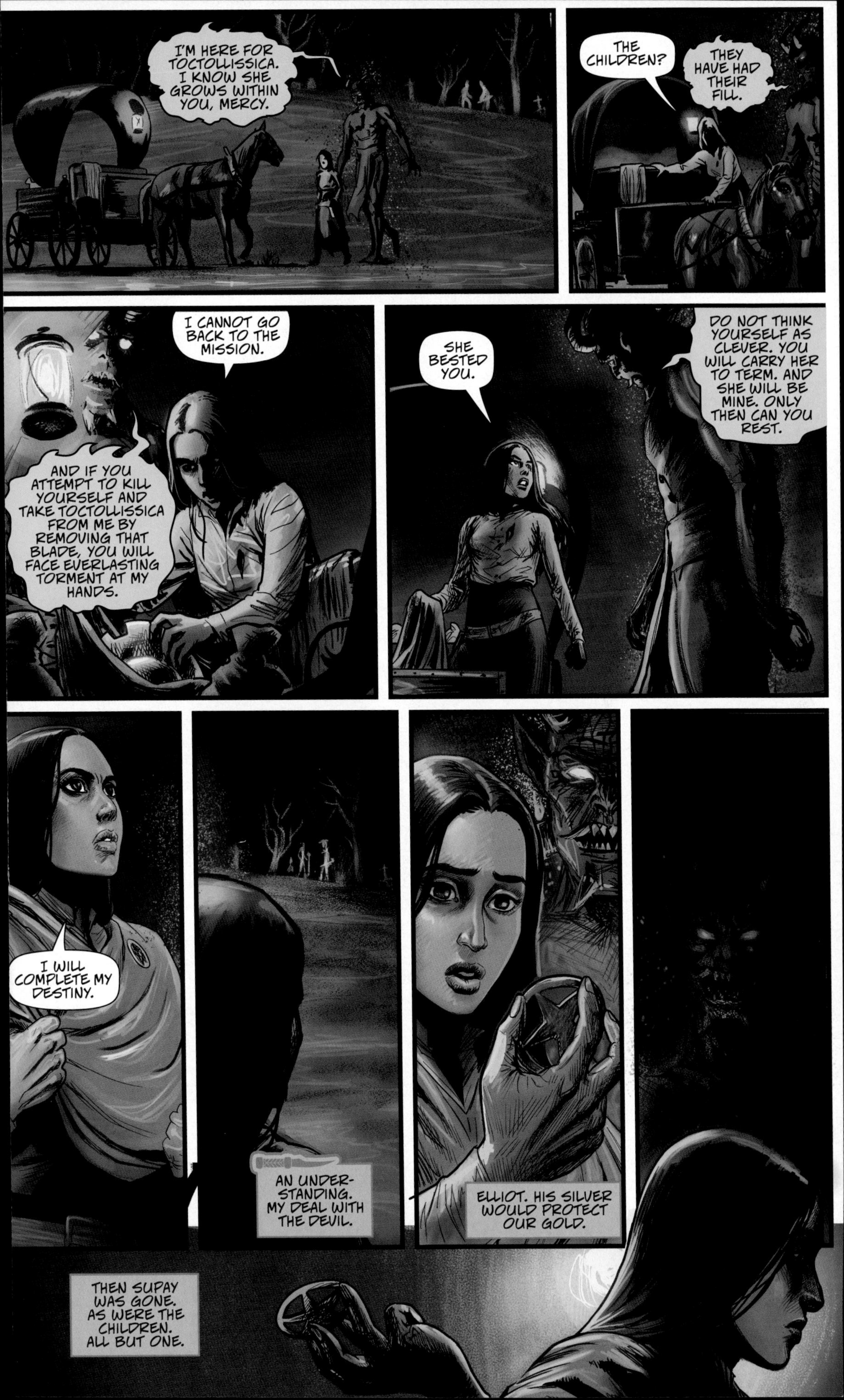
I'M HERE FOR TOCTOLLISSICA. I KNOW SHE GROWS WITHIN YOU, MERCY.
THE CHILDREN?
THEY HAVE HAD THEIR FILL.
I CANNOT GO BACK TO THE MISSION.
AND IF YOU ATTEMPT TO KILL YOURSELF AND TAKE TOCTOLLISSICA FROM ME BY REMOVING THAT BLADE, YOU WILL FACE EVERLASTING TORMENT AT MY HANDS.
SHE BESTED YOU.
DO NOT THINK YOURSELF AS CLEVER. YOU WILL CARRY HER TO TERM. AND SHE WILL BE MINE. ONLY THEN CAN YOU REST.
I WILL COMPLETE MY DESTINY.
AN UNDER-STANDING. MY DEAL WITH THE DEVIL.
ELLIOT. HIS SILVER WOULD PROTECT OUR GOLD.
THEN SUPAY WAS GONE. AS WERE THE CHILDREN. ALL BUT ONE.

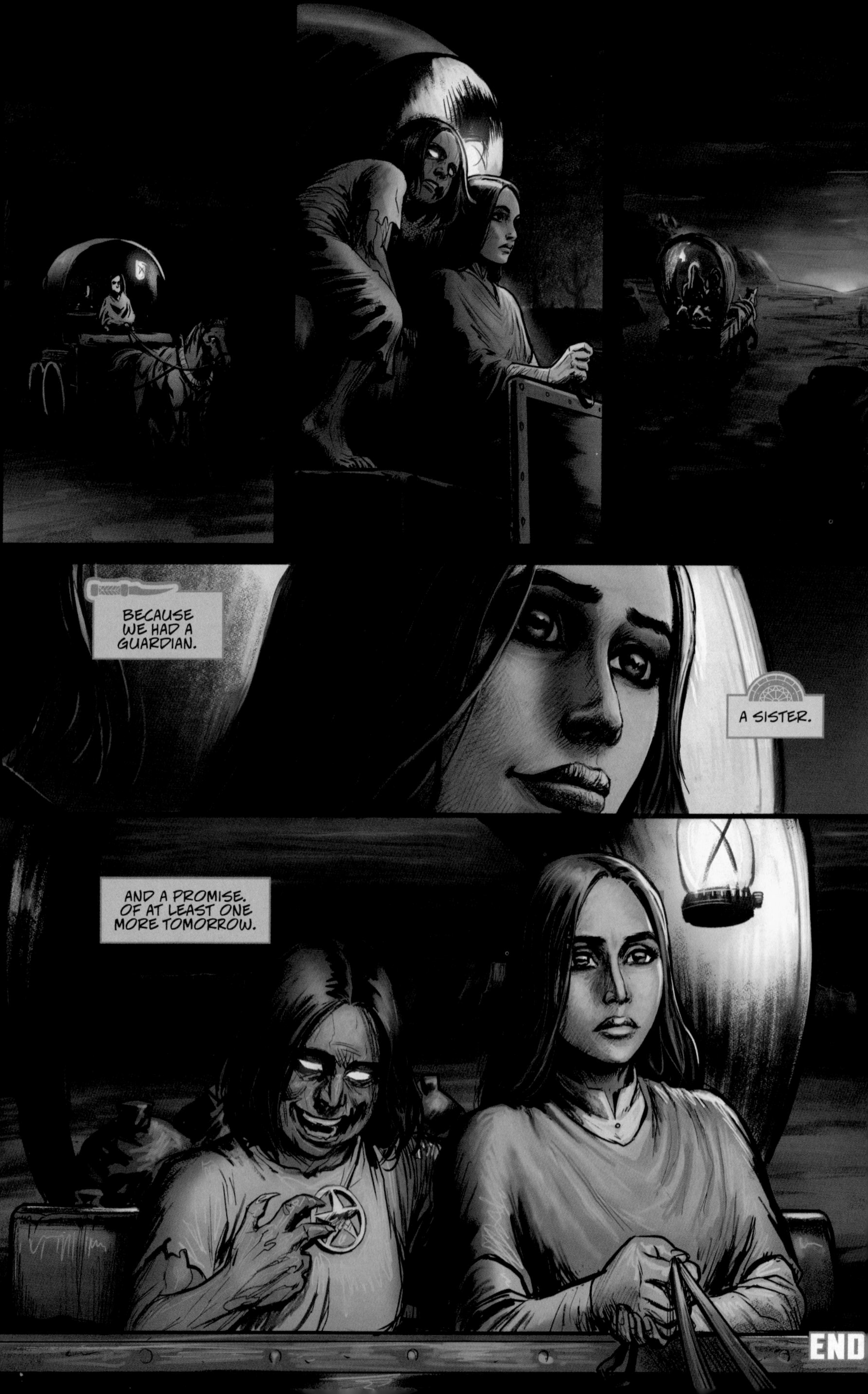
BECAUSE WE HAD A GUARDIAN.
A SISTER.
AND A PROMISE. OF AT LEAST ONE MORE TOMORROW.
END

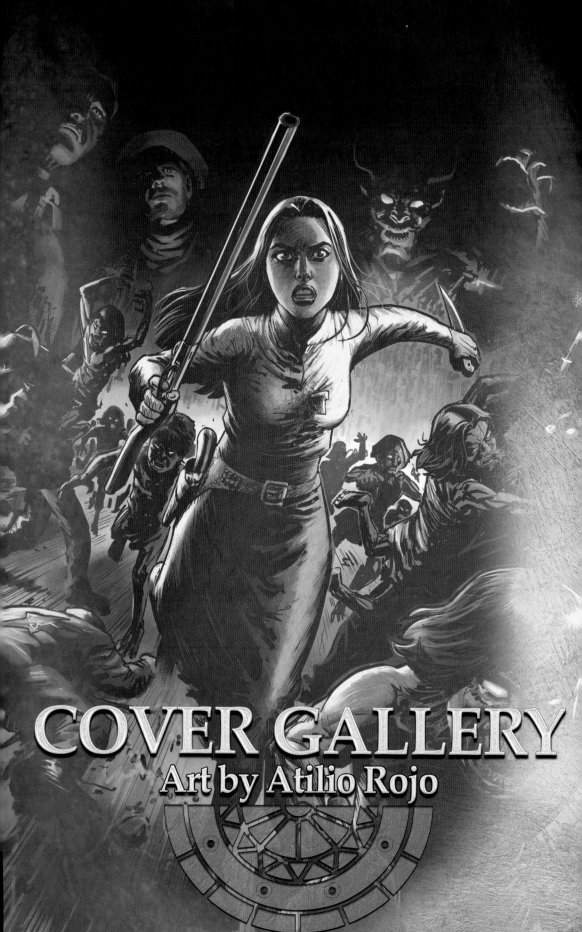

COVER GALLERY

Art by Atilio Rojo

Issue #1 Cover

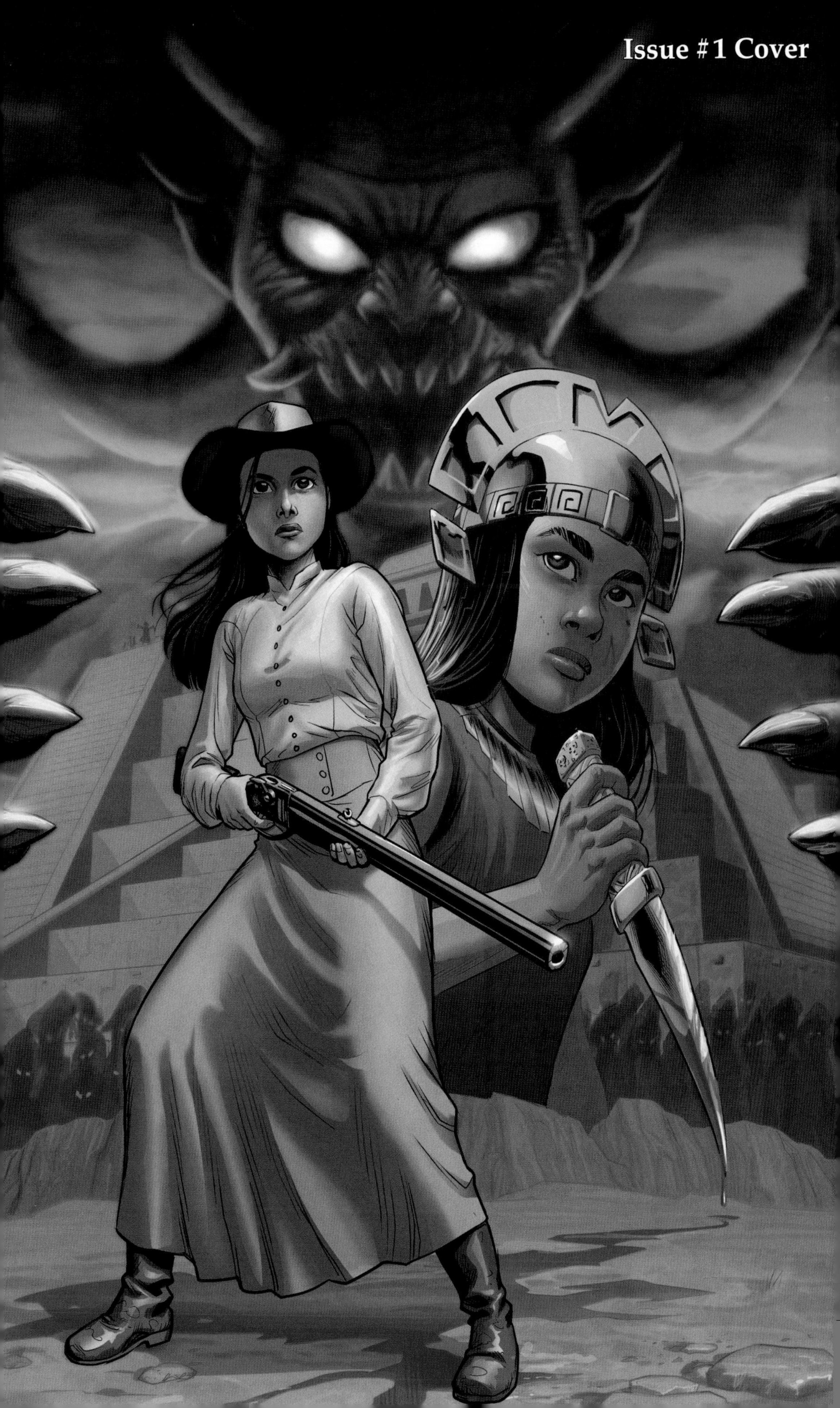

Issue #2 Cover

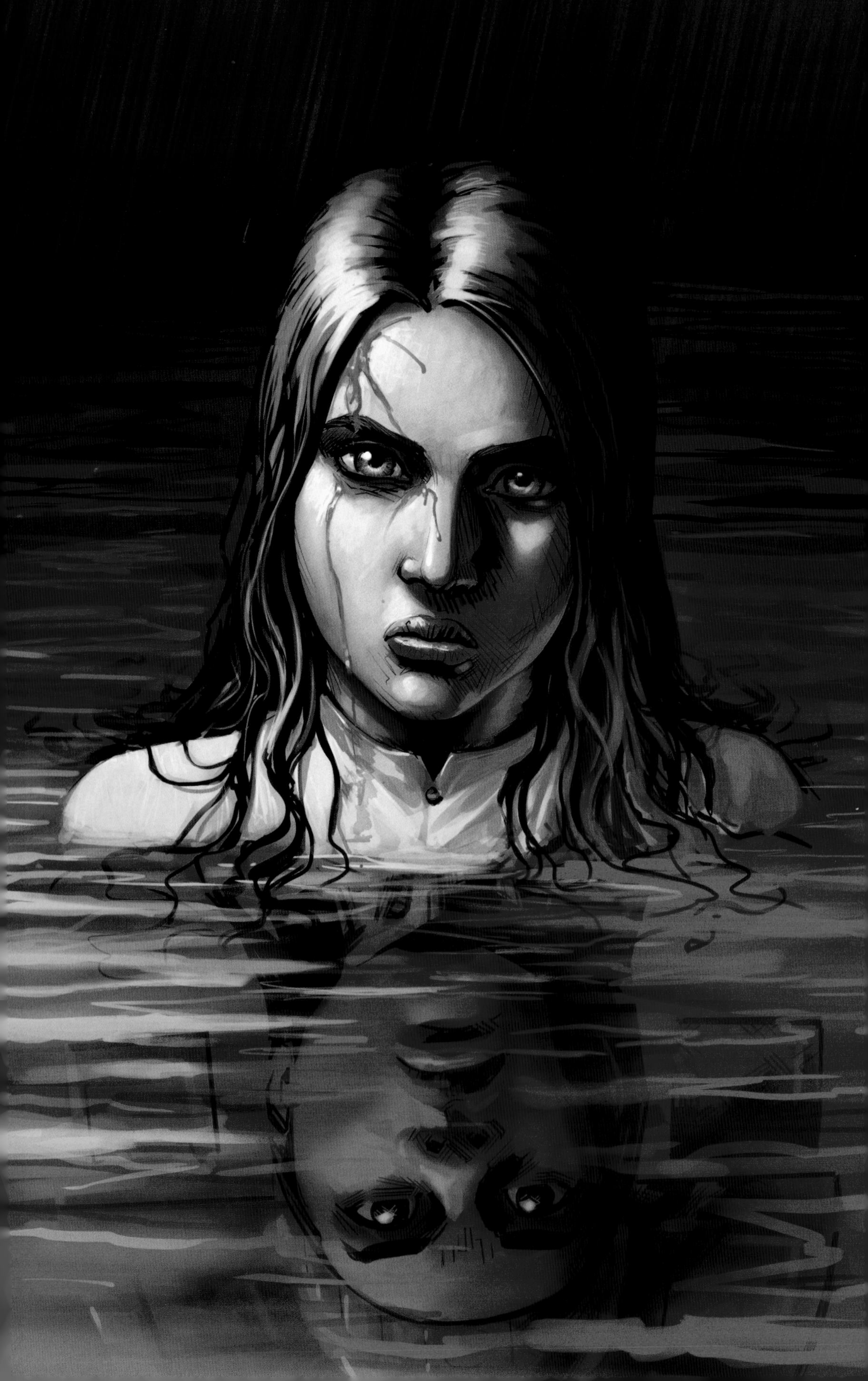

Issue #3 Cover

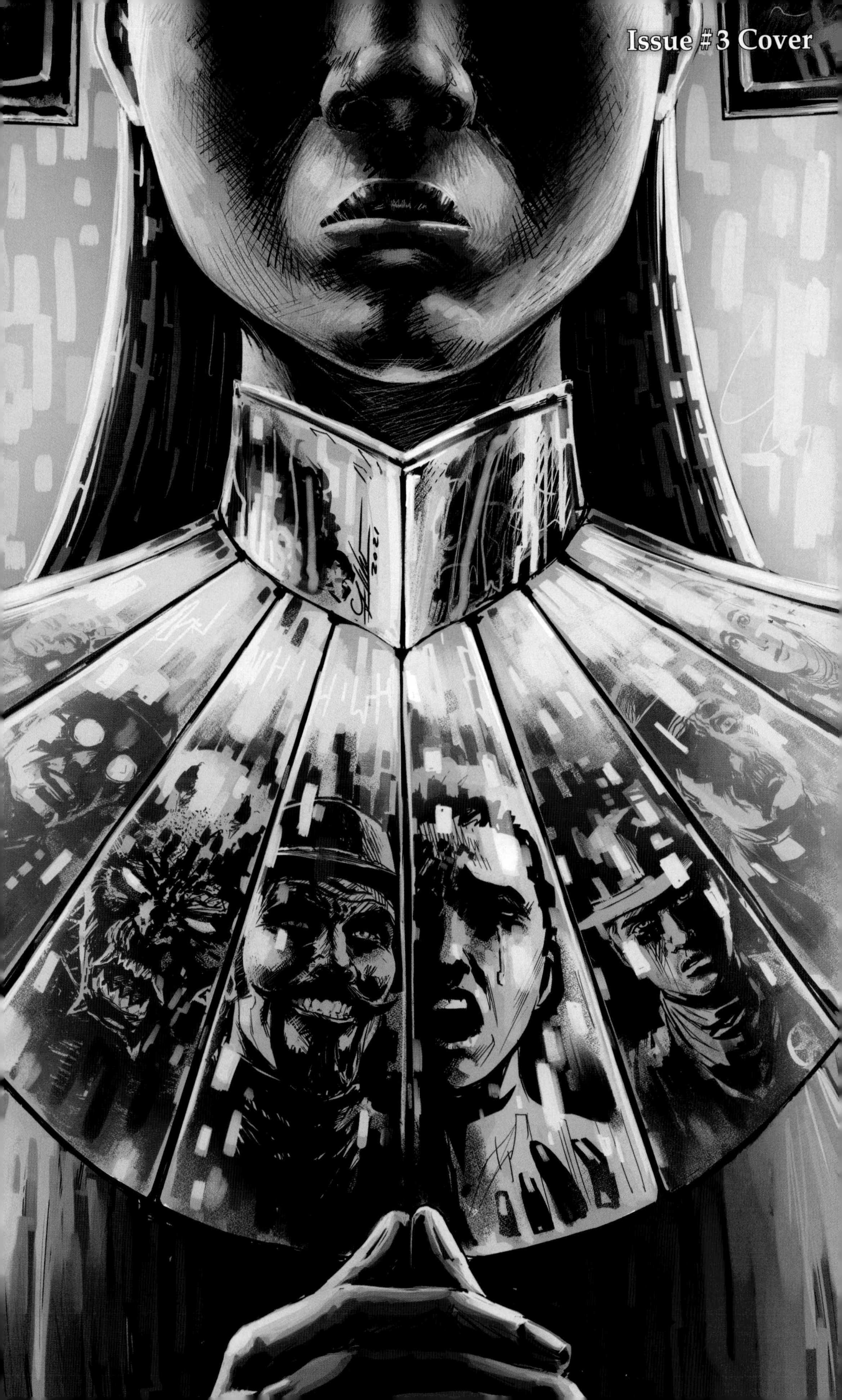

Issue #4 Cover

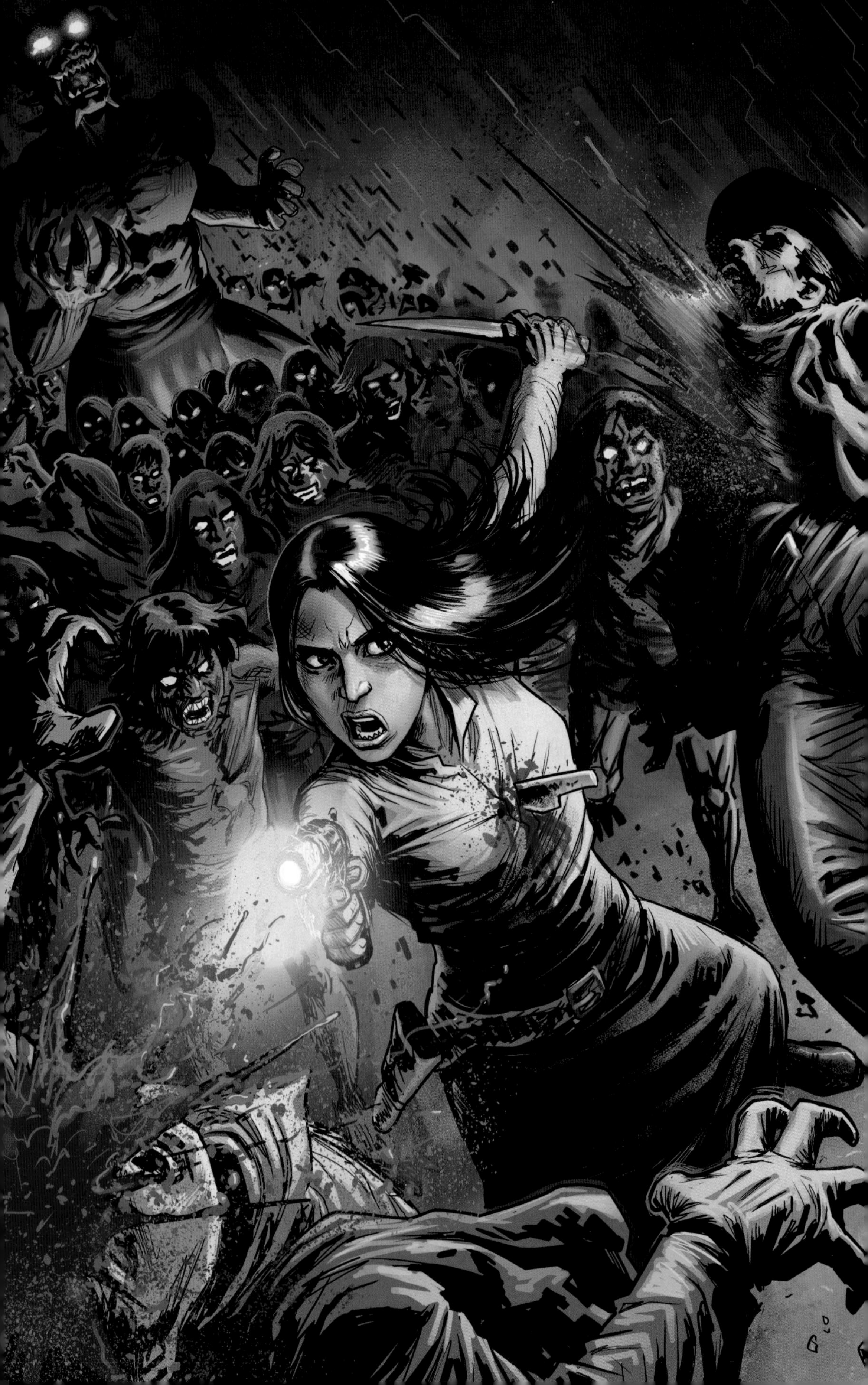

Issue #4 Unused Cover Art

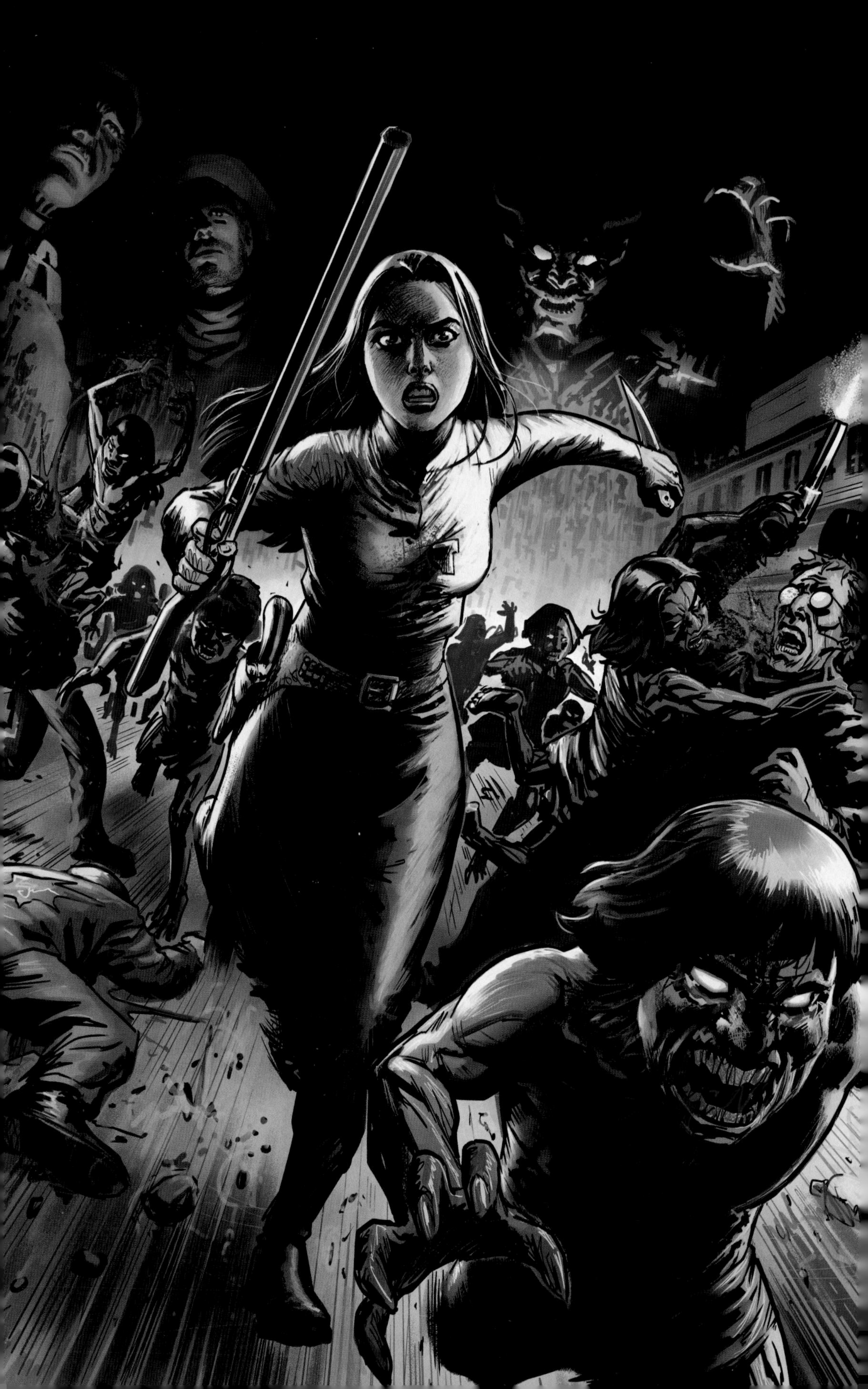

On St Mercy – John Zuur Platten

What inspired me to create *St. Mercy* is something I've been thinking about for a long time - and that is what happens when a character that would otherwise be perceived as weak faces adversity that would topple the most capable of heroes. I'd also been playing around with the idea of a reverse vampire myth. One of the most iconic ways to kill a vampire is to drive a wooden stake through their heart. I wondered what would happen if the only way to kill them was to remove that stake. So this is where the foundations of *St. Mercy* began.

As mentioned, I've always been very interested in mythical characters set against impossible odds. And I didn't want the kind of heroes you're used to seeing in these situations. Normally, when you see a story like this you have some type of musclebound superhero at its center. But I really wanted to go in another direction. I focused on characters who might be physically "weak" but were mentally and spiritually incredibly strong.

For me, the compelling thing about a character like Toctollissica is that although she's a relatively young girl, she's been chosen to take part in a very important ceremonial event for the Incans. She's going to be a human sacrifice in a ritual called the capacocha. Now, when we see it through a modern lens it seems horrifically brutal that children were being killed as offerings to the gods. But for the ancient Incans, this was a very honorable and important ceremony for their society. And children were thought to be the most perfect examples of humanity, and therefore, the best to sacrifice. These offerings would ensure prosperity for the tribes and were essential for the crops they cultivated, which were plentiful and diverse.

When we look back on ancient peoples, we see that they really had two lives that were much more intertwined than the people of today: their physical life and their spiritual life. Both of these lives were incredibly important to them. So as we look back, we think about the brutality of murdering a child. But to the Incans, being offered to the gods was a great and amazing honor. So in the story, Toctollissica is spending a year being treated like a rock star before she will meet her demise and then take her place with the gods. She's excited. She's embraced it. And then, she becomes frustrated when the shamans don't think she is ready. And this leads to chaos no one could have imagined.

This leads to the duality element of the story. Because when we do catch up with Mercy, it is in the boom years of the American Wild West. Opportunity and danger are daily realities. The law can only do so much to protect people. And there are more than enough outlaws to challenge authority and take advantage of the situation. Like Toctollissica, Mercy is also very much a character that has a spiritual life and is also very in tune with the events of the past. She and her father are the descendants of a long line of individuals that have protected the gold used in the Incan capacocha ceremonies throughout the centuries. Unlike other artifacts, this gold has been cursed.

So each heroine has both an obligation and a destiny to fulfill. And then, through no fault of their own, they are suddenly having to deal with these huge external threats. And because they are young women, they are being discounted and not considered a threat to the villains. However, their strength of character comes to the forefront, and both Mercy and Toctollissica, underestimated by their rivals, show how strong individual fortitude can be when challenged.

I liked the idea that Mercy would be considered a non-threat, so if you had a rough and tumble gang of cowboys ride into town the last person they think would be the biggest threat they'd have to face would be a 17-year-old young woman. Because Mercy is the one person to whom they should have been paying attention.

As for the setting, having Mercy exist in the American West was important because I wanted both her and Toctollissica to have relatively the same environment and social structure to deal with as their narratives unfolded. I wanted to have a character that was still young but was also dealing with adult issues and dealing with adult problems. Children of the West grew up much sooner and were functional adults in most ways by the time they'd reached their teens. They worked, they fought in uniform, they had families of their own. So although Mercy is only 17, she has many adult responsibilities, including helping to look after her father and also helping to run their small mission.

And then into this reality, we bring the gods in the form of Supay. The character has such a unique look - demonic and colorful. Atilio has done such a phenomenal job at envisioning Supay - staying true to the South American roots but also putting a more horrific spin on the ruler of the Incan underworld.

But gods don't deal with time the way humans do - theirs is an infinite span and they will play the long game. So although he has been defied by Toctollissica, Supay holds on to his grudge, knowing that eventually, he will have another chance. And when the gold is stolen from Mercy and her father, that chance arrives.

For me, this is where the story truly catches fire as three separate but connected realities crash into each other: The Ancient Incans, the American West, and the Spiritual Underworld. As the violence escalates, so do the more fantasy and horror elements of St. Mercy. As I was writing it, I felt that once the story goes over the crest, like a rollercoaster, there is no stopping it until it reaches the end.

Only then do we truly understand what Mercy and Toctollissica are willing to do for their beliefs and sense of honor as they are transformed into forces of nature.

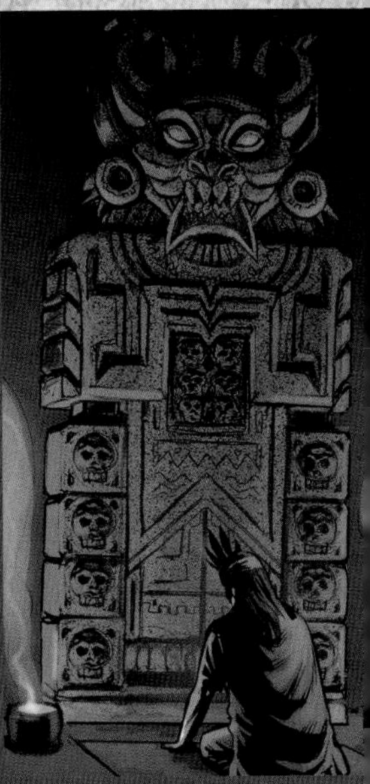

BACKGROUND ON THE INCAS AND TOCTO

My interest in Incan culture and the ritual sacrifice of children came about after I read an article about the capacocha and saw some very powerful images of mummified remains that had been preserved due to the harsh mountain climate of Peru.

https://www.newscientist.com/article/dn23954-mummified-inca-child-sacrifice-gives-up-her-secrets/

There is a peaceful and disturbing quality to both the story and the image of the youn 13-year-old girl who was at the center of the ceremony. I was drawn to her and wanted to kno more. There was also the spark of a story starting to develop in my head as researched the Incas, an why this particular form of sacrifice was so important to their culture.

Most of the documentation of the capacocha comes from the Spanish who would eventual conquer the Incas in a series of conflicts collectively known as the Conquest of Peru.

https://www.britannica.com/place/Latin-America/Conquest-of-Peru

But these accounts of the capacocha are almost all from an "adult", religious perspective the victors. Clinical. I wanted to see this extension of life through death from the viewpoint of th participants. I wondered what the highs and lows of being made ready for the gods would feel lik from the mummified girl's perspective. To me, she was both haunting and powerful. And so I gav her a name - Toctollissica - and started to imagine her journey.

It was during my research I discovered that being chosen to be part of the sacrificial ritua was considered a great honor. Young boys and girls were offered as tribute and sent from their trib homes to Cuzco (the head of the Incan Empire), where they would live in gilded shrines. Here, the existence would transform into one of luxury and excess as they were prepared for their eventu sacrifice.

And I knew that I wanted gold, which was central to Incan power, to play a central role the story of Toctollissica. This led me to introduce some creative liberties with the ritual - which wa usually done through strangulation or exposure to the elements, but also by blunt weapon beatings to something in which blood could more freely flow.

So I had the elements, but what was missing was how Tocollissica transcended all of those your boys and girls who had come before. And for that, I found the answer in Supay, the ruler of the Inca Underworld.

Compared to other demons, Supay was a revelation. Colorful and flamboyant and terrifyir in equal measures. Feared and loved (as are all gods). So he was definitely going to have to be part the story. The complex nature of people and their beliefs says as much about the followers as it do about their gods. In my mind, only powerful and imaginative people could "create" such a god Supay, and so Toctollissica would become my embodiment of the Incas.

But I wanted a unique confrontation between Toctollissica and Supay. What if she loved ar believed in her god with all of her heart, but being the immortal, omnipotent being he is, Supay didr reciprocate? What would happen? What chaos would ensue?

That was my starting point. And as *St. Mercy* started to come together, I realized that there was an opportunity in Toctollissica to see a character transition from believing in a god, to defying that god, and then perhaps, becoming a god herself. It was a story I had to tell.

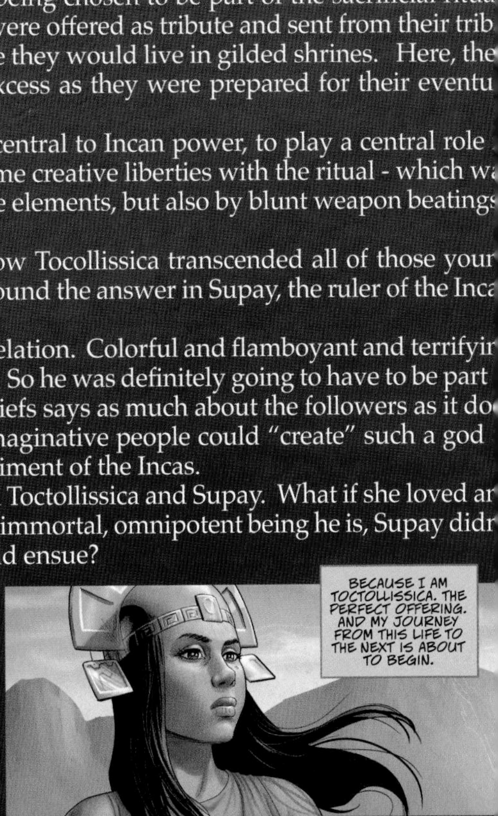
BECAUSE I AM TOCTOLLISSICA. THE PERFECT OFFERING. AND MY JOURNEY FROM THIS LIFE TO THE NEXT IS ABOUT TO BEGIN.

ST. MERCY AND
THE AMERICAN WESTERN

I've always been fascinated by westerns. When I was a kid, western shows were a staple of television, and I watched *Gunsmoke, Maverick,* and *The Rifleman* to name a few. The heroes were larger than life - confident in their morality and willing to fight to the death when necessary. They lived in a developing landscape where the rules of society were constantly being rewritten. Many characters of this genre of western were also veterans of the American Civil War, so they had experienced violence at a young age, and it had changed them as they reached their 30s and 40s.

Most interestingly of all to me was the sense of hope these shows used as an underlying theme to their narratives.

Western movies of the sixties and early seventies remain some of my favorite films. These include *The Good, the Bad and the Ugly, The Wild Bunch* (I have a personalized photo of Ernest Borgnine from the film that is one of my prized possessions), *True Grit, The War Wagon,* and *The Magnificent Seven.* I also have a love of more recent westerns, including *Unforgiven, Open Range, 3:10 to Yuma,* and *Hostiles.*

When I started to settle on the characters and worlds of *St. Mercy,* I realized that placing young Mercedes in a western setting would allow me to create a world for her that would be more reflective of Tocto's Incan society. These are both peoples that are in large part defined by their landscape. How they exploit it, and how they survive it, are central to their life stories. I also wanted that sense of untamed wilderness to be ever-present.

I'm fortunate in that I have an amazing resource close by here in Los Angeles - the Autry Museum of the American West. This museum has a spectacular collection of actual western artifacts combined with memorabilia from Hollywood's representation of the Wild West on the big and small screen. A few visits definitely served as inspiration and informed my research. The clothing, the wagons, the horses, the guns, the landscape - it all worked together to influence my creative process.

The museum has a massive gun collection, and that is where I decided I wanted Mercy to have a gun/rifle that would be an iconic weapon for her.

The Sharps Rifle, .45-100 caliber that was prominently featured in the excellent Tom Selleck film *Quigley Down Under,* became a component of the *St. Mercy* story because I wanted to show Elliot's mastery of the weapon as a way to provide some backstory for the character. I also realized early on that this would be a way for me to show some of Mercy's hidden competence with weapons that would eventually be revealed.

When Atilio and I first started talking about the art for the books, we were able to use the language of western cinema as a common reference point. I love the way Atilio has been able to use some of these visuals in the books - the close-ups of the narrowed, focused eyes just before the draw of the revolvers, the chaotic setting of the classic western saloon, the long, wide shots of horse and rider. The images are small stories in themselves, and I think they really help transport the reader to the world we've created.

As I was writing a female-centric story, I also wanted to know as much as I could about the role of women in the west. What I found interesting (and encouraging) was that although there was nothing like the equality we strive for today, women were very powerful influencers in not only men's lives but society in general. This dovetailed with the story I was constructing.

The western genre also helped set the tone of St. Mercy.

I knew that I wanted a violent world that wouldn't pull any punches, and this is where Sam Peckinpah comes into play, as he almost single-handedly changed what could be shared with an audience. Peckinpah directed *The Wild Bunch* (from a script by the director and Walon Green), and for its time, it contained an amount of bloodshed and violence that was shocking to most people. It also included villains as anti-heroes and a "good guy" that was a borderline sociopath. Instead of men of honor, *The Wild Bunch* features characters who have run out of anything other to fight for than money. And that's what makes the ending of the film that much stronger - honor, a sense of duty, and realizing they have reached the point of their own mortality, create characters that are unlikeable, and yet, we care about their journeys and empathize with their motivations.

My goal in writing the western elements of *St. Mercy* was to capture that same feeling in the world and the characters. Fatalism, violence, and yes, hope. I think that is why the western, though it has fallen out of favor at times (only to be resurrected again and again) continues to be a powerful genre for story-telling. It also represented the perfect metaphor for the trajectory of Mercy's and Tocto's lives and the challenges they face.

– John Zuur Platten

MEET THE TEAM

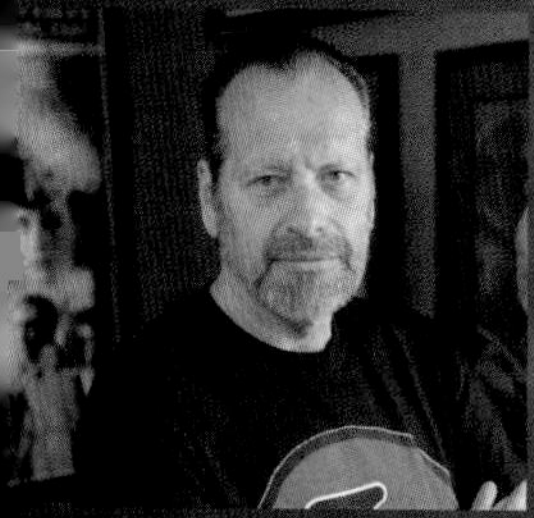

John Zuur Platten

John is a writer and designer who has shipped over 80 titles. With over 30 years of experience in the business, John has written for established franchises such as Jurassic World, Ghostbusters, The Fast and the Furious, and Riddick. He was a lead creative at Niantic Labs, creators of Pokemon GO. John has also written feature films, television, and graphic novels. His book on game writing is used in over 1000 universities around the globe.

tilio Rojo

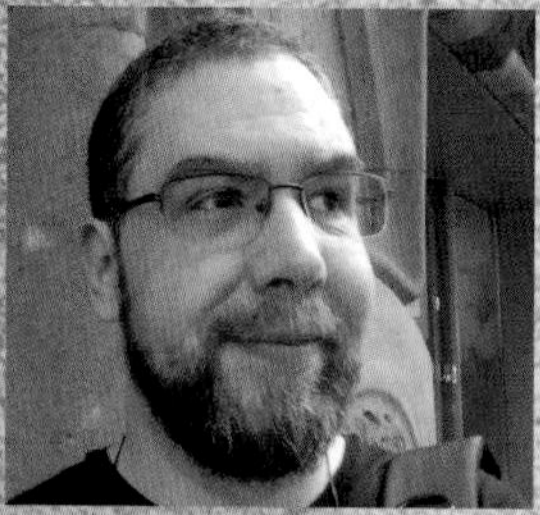

tilio Rojo started his sequential art career writing and drawing otic comics. Years later, he shifted to working in the American mics market, pencilling and inking IDW's Transformers— s, from erotic to robots. Fun! After accumulating more work new publishers including DC Comics, Rojo pencilled, inked, d colored Top Cow's IXth Generation. The artist has continued orking at Top Cow, providing covers for titles including Eden's ll, Samaritan, and Cyber Force.

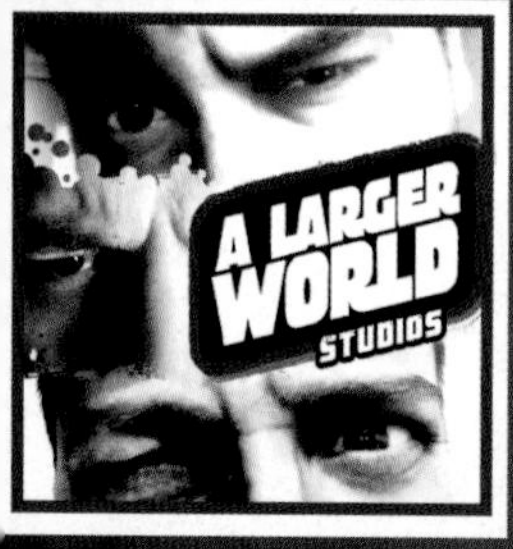
A LARGER
WORLD
STUDIOS

Troy Peteri

Troy and Dave Lanphear are collectively known as A Larger World Studios. They've lettered everything from The Avengers, Iron Man, Wolverine, Amazing Spider-Man and X-Men to more recent titles such as Witchblade, Cyberforce, and Batman/Wonder Woman: The Brave & The Bold. They can be reached at studio@alargerworld.com for your lettering and design needs. (Hooray, commerce!)

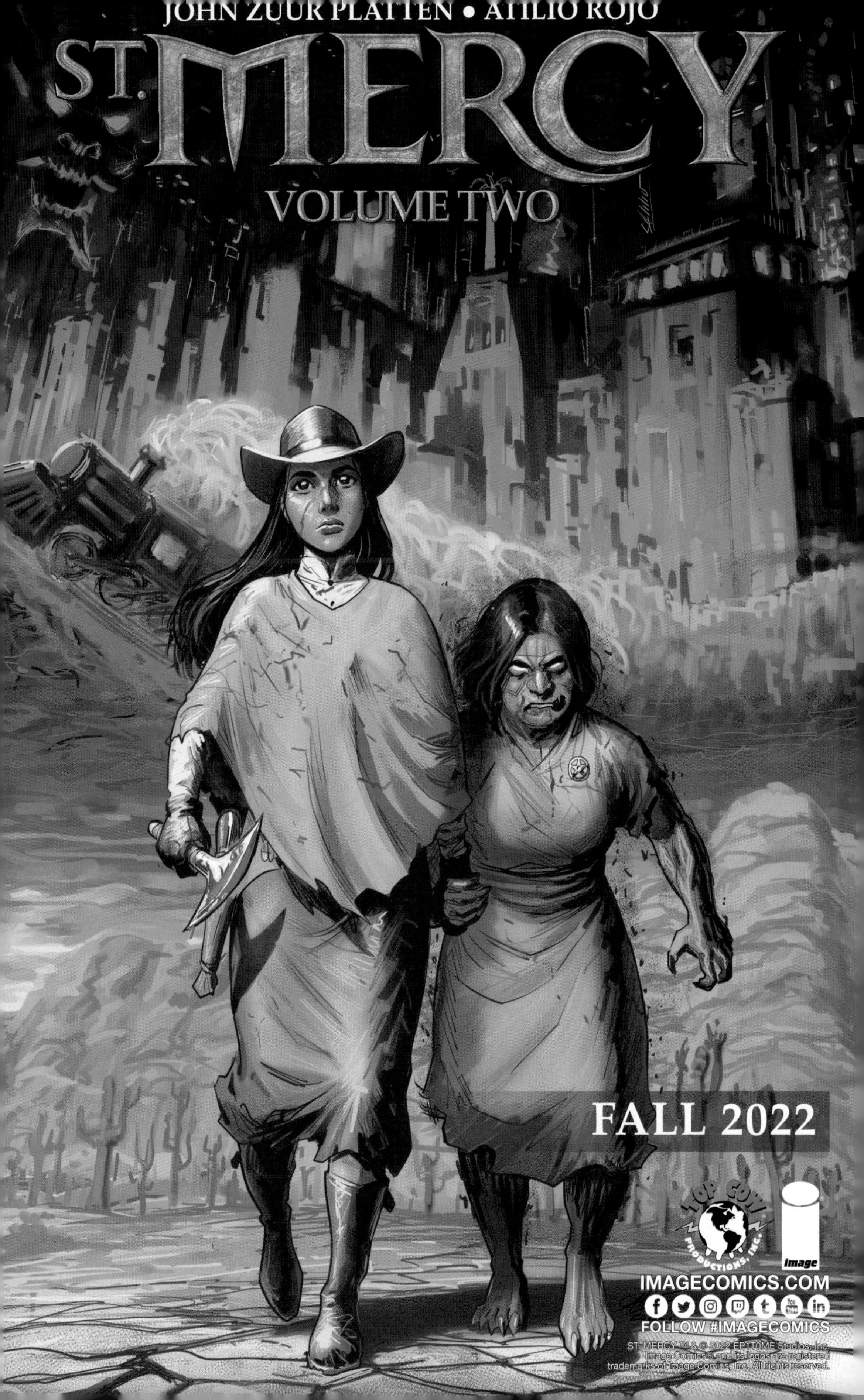

JOHN ZUUR PLATTEN • ATTILIO ROJO
ST. MERCY
VOLUME TWO
FALL 2022
IMAGECOMICS.COM
FOLLOW #IMAGECOMICS
ST. MERCY ™ & © 2022 EP1T0ME Studios, Inc.
Image Comics® and its logos are registered
trademarks of Image Comics, Inc. All rights reserved.

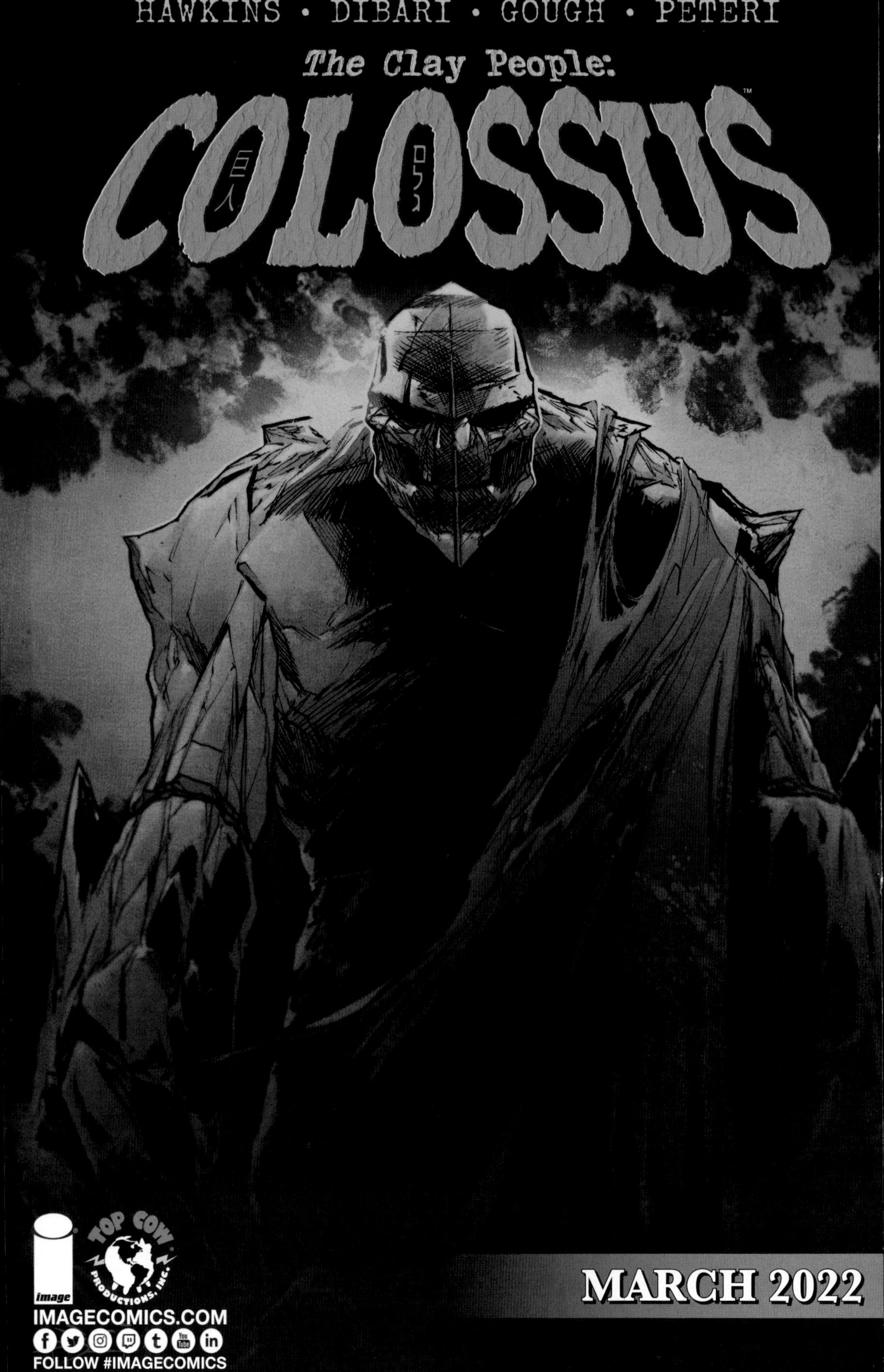
HAWKINS · DIBARI · GOUGH · PETERI
The Clay People:
COLOSSUS™
MARCH 2022
image
TOP COW PRODUCTIONS, INC.
IMAGECOMICS.COM
FOLLOW #IMAGECOMICS

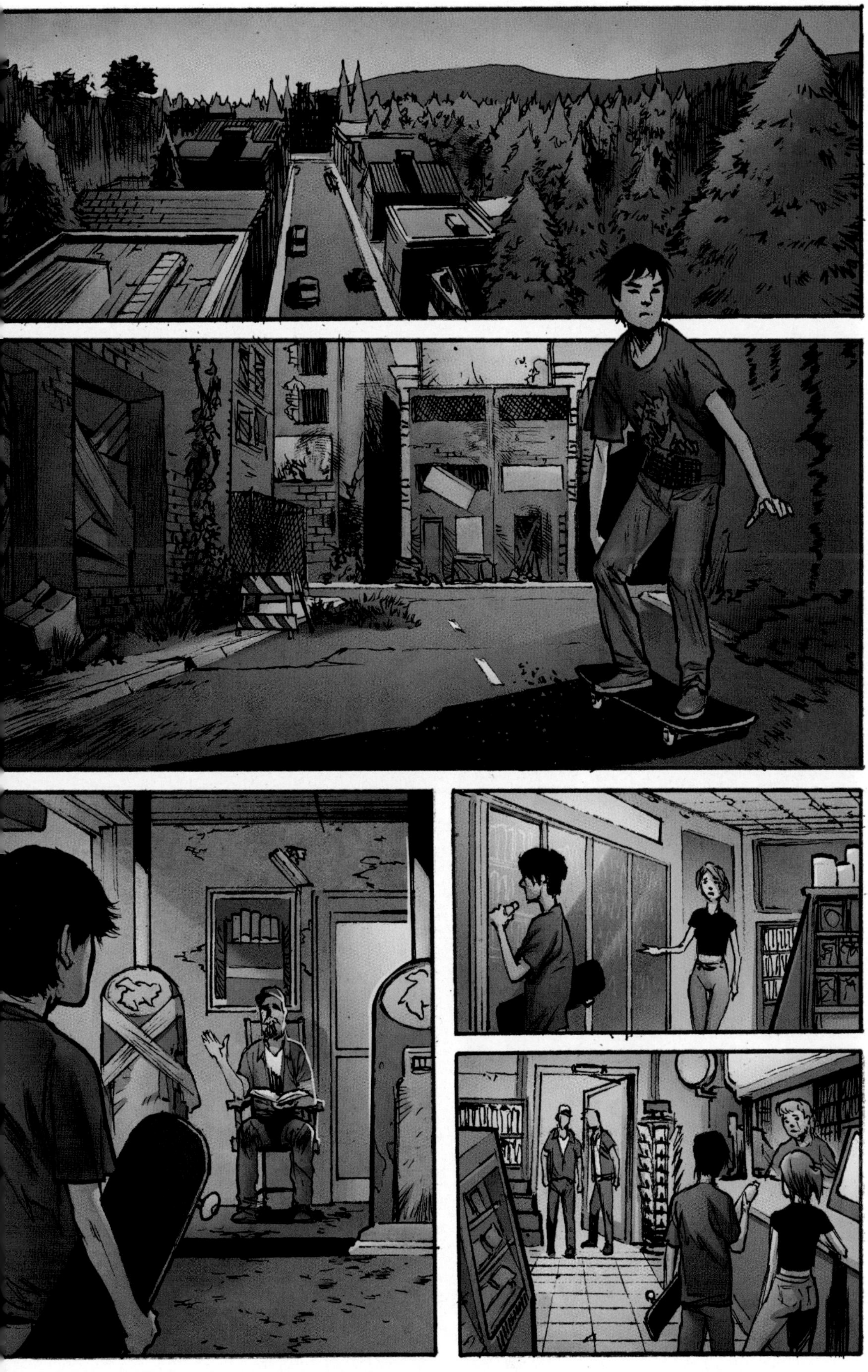

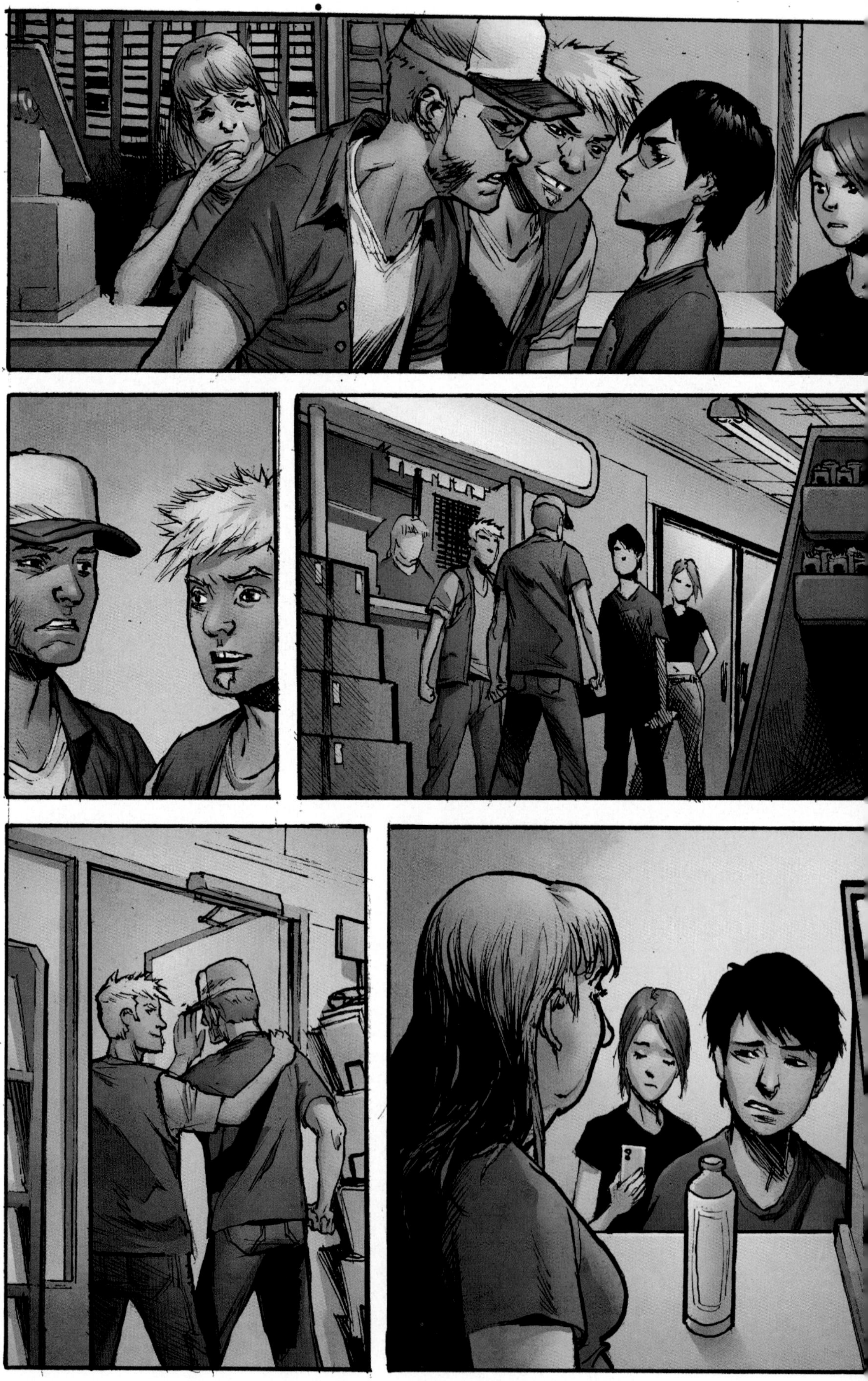

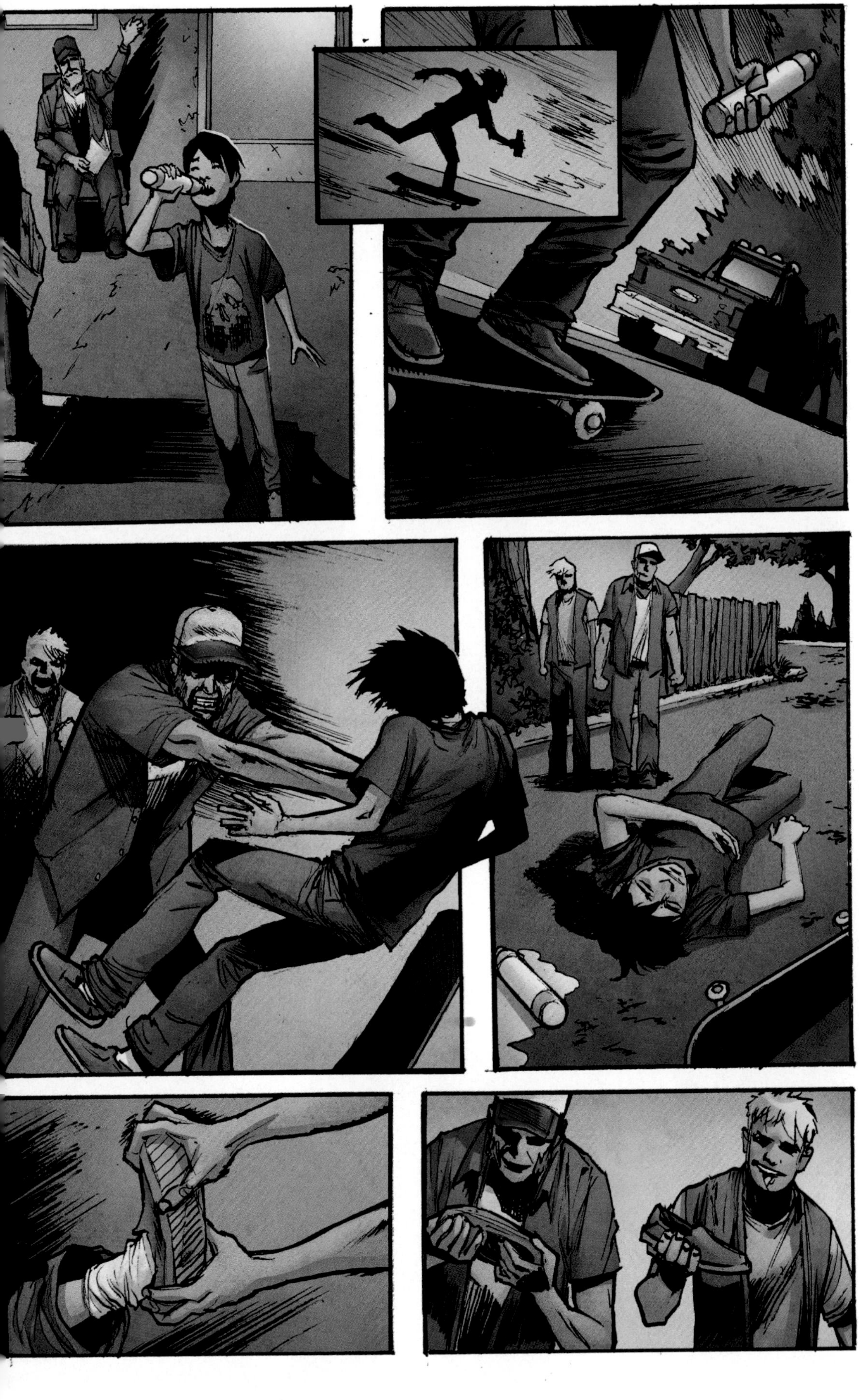

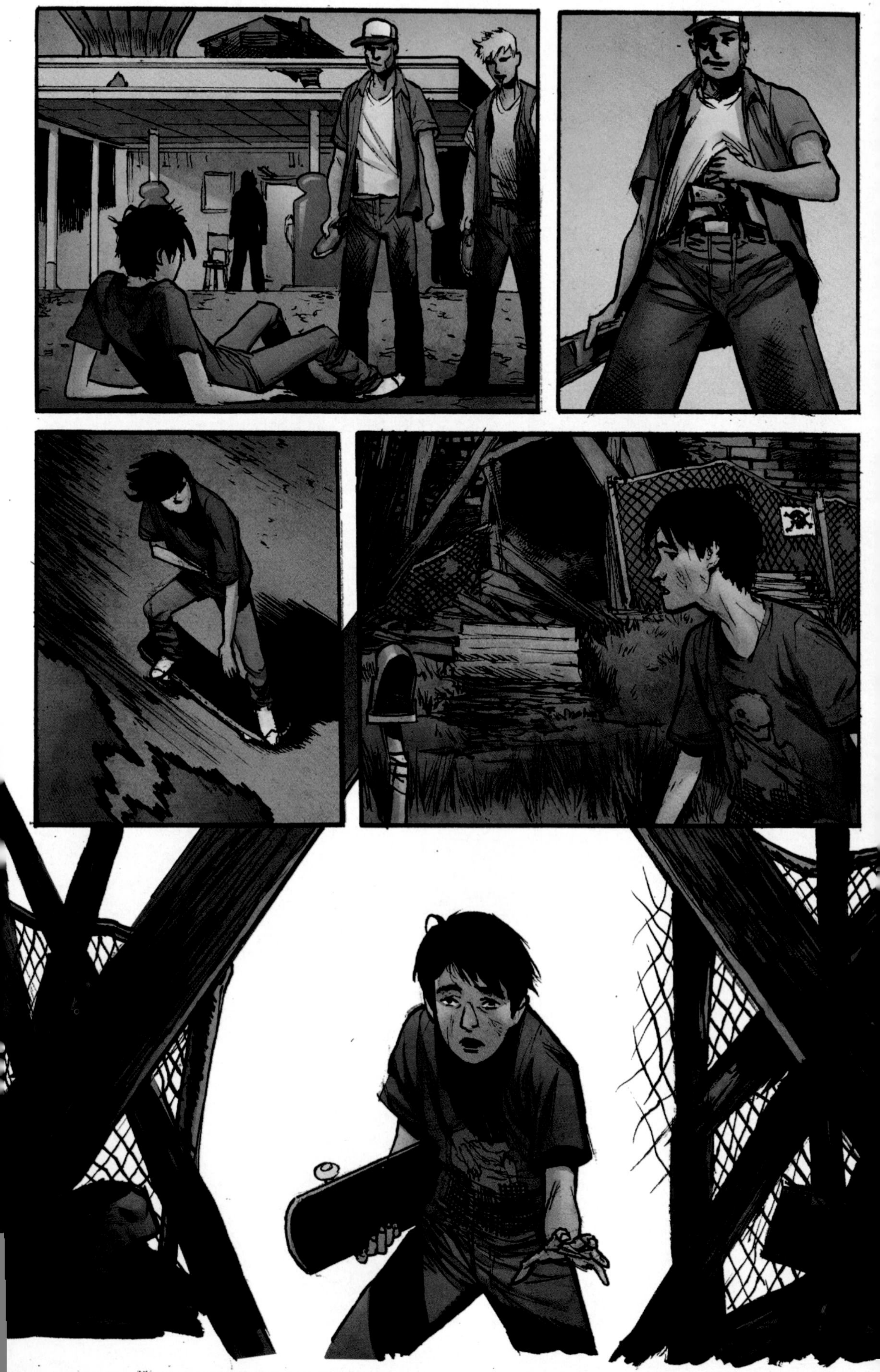

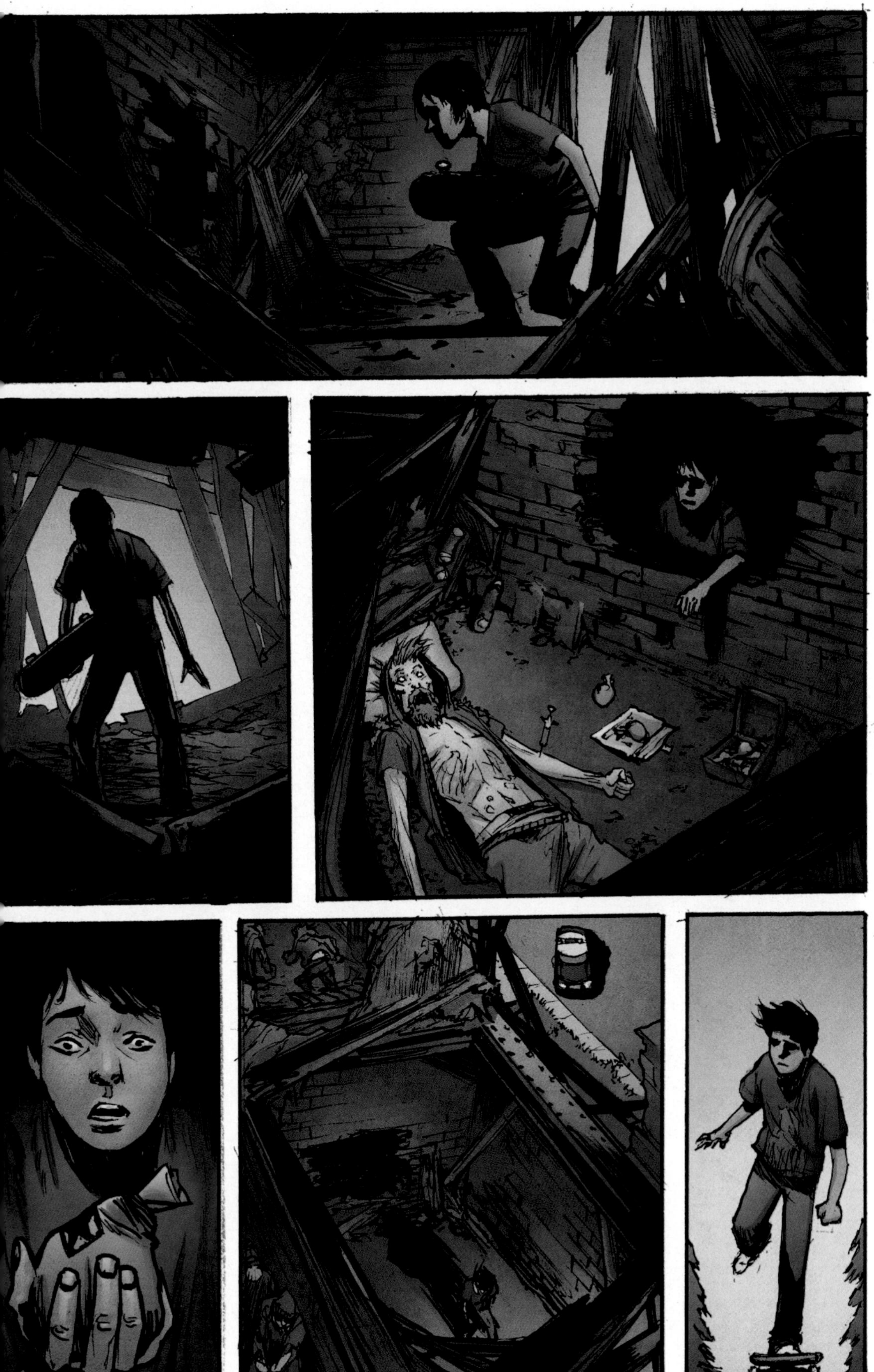

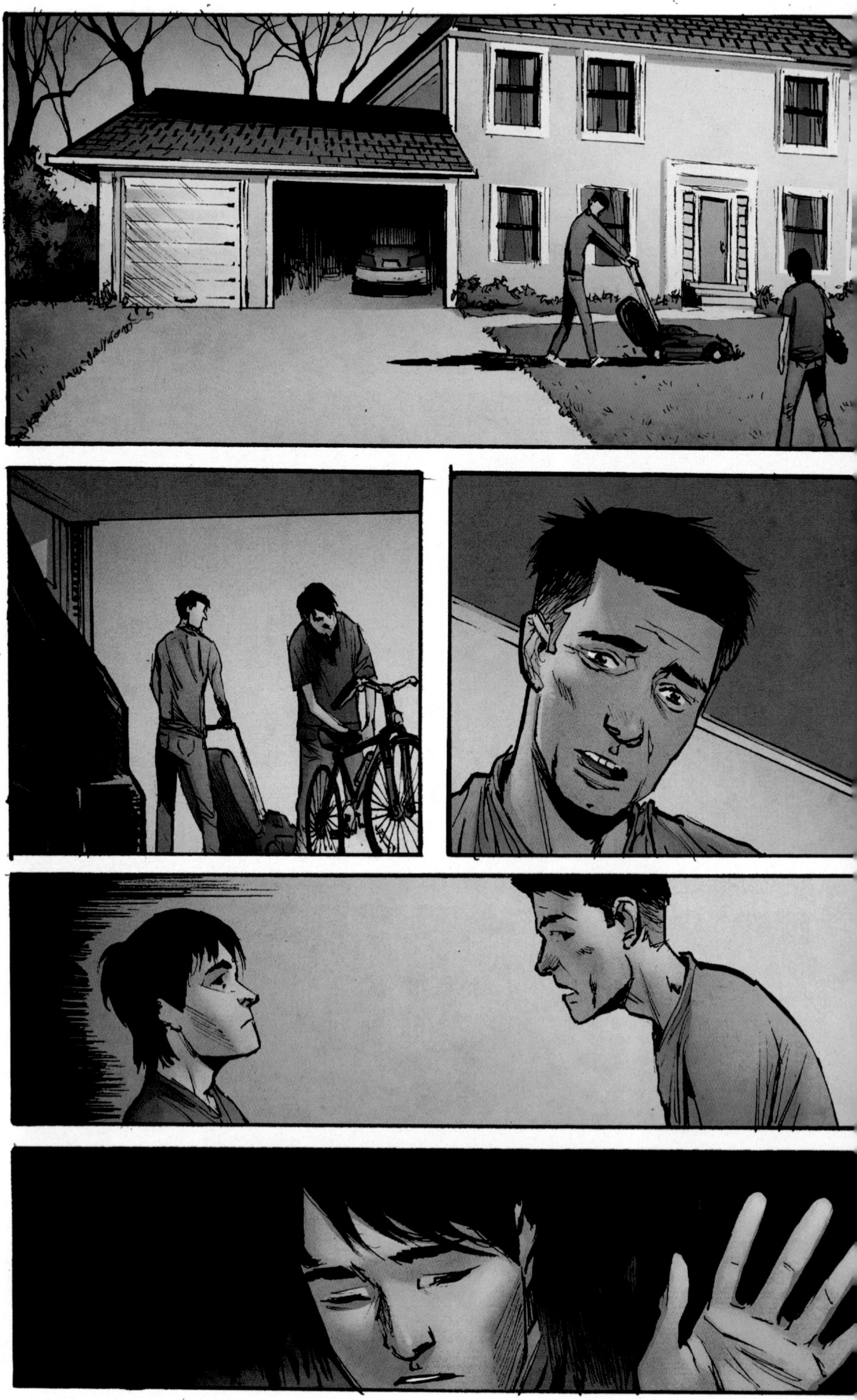

The Top Cow essentials checklist:

A Man Among Ye, Volume 1
(ISBN: 978-1-5343-1691-1)

Aphrodite IX: Rebirth, Volume 1
(ISBN: 978-1-60706-828-0)

Blood Stain, Volume 1
(ISBN: 978-1-63215-544-3)

Cyber Force: Awakening, Volume 1
(ISBN: 978-1-5343-0980-7)

The Clock, Volume 1
(ISBN: 978-1-5343-1611-9)

The Darkness: Origins, Volume 1
(ISBN: 978-1-60706-097-0)

Death Vigil, Volume 1
(ISBN: 978-1-63215-278-7)

Eclipse, Volume 1
(ISBN: 978-1-5343-0038-5)

The Freeze, OGN
(ISBN: 978-1-5343-1211-1)

Fine Print, Volume 1
(ISBN: 978-1-5343-2070-3)

Helm Greycastle, Volume 1
(ISBN: 978-1-5343-1962-2)

Infinite Dark, Volume 1
(ISBN: 978-1-5343-1056-8)

La Mano Del Destino, Volume 1
(ISBN: 978-1-5343-1947-9)

La Voz De M.A.Y.O.:
Tata Rambo, Volume 1
(ISBN: 978-1-5343-1363-7)

Paradox Girl, Volume 1
(ISBN: 978-1-5343-1220-3)

Port of Earth, Volume 1
(ISBN: 978-1-5343-0646-2)

Postal, Volume 1
(ISBN: 978-1-63215-342-5)

Punderworld, Volume 1
(ISBN: 978-1-5343-2072-7)

Stairway Anthology
(ISBN: 978-1-5343-1702-4)

Sugar, Volume 1
(ISBN: 978-1-5343-1641-7)

Sunstone, Volume 1
(ISBN: 978-1-63215-212-1)

Swing, Volume 1
(ISBN: 978-1-5343-0516-8)

Symmetry, Volume 1
(ISBN: 978-1-63215-699-0)

The Tithe, Volume 1
(ISBN: 978-1-63215-324-1)

Think Tank, Volume 1
(ISBN: 978-1-60706-660-6)

Vindication, OGN
(ISBN: 978-1-5343-1237-1)

Warframe, Volume 1
(ISBN: 978-1-5343-0512-0)

Witchblade 2017, Volume 1
(ISBN: 978-1-5343-0685-1)

For more ISBN and ordering information on our latest collections go to:
www.topcow.com
Ask your retailer about our catalogue of collected editions, digests, and hard covers
or check the listings at: **Barnes and Noble, Amazon.com,** and other fine retailers.

To find your nearest comic shop go to:
www.comicshoplocator.com